Ford Y-Block Engines
How to Rebuild and Modify

Charles Morris

CarTech®

CarTech®

838 Lake Street South
Forest Lake, MN 55025
Phone: 651-277-1200 or 800-551-4754
Fax: 651-277-1203
www.cartechbooks.com

© 2014 by Charles Morris

All rights reserved. No part of this publication may be reproduced or utilized in any form or by any means, electronic or mechanical, including photocopying, recording, or by any information storage and retrieval system, without prior permission from the Publisher. All text, photographs, and artwork are the property of the Author unless otherwise noted or credited.

The information in this work is true and complete to the best of our knowledge. However, all information is presented without any guarantee on the part of the Author or Publisher, who also disclaim any liability incurred in connection with the use of the information and any implied warranties of merchantability or fitness for a particular purpose. Readers are responsible for taking suitable and appropriate safety measures when performing any of the operations or activities described in this work.

All trademarks, trade names, model names, and numbers, and other product designations referred to herein are the property of their respective owners and are used solely for identification purposes. This work is a publication of CarTech, Inc., and has not been licensed, approved, sponsored, or endorsed by any other person or entity. The Publisher is not associated with any product, service, or vendor mentioned in this book, and does not endorse the products or services of any vendor mentioned in this book.

Edit by Paul Johnson
Layout by Connie DeFlorin

ISBN 978-1-61325-472-1
Item No. SA257P

Library of Congress Cataloging-in-Publication Data

Morris, Charles R.
  Ford Y-block engines : how to rebuild and modify / Charles R. Morris.
     pages cm
  ISBN 978-1-61325-061-7
  1. Ford automobile--Motors--Maintenance and repair. 2. Ford automobile--Motors--Modification. I. Title.

TL215.F7M667 2014
629.25,040288--dc23

                              2013035436

Written, edited, and designed in the U.S.A.
Printed in U.S.A.

Title Page:
A supercharged 322-ci Y-block is installed in this beautiful 1957 Ford Custom, which belongs to Rich Stuck of Brick, New Jersey.

Back Cover Photos

Top Left:
Here, the crankshaft is treated to a Magnaflux test for cracks. A magnetic powder is applied to areas of the crankshaft prone to cracks, such as oil supply holes, after which a magnetic field is introduced. The magnetic powder collects in any cracks; a crack in a crankshaft may not spell doom for the part. For a crankshaft the location, length, and depth of the crack are the determining factors.

Top Right:
With the piston and rod assembly seated against the crankshaft journal, remove the protective boots from the rod bolts. Check the connecting rod bearing clearance to be sure it is within specification. As done with the main journal, place a small piece of Plastigauge on the rod journal.

Middle Left:
The bowl areas under each intake and exhaust valve are blended. In doing so, you are not attempting to change the cylinder head's original configuration, but merely seeking to improve efficiency for a better-running longer-lasting engine.

Middle Right:
With the timing chain and gears in place, properly aligned and tightened, and camshaft end play checked, slide the oil slinger onto the snout of the crankshaft.

Bottom Left:
Use a feeler gauge to determine the gap between the tip of the valve and the face of the rocker arm. Each rocker arm has an adjuster that is turned until the proper gap has been achieved. You can feel a slight drag on the feeler gauge when lash is correct. Valve lash is set again with the engine hot after initial start-up.

Bottom Right:
Although not lighter than the stamped OEM valley cover, this cast-aluminum cover looks great and is less likely than an OEM part to leak due to bending from being overtightened. Using a proper sealant and snugging the hardware without overtightening keeps the top of the engine dry.

PGUK
63 Hatton Garden
London EC1N 8LE, England
Phone: 020 7061 1980 • Fax: 020 7242 3725
www.pguk.co.uk

Renniks Publications Ltd.
3/37-39 Green Street
Banksmeadow, NSW 2109, Australia
Phone: 2 9695 7055 • Fax: 2 9695 7355
www.renniks.com

CONTENTS

Acknowledgments 4
Introduction 5
What is a Workbench® *Book?* 8

Chapter 1: Engine Evaluation 9
   High Mileage 9
   Excessive Oil Consumption 9
   Low Oil Pressure 10
   Decrease in Performance 11
   Noises 13
   Diagnostic Tools and Techniques 15
   Spark Plug Inspection 15
   Ignition Timing Check 15
   Vacuum Test 17
   Compression Check 18
   Leak-Down Test 19
   Cooling System Pressure Test 20

Chapter 2: Pulling the Engine 21
   Hood 21
   Battery 21
   Fluids 22
   Wiring 22
   Distributor and Ignition 22
   Belts 23
   Lines and Hoses 23
   Hoist and Lift Brackets 23
   Driveshaft 23
   Transmission 23
   Engine Stand 24

Chapter 3: Preparing to Rebuild an Engine 28
   Facilities 28
   Safety is Crucial 29
   Organization and Planning 29
   Rationale for Rebuilding 30
   Tools and Equipment 30
   Machine Shop Services 33

Chapter 4: Engine Disassembly 34
   Valvetrain Disassembly 35
   Camshaft Removal 36
   Cylinder Head Disassembly 38
   Block Disassembly 40

Chapter 5: Inspection and Cleaning 44
   Professional Inspection 44
   Rocker Arm Assemblies 45
   Camshaft and Lifters 46
   Cylinder Heads 47
   Cylinder Block 52
   Pistons and Connecting Rods 59
   Crankshaft and Vibration Dampener 60

Chapter 6: Machining and Parts Selection 64
   Parts Sources 64
   Connecting Rods 64
   Rotating Assembly 69
   Cylinder Block 74
   Cylinder Heads 79
   Cylinder Head Resurfacing 83
   Valve Job 84
   Cylinder Head Assembly 87
   Piston and Connecting Rod Installation 89

Chapter 7: Assembly 90
   Safety and Cleanliness 90
   Specialized Tools and Products 92
   Bottom End Assembly 94
   Top End Installation 107

Chapter 8: High-Performance Y-Block Engine Build 111
   Racing Engines 114

**Chapter 9: Engine Installation, Start-Up and
          Break-In** 123
   Installation 123
   Priming the Engine 126
   Distributor Installation 127
   Priming the Fuel System 128
   Break-In 129

Epilogue 131

Appendix 132
   Torque Specifications 132
   General Engine Specifications 132
   Dampener Timing Settings 133
   Firing Order and Rotation 133
   Cylinder Numbering Order 134
   Cylinder Head Bolt-Tightening Sequence 134
   Cam Timing 135

Source Guide 136

Acknowledgments

Ask anyone who has ever rebuilt an engine and they will tell you without fail that it is not a solo task. Although one person can accomplish certain aspects of the rebuild, other skilled people are required along the way. A couple of friends helped me with the heavy work, such as removing the engine from the car. It usually takes at least two people just to safely remove the hood so extra help certainly comes in handy. In addition, a professional machine shop and parts source are a must. I chose Jordan Automotive Machine in Hainesport, New Jersey, for the machine work necessary to complete this project. Why? Well, first and foremost because proprietor and ASE Master Engine Machinist Gil Jordan speaks Ford fluently. In my opinion, having experience with the idiosyncrasies of Ford engines is paramount to a successful rebuild.

The great news is that throughout this book you'll see references to certain engineering features unique to the Y-block V-8 engine family. You need to recognize these and perform these specific procedures because if they are ignored during the machining and assembly phases, it spells disaster for your project.

This book is the result of much collaboration with my friends Richard Stuck and Jerry Christenson. Rich owns both engines covered, including the beautiful supercharged 1957 Custom. He is also the proud owner of the multitude of rare Y-block parts depicted. Jerry kindly lends his wealth of knowledge, which was accumulated over decades of building and successfully drag racing Y-block-powered Fords. I must admit that I took my very first trip down a drag strip at the wheel of a Y-block-powered 1954 Ford. My experience and forte has always been with the FE series engines, but it's fascinating to me that my Y-block friends are fond of referring to the FE as "second-generation Y-blocks." So, having two friends with so much experience with this engine family has been a great help. As I say, "Rich and Jerry liked Y-blocks before Y-blocks were cool," and that is a good thing.

Joel Naprstek, another friend, always can be depended upon to lend his talents to my projects. He is one of America's most talented automotive artists, and I thank him for his contribution of line art.

Also deserving of recognition is Tim McMaster, who continues to put Y-block-powered vehicles in the record books decades after they were declared obsolete.

INTRODUCTION

Ford's Y-block engine series has now gained its deserved recognition and consequently has also gained a new lease on life. For a number of years, this venerable engine was maligned and largely overlooked as an antiquated V-8 with little performance potential. That is certainly not the case now. Much of that has to do with the performance aftermarket ignoring the Y-block even during its heyday in the mid-1950s. Although the engine family has always had its share of loyal devotees, most agree that those who loved the Y-block were far more likely to be the restorers of classic Thunderbirds and other 1950s Fords than the segment of the automotive hobby known as "hot rodders."

Looking back through the decades that have passed since a version of the Y-block V-8 carried the banner for Ford performance (in a time when performance related directly to sales figures), one is sometimes hard-pressed to find an accurate, or unbiased, accounting of just how well Fords powered by this engine series performed. Granted, some things adversely affected the engine's reputation, such as lubrication problems, but these had more to do with available products and lack of proper maintenance than the design itself.

The time has come to set the record straight and to provide a complete and thorough guide for rebuilding these excellent engines. After all, I want to keep as many examples of this fine engine motoring down the highways of America as possible. In this book, I provide a step-by-step rebuild of a stock 292. In doing so, you learn the features of this particular engine series. In addition, through the use of a combination of modern parts and techniques, you learn how to perform a rebuild of a Y-block V-8 engine that is both strong and reliable.

Rather than simply rebuilding a stock engine and making references to performance modifications along the way, I feature a second engine. It was rebuilt using the latest performance parts and technology that were developed specifically for this engine series. This engine is a 322-ci, supercharged Y-block that is based on a 1957 vintage 292-cylinder block.

I have a cadre of longtime, diehard Y-block drag racers, one of whom is my friend Jerry Christenson, as well as the "traditional hot rod" movement to thank for the development of modern performance parts. These hot rodders have stood behind this engine platform and have helped

Ford's 239-ci OHV Y-block V-8, first offered in 1954, produced 130 hp with a 2-barrel carburetor. They may not look modern by today's standards, but the first Y-blocks were a major step forward for the company compared to the flathead engines they replaced.

INTRODUCTION

to resurrect it. This engine series was shunned for many years but was the mainstay of the performance industry and is now capable of delivering astounding amounts of horsepower. It also does so more reliably than other engines that have been revered in the performance world for years.

With the introduction of the first mass-produced V-8 engine in 1932, Ford Motor Company launched a new era in American automobile production. Ford's legendary valve-in-block flathead V-8 proved itself to be strong, reliable, and most important, inexpensive to produce. With millions of the venerable V-8 produced from 1932 to 1953, to merely refer to the flathead as a successful engine series is an injustice. Not only did the flathead, in various forms, power multitudes of passenger cars, trucks, and even military vehicles, it left a legacy of performance everywhere, from the Indianapolis Motor Speedway to the back roads and abandoned airstrips of America, where the fledgling hot rod hobby was born. Well into the third decade after its introduction, Henry's flathead V-8 still powered hot rods and race cars. By 1948, Ford's management recognized the need to develop a new engine series to replace the flathead in order to keep pace with the competition.

In 1945 Henry Ford II was named company president and embarked on a mission to restructure and modernize the company. Ford tapped Harold Youngren, vice president of engine design, along with talent recruited from throughout the auto industry, to lead Ford into the future. Victor Raviolo, Robert Stevenson, Allen Cleveland, and Paul Clayton were tasked with the development of a new engine family. This engine platform included 8- and 6-cylinder engines using an overhead-valve (OHV) design.

Ford launched the first examples of its new OHV engines in 1952 with the introduction of a 215-ci in-line 6 and a 317-ci V-8 that was destined for the Lincoln. There was a Y-block version for Lincoln but this engine was substantially different than the Ford Y-block. It was cast and machined to accommodate hydraulic valve lifters. In addition, the cylinder heads used a conventional vertical port arrangement, which differed from the 1954 and up versions of the engine family.

Ford still intended to remain the leader of the first of the "low-priced three": Ford, Chevrolet, and Plymouth. The new Ford Y-block was intended to keep Ford in front of the pack. Victor Raviolo and his team forged ahead to develop an OHV V-8 engine that met the performance and design requirements for the Ford and Mercury lines. Ford's engineering goals for the new engine series were to build an engine that matched its predecessor in height, width, length, weight, and cubic-inch displacement. In addition, the cast cylinder block design provided maximum strength and allowed for later increases in displacement and compression. It featured a short-stroke rotating assembly, and, unlike the flathead, an OHV arrangement. Finally, the simplicity of design reduced manufacturing costs.

Before its 1954 introduction, Ford built and tested 200 experimental Y-block versions of the engine, and these test engines proved to be strong and reliable during the

From 1954 to 1958, Ford Y-block engines were equipped with some artistic valve cover logos that identified the engine. The valve covers on the 1959 to 1962 engine series were not adorned with these decals.

INTRODUCTION

50,000 hours on the dynamometer. The new engine series became known as the Y-block, because it had a new deep-block design, and was Y-shaped when viewed from the front. The dyno and highway tests totaled more than 700,000 miles.

In keeping with design goals, the new engine displaced 239 ci (the same as the 1953 Ford flathead) with a bore of 3.50 inches and a 3.10-inch stroke. With a 2-barrel carburetor and 7.2:1 compression, the new engine developed 130 hp, eclipsing its predecessor's 110. The 256-ci version of the engine, used to power the Mercury line, pumped out 161 hp and was fed by a 4-barrel carburetor.

Ford's plan for the new engine family was referred to as "High Futurity," which translates to 10 years of progressive increases in output. Output, in this case, referred to higher compression ratios, cubic-inch displacements, horsepower, and torque.

For 1955, Ford increased the cubic inches to 272, with the 292 available in Thunderbird and Mercury cars. The 312-ci Y-block was introduced in 1956; it powered all Mercurys, and, along with the 272 and 292, was offered in the Ford line. In 1957 the 272-, 292-, and 312-ci versions of the Y-block were offered across the Ford line, while the Mercury family depended entirely on the 312.

As it turned out, the High Futurity plan for the Y-block only remained until 1957, and, by that year, the engine family reached its pinnacle of development. By 1958, the 272 was gone from the option list and the 292 was the only Y-block available in Ford cars. The Mercury received the 312 and the Thunderbird received the new 352-ci FE series engine. The 1959 and 1960 Y-block offerings for Ford and Mercury were a repeat of 1958.

Although the 292 Y-block soldiered on in Fords until 1962 and the 312 in Mercury passenger cars until 1960, further development had virtually ceased by 1958, when it was relegated to second-fiddle status by the introduction of the FE engine family.

WHAT IS A WORKBENCH® BOOK?

This Workbench® Series book is the only book of its kind on the market. No other book offers the same combination of detailed hands-on information and revealing color photographs to illustrate engine rebuilding and modifying. Rest assured, you have purchased an indispensable companion that will expertly guide you, one step at a time, through each important stage of the rebuilding process. This book is packed with real-world techniques and practical tips for expertly performing rebuild procedures, not vague instructions or unnecessary processes. At-home mechanics or enthusiast builders strive for professional results, and the instruction in our Workbench® Series books help you realize pro-caliber results. Hundreds of photos guide you through the entire process from start to finish, with informative captions containing comprehensive instructions for every step of the process.

The step-by-step photo procedures also contain many additional photos that show how to install high-performance components, modify stock components for special applications, or even call attention to assembly steps that are critical to proper operation or safety. These are labeled with unique icons. These symbols represent an idea, and photos marked with the icons contain important, specialized information.

Here are some of the icons found in Workbench® books:

Important!
Calls special attention to a step or procedure, so that the procedure is correctly performed. This prevents damage to a vehicle, system, or component.

Save Money
Illustrates a method or alternate method of performing a rebuild step that will save money but still give acceptable results.

Torque Fasteners
Illustrates a fastener that must be properly tightened with a torque wrench at this point in the rebuild. The torque specs are usually provided in the step.

Special Tool
Illustrates the use of a special tool that may be required or can make the job easier (caption with photo explains further).

Performance Tip
Indicates a procedure or modification that can improve performance. The step most often applies to high-performance or racing engines.

Critical Inspection
Indicates that a component must be inspected to ensure proper operation of the engine.

Precision Measurement
Illustrates a precision measurement or adjustment that is required at this point in the rebuild.

Professional Mechanic Tip
Illustrates a step in the rebuild that non-professionals may not know. It may illustrate a shortcut or a trick to improve reliability, prevent component damage, etc.

Documentation Required
Illustrates a point in the rebuild where the reader should write down a particular measurement, size, part number, etc. for later reference or photograph a part, area, or system of the vehicle for future reference.

Tech Tip
Tech Tips provide brief coverage of important subject matter that doesn't naturally fall into the text or step-by-step procedures of a chapter. Tech Tips contain valuable hints, important info, or outstanding products that professionals have discovered after years of work. These will add to your understanding of the process, and help you get the most power, economy, and reliability from your engine.

CHAPTER 1

ENGINE EVALUATION

A number of factors are involved in deciding if your stock engine needs to be rebuilt. In this chapter I list common symptoms associated with a worn-out engine and some simple diagnostic steps to make an informed decision. A thorough inspection (particularly leak-down and compression tests) of your engine will help you determine its state of health and whether or not you need to rebuild it.

High Mileage

Today, many newer engines have 100,000 or more miles but it is highly unlikely to find a Y-block Ford V-8 with 100,000 miles or more. This has less to do with the overall design and strength of the engine series than it does the maintenance practices, materials, and systems used in engines designed in the 1950s. Quite simply, the advances in design, materials, manufacturing techniques, fuel delivery, and ignition systems found in today's engines far overshadow anything even dreamed of as little as two decades ago let alone the 1950s. These advances include digital ignition, electronic fuel injection, engine management computers, and a myriad of sensors to monitor every aspect of engine performance. Although Y-block-powered vehicles are collectible and desirable today, in the 1950s and 1960s, they were used primarily as daily transportation for families and not seen as treasures in need of long-term preservation.

Excessive Oil Consumption

A car with high-mileage and/or a poorly maintained Y-block uses oil and requires a rebuild. As a general rule, if your engine uses a quart of oil for every 1,000 miles or less, it is consuming an excessive amount.

This Y-block has had a long service life. It needs to be thoroughly inspected and evaluated to determine whether a rebuild is necessary. You should perform leak-down and compression tests to verify the basic health of the engine. Some Y-blocks may have excellent valve sealing and piston ring sealing, which means that a complete rebuild is not required.

CHAPTER 1

Take note that I'm referring to an engine that "uses" oil, as opposed to "burning" it. You need to determine the root cause of the problem, rather than assuming your engine is burning oil.

Carefully and methodically examine the block, heads, intake, and all parts of the engine for oil leaks. A leaking rear main seal, valley pan gasket, or valve cover gasket that leaves a few drops of oil on your driveway can contribute greatly to oil consumption because engine leaking is constant and often much greater when the engine is running.

For example, I recently noticed drops of oil under the draft tube in my engine so I looked into it. With the engine running, it appeared that the oil was leaking directly from the road draft tube itself, which seemed highly unlikely because it was a recently rebuilt engine. Closer examination revealed two fasteners had not been correctly tightened. In fact, the two heavy-duty Phillips-head screws that secure the road draft tube to the side of the block had somehow worked loose. A little thread sealer and aggressive tightening resolved the problem and soon the underside of the engine was dry. The 312-ci engine uses the old-style rope rear main seal only; the engine has a greater chance of leaks with this type of seal.

Internal oil loss may be the result of worn or cracked valvestem seals or guides, problems that are correctable without having to completely rebuild the engine. All engines have lubrication issues because of the clearance between the stems of the valves and their guides. Over time the clearance increases and oil is allowed to pass down the valvestem and into the combustion chamber where it is burned off. Likewise, the rubber seals on the valvestems typically become brittle and crack over time so oil is allowed to flow past the valveguides. You don't have to remove the heads to replace the valvestem seals, and this may greatly reduce internal oil consumption.

There are two ways to replace the valvestem seals without removing the heads. First, you can move the piston to top dead center (TDC) and stuff rope down the plug hole to keep the valve from dropping while you use a lever-type compressor to free the valvespring. Second, you can use compressed air applied through a fitting in the spark plug hole to pressurize the cylinder, and then use a lever-type compressor to free the valvespring.

A puff of blue smoke from the exhaust pipe immediately after engine start-up is a common indicator that an engine has worn valve seals. A cracked fuel pump diaphragm is another cause of internal oil loss. When this occurs, the fuel pump's internal vacuum sucks oil from the crankcase into the fuel stream of the carburetor, and this produces continuous blue smoke from the exhaust. Some owners may be alarmed and think that the engine has suffered a catastrophic internal failure because of the blue smoke. That is not the case unless the smoke is accompanied by the ominous sounds related to internal parts failure.

Low Oil Pressure

A drop in engine oil pressure may be caused by wear to rod bearings, wear to main bearings, a bad oil pump, or any combination of these. Sadly, during the era of the Y-block Ford V-8, some great mind in the auto industry decided to unburden the motoring public from the responsibility of having to read a gauge that actually displays engine oil pressure. A warning light replaced the time-honored gauge, and this light was electromechanically activated when engine oil pressure dropped below a preset limit. This warning light quickly became known as an "idiot light," and my firm belief is that the term was derived from someone possessing at least a modicum of knowledge on how to properly monitor and maintain the average internal combustion engine. You must wonder how many engines expired over the years as a result of uninformed motorists believing in the powers of that magic light.

The following is from the 1956 Ford car shop manual as it relates to the oil pressure indicator light: "As the engine comes up to speed, the oil pressure increases, and after the pressure has risen to a *safe value*, the oil pressure activated

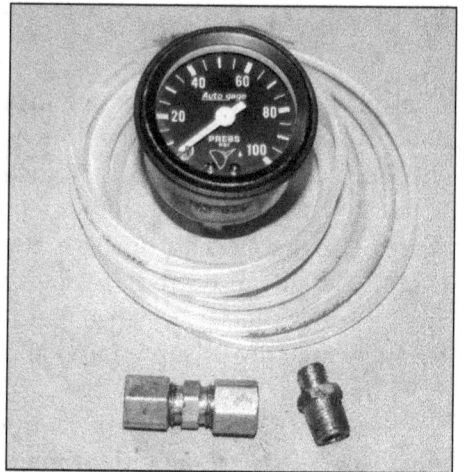

I keep an inexpensive aftermarket oil pressure gauge and an assortment of adapter fittings in my toolbox. This simple gauge has served me well over the years when working with cars that were not equipped with such a gauge from the factory or to diagnose a faulty factory gauge or sending unit.

10   FORD Y-BLOCK ENGINES: HOW TO REBUILD AND MODIFY

ENGINE EVALUATION

switch opens up, allowing the light to go out. As long as oil pressure is maintained, the indicator light remains out. If at any time the oil pressure in the system drops below *about 7 pounds*, the switch closes, and the light comes on." I don't know about you, but this does little to instill confidence that my engine is being properly monitored in this critical area.

Of course, if you come from a hot rod background, you installed an aftermarket oil pressure and water temperature gauge almost immediately after buying your car. On many occasions the first indication that a Ford V-8 engine was losing oil pressure was the clattering caused by the hydraulic valve lifters as they began to collapse. If you drove Fords powered by the Y-block V-8, which had no provisions for hydraulic valve lifters, the first indicative sounds of low oil pressure were often far more ominous because catastrophic damage to the engine had already occurred.

Use one of these specially designed sockets to remove the engine oil pressure switch. Craftsman, for example, has them in several sizes to fit different switches. Removing the switch by using locking pliers such as Vise-Grips or simple pliers may damage it.

If you are restoring a car to exacting standards, I recommend installing a full-time dedicated electric or mechanical oil pressure gauge under the dash. I keep an inexpensive aftermarket version and an assortment of adapter fittings in my toolbox so I can diagnose oil pressure problems on vehicles with idiot lights.

All I need to do is remove the oil pressure sender, which is located on the driver's side of the cylinder block just to the rear of the oil filter. I install the necessary adapter fittings in place of the oil pressure light switch and connect the mechanical gauge in order to take accurate oil pressure readings. Readings should be taken when the engine is cold, and then again, when it has reached normal operating temperature. With the engine at normal operating temperature, pressure readings of more than 20 psi at idle are adequate. You should see an immediate increase in pressure with no fluctuation as engine RPM increase.

If your engine has low oil-pressure readings, a number of things may be the cause, such as dirty oil with decreased viscosity or a clogged filter or passage in the engine's lubrication system. This is common in Y-block engines. More critical indications include excessive main or connecting rod bearing clearance. Although it isn't a common failure, the oil pump or the drive that runs off the distributor may also be at fault. I make it a practice to replace the oil pump driveshaft with a heavy-duty replacement and carefully check the oil pump's internal rotors for indications of wear or excessive clearance whenever I rebuild an engine. The dollars spent in this area reap dividends in engine life for years to come.

Decrease in Performance

If your engine has experienced a decrease in fuel economy and engine performance, it does not necessarily mean it is worn out and is in need of a rebuild. Many factors can contribute to a loss of power and fuel economy, some of which do not relate directly to the condition of the engine. You need to thoroughly and methodically inspect, test, and evaluate each major system of the engine. Once you've inspected each of them, you should conduct a compression and leak-down test to verify the current state of your engine. A clogged or restricted exhaust system could be the cause. Ascertain whether the exhaust manifold heat riser is free and not stuck in the closed position. Visually examine the exhaust pipe, and verify that it is not kinked or collapsed. An old, dirty, and clogged fuel filter, air filter, carburetor, or automatic choke restricts air and fuel flow to the engine. This produces changes to the air/fuel mixture and causes a loss of power and fuel mileage.

If your Y-block Ford or Mercury is a 1954–1956 model, remember that the oil in your oil bath air cleaner needs to be changed at fairly frequent intervals. Ford recommended changing the air cleaner oil every 2,000 miles.

In addition, if your fuel tank and lines are original, your classic Ford or Mercury may be suffering from five decades of rust, dirt, and corrosion. If this is the case, these parts desperately need to be replaced. In addition, the ethanol-based fuels we are forced to use have proven to be corrosive and destructive to older automotive fuel systems. I have found rubber fuel lines deteriorated from the inside while still appearing outwardly fine. Modern fuels have also destroyed Viton-tipped carburetor needles.

A worn-out or incorrectly adjusted clutch or a malfunctioning automatic transmission can slip and be responsible for decreases in power and fuel mileage.

The ignition system can also cause decreased performance and fuel mileage. If your engine is still equipped with its original breaker points style of ignition system, breaker points gap, a bad condenser, faulty plug wires, or a dirty or cracked rotor or distributor cap can substantially degrade performance. These symptoms can also mimic other more serious problems. Something as simple as a disconnected or broken vacuum hose leading from the carburetor to the distributor's advance unit can lead you to believe your engine is on its last legs.

Timing chain and gear damage or wear can also decrease performance. A stretched timing chain and worn timing gears cause a change in the valve timing. If the chain has been severely stretched the engine no longer runs.

Damaged or burned intake or exhaust valves, a buildup of carbon deposits in the combustion chamber, weak valvesprings, and excessive camshaft lobe wear adversely affect engine performance. Solid valve lifters are installed in all Y-block engines, and the valve system reacts to changes in adjustment, or lash, of thousandths of an inch. In extreme cases, incorrect valve lash adjustment causes damage to related valvetrain parts.

A blown or leaking head gasket is a common engine problem that manifests itself through an immediate loss of power. Although this is considered a serious engine problem when detected, the engine should not need a complete overhaul if repaired in a timely fashion. The factory equipped all Ford Y-block V-8 engines with steel-shim head gaskets. Corrosives in the cooling system can take their toll on them over the years. It is prudent to replace the original-style gaskets with modern composite gaskets when rebuilding your engine.

Safety First!

My motto is: Safety first, here, now, and always. Working around the moving parts of a running engine can be dangerous, and you need to take all precautions to protect yourself and prevent accidents. If you are absorbed in the task of diagnosing a problem or tuning the engine, it is easy to become distracted and get hurt.

Before starting the engine perform a walk around, as the pilot of an aircraft does before takeoff. You should identify anything that could potentially contact the moving parts of your engine, particularly the fan, belts, and related accessories. Pay particular attention to your clothing, and avoid wearing loose-fitting clothes or jewelry that might become entangled in moving parts and cause injury. Wear safety glasses or goggles to protect your eyes against flying debris or liquids.

Do not start the engine until you are satisfied that it is safe to do so and remain vigilant and aware at all times while the engine is running. It is always a good idea to set the parking brake and chock the wheels of a car that is running when no one is behind the wheel. ∎

Before working in or around your car, make sure to chock the wheels and set the parking brake. A few simple precautions taken before beginning work may prevent injury to you and damage to expensive equipment.

A fully charged and easily accessible fire extinguisher is the most important tool in your home garage.

ENGINE EVALUATION

A marked decrease in engine performance may be related to something as simple as a dirty or stuck automatic choke. Ensuring that the choke is functioning properly is one of the simplest diagnostic tests and requires no specialized tools.

Noises

Your engine is full of moving parts, and all of them have the potential to make noises that signal a problem. Due to the harmonics involved, engine noises can be very difficult to pinpoint. You should first determine if the noise is at engine speed or at half engine speed. As a general rule, noises that are at lower engine speeds usually emanate from the valvetrain with the exception of fuel pump noises and a condition called piston slap. Noises at higher engine speeds normally indicate a problem in the bottom end, or crankshaft area, of the engine.

Using an ignition timing light is an easy way to determine the engine speed when the noise occurs. Connect the timing light to a spark plug wire and start the engine. If you hear the noise once for each time the light flashes, the noise is at half throttle. If the noise occurs twice for each flash of the light, it indicates that the noise is at full throttle. Once the engine speed has been determined, you can set about locating the noise. The cylinder block can harmonically transmit internal noises, so it may be difficult to locate the source without some type of listening device. A mechanic's stethoscope is often used to pinpoint engine noises, but if you don't have one, a length of plastic tubing or a long screwdriver can get the job done quite well.

As a teenager I learned the value of using a screwdriver to locate the source of engine noises. A mechanic had diagnosed a noise in the engine of a friend's 1956 Ford as emanating from a faulty piston wrist pin. Luckily for us, a local hot rodder had schooled me in the technique. He placed the end of a long screwdriver against the engine while touching the handle end to his ear in order to pinpoint internal noises. He recommended using a screwdriver with a wooden handle, and I keep one in my toolbox to this day.

In that particular case, the fuel pump eccentric was the source of the noise and not the more serious wrist pin as originally diagnosed. The technique is to move whatever you are using as your probe (screwdriver, length of plastic tube, or stethoscope) from place to place until the source of the sound is located.

If the noise is coming from a particular cylinder, the piston and connecting rod assembly could be causing it. Place the tip of your probe next to each spark plug to locate and isolate it. If the noise is coming from the top of the engine, the valvetrain or related parts are most likely the cause. Remove the valve cover and visually inspect the valvetrain to pinpoint the problem. Do this while the engine is shut off and while it is operating. With the engine turned off check for signs of a bent pushrod or broken valvespring. With the engine running, ascertain that the pushrods are all spinning and check for a rocker arm that may not be opening its valve as far as the others. Should either be the case, you may have an excessively worn camshaft lobe(s).

During the years they were in production, the Y-block Ford engines suffered from an oiling problem. Copious amounts of sludge are often discovered under the valve covers. When this condition exists, chances are the lack of proper lubrication has caused damage, scoring rocker arm shafts and rockers.

I recall hearing rocker arms on a Y-block making a sound when running that was akin to a rusty gate hinge. It was times

Automotive stethoscopes allow you to isolate and identify internal engine noises that cannot be easily pinpointed because of harmonics. The Lisle tool company offers easy-to-use stethoscopes; they are available at Napa Auto Parts stores.

CHAPTER 1

Over the years the dreaded sludge buildup has led to the demise of many Y-block engines. Sludge buildup in the road draft tube and filter of an engine prevent the engine's crankcase from properly venting noxious gasses and moisture, which can lead to serious problems.

One of the engineering shortcomings of the Y-block V-8 that contributes to the accumulation of sludge is this lip under the valve covers. This problem can be corrected by removing these lips, which are spot welded in place. You still maintain your engine's original look. Eastwood offers a special bit for a hand drill, which effectively removes the spot welds. Aftermarket valve covers do not have this lip.

These passages in the cylinder heads are clogged with sludge. They are the only way for the Y-block to deliver vital oil to the top end of the engine. Once they have become blocked, failure of valvetrain parts is soon to follow.

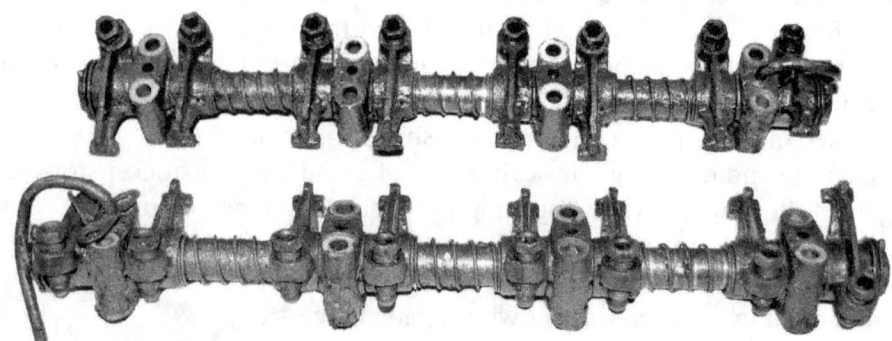

Sludge accumulation on rocker arm assemblies is very common. It causes oil starvation to moving parts and their ultimate failure.

Delving a little deeper into an engine that fell victim to sludge buildup reveals a deadly accumulation in the lifter valley. Such accumulations of sludge affect the engine's ability to lubricate moving parts and dissipate internal heat.

like this that "old school" mechanics installed a top oiler, also referred to as a Tennessee Oiler kit. Mechanics tapped into the side of the blocks to install them. These commercially produced Rube Goldberg–type contraptions diverted oil around the clogged internal passages and remedied the problem. A copper tube was plumbed into the valve cover where it routed the oil. If you come across a Y-block with one of these devices, chances are it is in serious need of a rebuild.

Piston Slap

Excessive clearance from the piston to the cylinder wall causes piston slap, which manifests itself as a hollow noise that's most prominent when the engine is cold and under a load. Piston slap causes wear due to poor lubrication or high mileage or, in extreme cases, a collapsed or broken piston skirt.

ENGINE EVALUATION

If the sound goes away soon after the engine warms up, it is an indication that the condition is not severe. The Y-block came equipped with cast-aluminum pistons, but if forged-aluminum pistons have been installed, they are more prone to slap until the engine has warmed up. This is due to the increased piston-to-wall clearance required when using forged pistons because of their rate of expansion. An easy method of determining if the noise is piston slap is to retard the ignition timing a few degrees while the engine is running.

Remember that Ford distributors have a counterclockwise rotation so slowly turning the distributor in a counterclockwise direction retards the timing. By retarding the timing, you are reducing the load on the pistons caused by combustion. If piston slap is the culprit the noise should diminish.

Wrist Pin Noise

Wrist pin noise is most prominent at idle or low speed and manifests itself with multiple knocking sounds that are quite distinct. If your engine has developed wrist pin noise, the bushing at the small end of the connecting rod may be failing, or the pin, which is retained by lock rings, may have come loose from the piston.

Bearing Noise

Engine bearings with excessive clearance or wear cause a knocking sound, and it is most pronounced when the engine is first started, either hot or cold, before a sufficient level of oil pressure has been reached. Bearing noises also manifest themselves under hard acceleration, but should not be confused with detonation, a condition that produces more of a rattling sound. Main bearings knock at half engine speed with the somewhat muffled sound coming from deep within the cylinder block.

Connecting rod bearings also knock when clearances are excessive or if there is insufficient oil pressure. A connecting rod bearing knock is most prominent upon deceleration after the engine has been run at a constant speed for a while.

Piston rings that are broken, or have lost the tension required to hold them tight against the cylinder wall, create a chattering sound that is most noticeable under acceleration. The easiest way to diagnose a piston ring problem is to conduct a compression check on the engine.

Diagnostic Tools and Techniques

Now that I have covered some of the problems that your engine may be experiencing, it's time to diagnose the overall condition of the engine and describe the tools used to pinpoint potential problems. Using this information you should be able to confidently assess the need for a rebuild.

Here is a good tip: Start simple and perform a comprehensive visual examination of the engine. Don't overlook the obvious. Some of your engine's simplest parts reveal information that speaks volumes about what has been taking place under the hood.

Spark Plug Inspection

Spark plugs are the window to what is occurring in each of the engine's cylinders, so it's smart to keep them in order as removed to assist in isolating potential problem areas. First, check that the proper heat range spark plugs for your application are in the engine. Something as simple as incorrect spark plugs can adversely affect performance and fuel economy. Once you verify that your engine is fitted with the correct spark plugs, i.e., the proper heat range for your application, conduct a visual inspection of each spark plug. There are several things to look for.

A wet, black insulator indicates excessive amounts of oil in the combustion chamber or a plug is not firing and has been fouled by fuel. You can ascertain the latter by conducting a sniff test to determine the presence of raw gasoline.

Bubbling or blistering of the insulator is an indication of excessive heat in the combustion chamber and is usually attributed to an overly lean fuel mixture.

If the plugs show a dry black or dark gray coating, the fuel mixture may be too rich, or there could be a problem with the ignition.

A serious problem such as a blown head gasket may also exist if two spark plugs from adjacent cylinders show a white foamy deposit while the other plugs in the engine are burning clean. A properly burning spark plug shows a uniform, light brown color across the ceramic insulator.

Ignition Timing Check

I have made many references to ignition timing, such as setting your engine to TDC and rotating 90 degrees in a clockwise direction. Here's how to take these readings on an engine. The Y-block Ford V-8 engine series timing increments are machined into the face of the vibration dampener. You read them from the passenger's side of the engine when they align with a pointer affixed to the timing cover.

CHAPTER 1

A timing light is essential for properly tuning most engines. It can also be used to diagnose problems with distributor advance. I have been using the same Craftsman timing light since the early 1970s.

This specialized distributor wrench allows access to the bolt that secures the hold-down clamp on the distributor. On engines such as the Y-block with a rear-mounted distributor, this tool is a time-saver. Summit Racing offers these specialized wrenches through their catalog.

Clean the Dampener

Use a good cleaning solvent to clean the dampener so the marked increments are easier to read. You need to remove years of dirt and grime from the outside circumference of the dampener. You may find that it is easier to access the dampener from under the car (on the Y-block series engines you still have to deal with the front motor mount bracket, so it can be a little challenging) and necessary to turn the engine over in order to clean the entire surface of the dampener.

You can disable the ignition and use a remote switch to activate the starter and turn over the engine. However, I often attach a socket and breaker bar to the crankshaft bolt and turn over the engine manually so I have more control of where the dampener stops in its rotation. If you choose to turn the engine manually, remove the spark plugs so you are not fighting compression.

After you clean the dampener, the timing marks should be clearly visible. (You can use two different colors so they are easier to distinguish later.) TDC is marked on the dampener as TDC or the numeral zero. Refer to the TDC chart (and the timing increments marked as 2-4-6-8-10) on page 135.

You can highlight the TDC line using a colored chalk marker. Automotive touch-up paint also shows up well and does not wear off easily.

Next, use a straightedge to divide the dampener into sections 90 degrees apart and place a short paint mark at each point. This makes it easy to move the engine through its rotation 90 degrees at a time.

The final step is to mark the timing increment that corresponds with the manufacturer's specifications for your particular year, model, and engine. For this step you may want to use a white marker or paint so that it contrasts with the TDC and 90-degree markings and causes no confusion.

With the vibration dampener clearly marked, you are now ready to check ignition timing, verify TDC, and make accurate 90-degree rotations of the crankshaft.

Check the Breaker Points

The stock ignition system on your Y-block and other V-8s of the era is a breaker-points system. You must first check breaker point gap/dwell angle before checking the timing. Often the gap on the points is too small, or close. This is often caused by normal wear on the rubbing block, which contacts the distributor cam, retarding ignition timing.

Use a dwell angle meter or simple feeler gauge to set the gap/dwell angle. If your engine has been upgraded to an electronic system (such as PerTronix Igniter or MSD), disregard the previous step.

With the points set, you are ready to check timing.

Use a Timing Light

Attach the timing light to the number-1 spark plug lead. In a Ford engine, the number-1 cylinder is located closest to the grille and farthest from the firewall on the passenger's side of the engine.

Disconnect and plug the vacuum advance hose from the distributor. Loosen the hold-down clamp at the base of the distributor, and then make a thorough check to ensure that nothing is too near any moving parts before starting the engine. With the engine running at normal idle speed, trigger the timing light

ENGINE EVALUATION

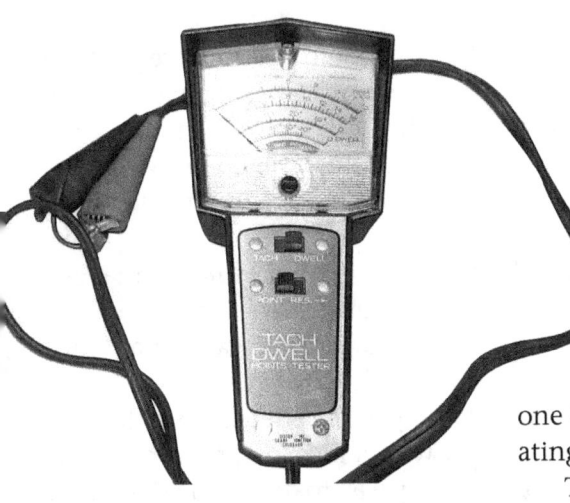

A dwell meter is also referred to as a dwell tachometer because it has a tachometer feature. It is essential for properly tuning any engine that has a points-style ignition system. With the advent of electronic ignition systems in American automobiles in the early 1970s, dwell tachometers were no longer required for engine tuning and have become scarce. Actron offers a dwell/tach/volt analyzer (PN CP7605).

to initiate the flash and aim it at the timing pointer.

The strobe effect of the light causes a stop-action view of the vibration dampener as it rotates, allowing you to see the relationship between the timing increments on the dampener and the pointer. Rotate the distributor slightly until they are aligned.

Carefully tighten the distributor hold-down clamp, and recheck the timing to make sure it has not moved. Now reattach the vacuum advance hose to the distributor, and activate the timing light again.

You should see the timing advance slightly on the dampener. If there is no advance, there may be a problem with the distributor's vacuum advance or low engine vacuum, which results in a loss of power and fuel economy.

Vacuum Test

A simple vacuum gauge is a valuable diagnostic tool and can reveal a number of mechanical problems from minor to major. When an engine is running it creates vacuum in the intake manifold. A vacuum test reveals any time one or more cylinders are not operating at peak power.

To check engine vacuum, connect the gauge to a port on the intake manifold, or carburetor, and start the engine. The vacuum reading should be 16 to 18 degrees of mercury at idle. Keep in mind that vacuum readings are lower at higher altitudes; they are also lower if a camshaft with a more radical profile (more overlap) than stock is installed.

A low initial vacuum reading may be indicative of nothing more serious than incorrect ignition timing, so get out that timing light and check, and/or adjust timing as needed. If you are getting slow fluctuations on the vacuum gauge, it may indicate a fuel mixture that is too rich. Try increasing the idle speed or turning the idle mixture screws on the carburetor in to correct the problem. If the gauge shows a consistently low vacuum reading, the engine could have a blown intake or cylinder head gasket that requires further diagnostic work.

With a vacuum gauge hooked up, revving the engine should produce a drop in vacuum with a steady reading on the gauge. If the needle shows a fluctuation, it could indicate that valvesprings are weak.

Cranking Vacuum Test

With the engine at normal operating temperature, you can perform

A vacuum gauge reveals engine problems. It is most useful for fine-tuning early carbureted engines. Summit offers a vacuum test gauge that may also be used to check fuel pump function.

cranking vacuum tests. First disable the ignition so that the engine doesn't start, and then crank the engine with the assistance of a helper or remote starter. The reading on your vacuum gauge should remain steady. A fluctuation of the needle indicates a problem in one or more of the cylinders. In this case, the problem could be as simple as valve adjustment in an engine with mechanical valve lifters or a collapsed lifter in those equipped with hydraulic lifters.

Note: All Y-block V-8 engines use mechanical valve lifters. It could also indicate a wiped camshaft lobe, leaking valves, worn piston rings, a damaged piston, or blown head gasket. A damaged camshaft lobe(s) sends a hollow popping sound through the carburetor under load.

Power Balance Test

You can pinpoint a problem cylinder(s) by checking the power balance between them. Most engine analyzers have the capability of conducting a power balance test, but few of us own such expensive pieces of equipment. Fortunately, there is an alternative means for analyzing power balance. A pad, pencil or pen, and tachometer (a dwell tachometer suffices) are the only tools needed for this test on a breaker-points ignition system.

Start the engine and increase throttle until 1,000 rpm is reached. Use a pair of insulated-handle pliers to remove the spark plug caps one at a time and disable the cylinders. Be careful not to contact the live ends of the plug wires as they continue to carry current even when disconnected. Note the RPM drop, and then reconnect the plug wire. Repeat this process until you have disabled each cylinder and noted the RPM on each.

A healthy or properly operating cylinder creates a greater RPM drop when the spark plug wire is removed. When a cylinder is down on power, it contributes less to engine power. Thus, any cylinder that is down on power reveals itself by a smaller decrease in RPM.

This method should only be used to disable cylinders on engines that have conventional points-type ignition systems. Disconnecting a plug wire in a vehicle equipped with electronic ignition may cause a power surge that can damage the ignition. There are commercially available test kits that allow you to disable those cylinders by shorting out the plug wire without risking a power surge.

Compression Check

A compression test is the simplest and least expensive means of determining how well a cylinder is sealing. Be certain that the engine has reached its normal operating temperature before checking compression. For this test you need paper, pen or pencil, and a compression gauge. Be aware that when you are conducting a compression check, a combustible mixture of air and fuel is blowing out of the cylinders under pressure, and any spark or flame can result in an explosion. Make sure your work area is well ventilated and free of any ignition sources.

Disable the ignition, remove the spark plugs, and block the throttle in the open position, then install the compression gauge in the cylinder to be tested. Using a remote starter, or an assistant, crank the engine a minimum of three complete revolutions and note the highest reading on the gauge. Repeat this process until all the cylinders have been checked and the readings recorded.

The maximum reading for this test is not as important as the percentage of difference between the readings for each cylinder. All cylinders should read above 100 psi, with 160 to 165 psi being the norm for the Y-block V-8 engine series. Each reading should be within 75 percent of the highest, while 90 percent or better is optimum. If you find two adjacent cylinders that read considerably lower than the rest, chances are a head gasket has blown between the two cylinders.

If you experience a single cylinder with a low compression reading, an easy way to determine if the cause is related to the piston ring or valve is to squirt approximately a teaspoon of oil into the cylinder via the spark plug hole and repeat the test.

If the pressure reading increases, the piston rings are not seating to the cylinder wall. If there is no change, it is likely that a valve is not seating properly, or you have a blown head gasket.

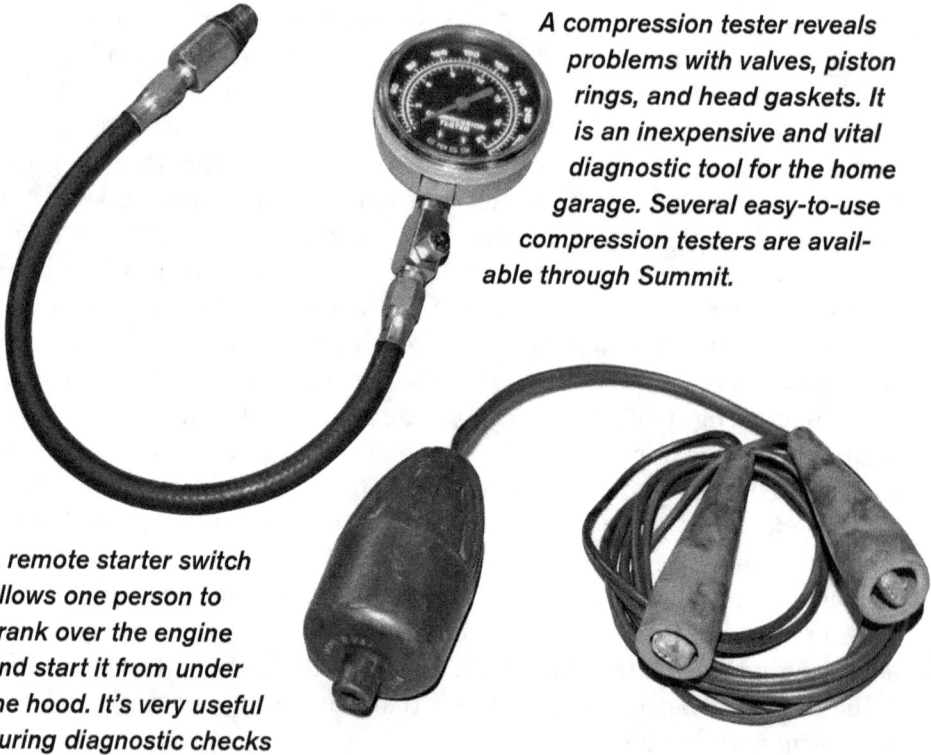

A compression tester reveals problems with valves, piston rings, and head gaskets. It is an inexpensive and vital diagnostic tool for the home garage. Several easy-to-use compression testers are available through Summit.

A remote starter switch allows one person to crank over the engine and start it from under the hood. It's very useful during diagnostic checks and setting the engine on TDC for timing purposes. Actron tools, available at Pep Boys and other auto parts stores, manufactures a sturdy simple-to-use remote starter switch.

ENGINE EVALUATION

You can perform a compression check on the cylinders after removing the coil wire and thus disable the ignition. Remove the spark plugs from the engine and thread the compression tester fitting into the spark plug opening of the cylinder being tested. Crank the engine through several revolutions to obtain a reading on the gauge. Make notations of the readings for each cylinder, and when the test has been completed, check your results against manufacturer specifications. Pay attention and look for any wide variations in readings between cylinders. This simple test can reveal and isolate a variety of engine problems. Specifications usually call for the compression readings to be taken when the engine is at operating temperature.

Leak-Down Test

A leak-down test is a more sophisticated means of checking how a cylinder is sealing than a compression test. It uses an external pressure source to test the rate at which a cylinder loses pressure. Because a leak-down leak tester is a more sophisticated tool, there aren't many in home shops, but you can perform this test at home by using an air tank and spark plug hole adapter (with the exception of reading the actual percentage of leak down).

To perform a leak-down test the piston of the tested cylinder must be at TDC on its compression stroke, so that both valves in the cylinder are closed. This test is easiest to perform by following the engine's firing order, so start by bringing the number-1 cylinder up to TDC on the compression stroke.

Next, disable the ignition by removing the coil wire, remove the spark plugs, and install a compression gauge in the spark plug hole.

Next, take off the radiator cap and engine breather/oil filler cap and block the throttle in the open position to assist in identifying what is leaking. If a leak is present remove the compression gauge. Fill the cylinder with compressed air using an adaptor between the hose and the spark plug hole. Caution: Keep hands away from the fan, belts, and pulleys during a leak down test, because if the

A Seized Y-Block

This is the sad tale of a Y-block left to sit. Once upon a time there was a one-owner, 1960 Starliner, powered by a 292-ci Y-block V-8 and backed up by a 3-speed overdrive transmission. The good news is that the original owner of the car stored it in a barn for many years after he had stopped driving it. The bad news is that a young man bought the car, probably with good intentions, and ended up doing nothing with it for an additional period of time.

Enter current owner Frank Pape of Burlington, New Jersey. Already the proud owner of a 1960 Sunliner, Frank immediately recognized the potential in the once-proud Starliner and purchased the dead car. He assessed the car's mechanical condition and soon discovered that the engine didn't turn over. After spraying the cylinders with penetrating oil, and allowing a reasonable soak time, the engine still didn't turn over.

Here's a tip: If after soaking the cylinders with penetrating oil, removing all the spark plugs, and attempting to turn the engine manually with a breaker bar it still doesn't turn, chances are you have a serious mechanical problem on your hands.

The fact that the car was equipped with a standard transmission left one old-school option to free up the stuck 292. Frank decided to tow the car at low speed with the transmission in second gear and pop the clutch. He hoped that the shock of the drivetrain engaging against the flywheel would force it to turn over. No such luck. The only option left at this point was to remove at least one cylinder head to see if the root of the problem was visible.

Although this engine may have been in running condition when the car was originally parked, water was now in the cylinders. This could have happened because of a blown head gasket, the carburetor being exposed to rain, or a lack of antifreeze causing the block to crack through a water jacket. Whatever the root cause of this tragedy, it is readily apparent that this car is in the market for, at the minimum, a new long-block as part of the restoration process. In this case, proper winterizing could have easily prevented the costly problem that confronted Frank.

CHAPTER 1

piston is not at TDC, introducing air pressure into the cylinder may cause the engine to turn over. The cylinder should hold pressure and not leak down at a rate of more than 5 to 10 percent. More leak down than that indicates a problem in that cylinder.

With this method, you do not have a gauge to determine percentage of leak down. You can still make a fairly accurate assessment of any leakage by performing a few simple checks.

Listen for air escaping through the breather, carburetor, oil filler, dipstick tube, exhaust pipe, or radiator. Note that a small amount of air escaping through the breather is common in worn engines.

If you hear air escaping through the carburetor, an intake valve is leaking. Air coming from the exhaust indicates an exhaust valve is at fault. To be doubly certain that neither of the valves are leaking be sure that the cylinder being checked is still at TDC on the compression stoke.

If a blown or leaking head gasket is the problem, air leaks into a cylinder adjacent to the one being tested or through the cooling system via the radiator filler neck.

Air leaks at the dipstick tube or breather are indications that the piston rings are not sealing properly against the cylinder walls.

Once you have completed the test on the number-1 cylinder and noted the results, you can proceed through the firing order: 1-5-4-8-6-3-7-2, testing each cylinder as you go by rotating the engine clockwise to the next 90-degree mark on the dampener. Verify the cylinder by removing the distributor cap, and confirm that the rotor is facing toward the position on the cap that holds the plug wire for that cylinder.

Cooling System Pressure Test

Blown or leaking head gaskets that have adjacent cooling passages in the cylinder block also show up during a cooling system pressure test. A head gasket problem reveals itself as air and/or coolant escaping into the affected cylinder. This simple diagnostic test also identifies other leaks in the cooling system.

A pressure tester is designed to perform this test. Simply install the tester in place of your radiator cap, pump up the pressure, and check for leaks.

Use a cooling system pressure tester to detect cooling system leaks; it is a good way to reveal leaking or blown head gaskets. Fit the pressure tester in place of the radiator cap, and apply pressure to the cooling system by squeezing the bulb attached to the device. With the cooling system pressurized, look for fluid leaks around the cylinder heads or any drops in pressure (as indicated on the gauge) that are indications of existing problems. If you remove the oil filler cap while conducting a cooling system pressure test you will hear air leaking internally. A hissing or gurgling sound that emanates from the oil filler neck once the cooling system has been pressurized is a strong indication of an internal leak.

Identifying a 312

How do you identify a 312 Y-block from the outside? You cannot. I am sorry to yank the rug from under your feet, but one of the unusual features of the Y-block is that its serial number cannot specifically identify it. The Ford system assigns a basic casting number to parts. All cylinder blocks, for example, are 6015.

Unfortunately, the prefix and suffix aren't any help either because they don't distinguish between a 312 and a 292 block. Ford used nine different casting numbers for the 292, and some of them are shared with the 312 block.

Here's a summary of Ford and Mercury cars that were fitted with the 312. In 1956 all Mercurys, some Thunderbirds, and some Ford cars received the engine. In 1957, all Mercurys, with the exception of those equipped with the 368, some Thunderbirds, and some Ford cars received this engine. From 1958 to 1960, only Mercurys housed the 312. Ford did not install the 312 in trucks.

So how can you be sure if a particular Y-block is actually a 312? The only way to be absolutely certain is to remove the oil pan. With the oil pan off here is what to look for: First, 312 main bearing caps are stamped ECZ, while all other Y-blocks are stamped EBU. Second, the rear flange of the 312 crankshaft has what can best be described as a button on its outside circumference (step 8 on page 62). ■

CHAPTER 2

PULLING THE ENGINE

After you have conducted a thorough inspection and evaluation of the engine, you know whether it needs to be rebuilt or not. Almost all engine analysis can be done with the engine in the chassis. At this stage, you've determined that the engine does indeed need a rebuild and must be pulled from the chassis, so proper planning and preparation is a must.

Keep in mind that you are about to jack up a vehicle weighing nearly two tons, disconnect lines carrying hazardous and potentially flammable liquids, and ultimately lift an engine that weighs more than 600 pounds. Make sure the vehicle is on a level surface. You should get some help to perform this procedure so you can safely and carefully remove the engine from the chassis. A good arrangement is to have one person spot the engine and steady it, while the other operates the engine hoist. You may jack up your car during the engine rebuilding process but do not work under the car when it's only supported by a floor jack. You need to have jack stands at each corner of the vehicle if you're working under it. Always chock the wheels so your car doesn't move. If you are removing the engine and transmission together as a unit, now is the time to remove the driveshaft, transmission linkages, speedometer cable, and neutral safety switch wiring.

Hood

Removing the hood provides additional working room and light, so I do this early in the process. Taking the hood off and safely stowing it is a two-person job at minimum. I recommend using old blankets to pad the area of the cowl vent, which is at the back of the hood in front of the windshield. Also use covers on both fenders to protect the paint.

Battery

Loosen the bolts that secure the battery cables to the terminals, and remove the cables. You should remove the battery from the car and store it in a safe place, keeping it out of the way of an errant swing of the engine as it is lifted from the car. Safely store the battery on a plastic

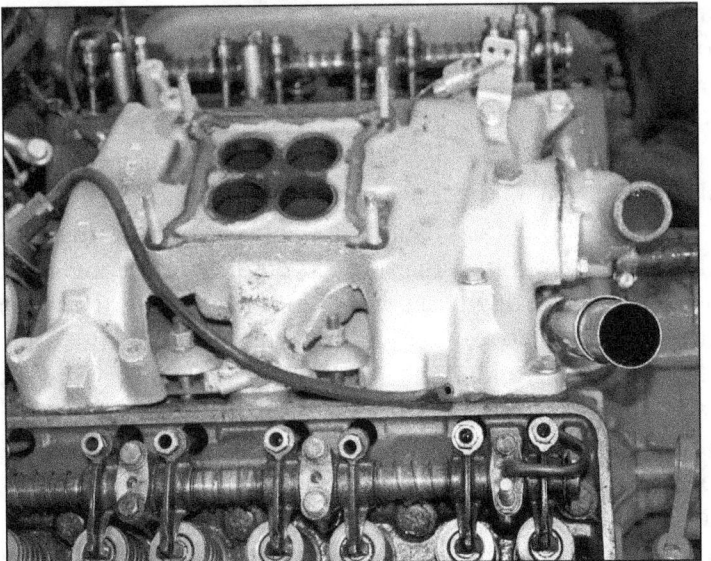

You need to methodically and carefully examine the top end of the engine. Look for telltale signs of wear and damage, such as oil seeping between the head and the block. This indicates a blown head gasket. Carefully look at the rocker arms, springs, and keepers. If you see a collapsed spring, catastrophic engine damage may have occurred.

CHAPTER 2

or wood shelf where it is not exposed to extreme temperatures. This could ruin the battery.

Fluids

A Y-block (and any other gas engine) contains hazardous, flammable fluids and chemicals that need to be properly disposed of before you start the rebuild process. After you have drained the oil, radiator fluid, transmission, and possibly power steering fluid from your vehicle, make sure they are properly recycled.

Oil

The typical Y-block engine holds 6 quarts of oil so make sure your drain pan has more than enough capacity. You can drain the oil with the engine in the car or on an engine stand. If you drain the oil with the engine in the car, make sure the car is properly supported by ramps or jack stands.

After draining the oil, inspect it. If it's golden and clear, the oil is relatively fresh. If it's black, you know it's old, but look for metal shavings or anything else unusual. If it's milky or discolored, most likely coolant mixed with the oil. You could have a cracked block or another problem.

Radiator

In some applications, you may need to remove the fan shroud before you can remove the radiator from its mounts in the core support. Starting at the front of the engine, remove bolt-on parts, the fan, drive belts, and the generator or alternator. Use tags and a Sharpie to mark the location of the wires before you disconnect them. This helps determine the location of the wires during the reassembly process and the position of the power steering pump (if applicable).

A 5-gallon bucket or large multi-gallon drain pan is good for this job. Keep in mind that opening the radiator petcock does not allow all the coolant to drain from the block. This has to be dealt with separately. If there is no petcock in the side of the block, remove the lower radiator hose, which allows most of the coolant to drain.

The old rubber hoses often become stiff and brittle. After many heat cycles, they may be almost bonded to the outlet of the radiator. Place a small flathead screwdriver under the lip of the hose, and run it around the circumference of the hose end. Squeeze the hose, and work it back and forth until it comes loose. If that doesn't work, you may have to cut it off with a utility knife.

Once the coolant has been drained into the catch bucket or pan, transfer it to a clean container, such as a one-gallon milk jug. Do not mix the coolant with oil or any other chemical. Many oil change outfits and auto parts stores recycle these chemicals for free but not if they are mixed together.

Power Steering

If your Y-block has never been rebuilt or has high mileage, you have the choice of either disconnecting the power steering pump lines and removing the pump or securing it to the side. If you disconnect the lines, remove the power steering pump and drain the fluid into a container. The fluid is most likely beyond its service life, and the reservoir needs to be refilled with fresh fluid.

Power steering pump lines are often flexible enough to allow the pump to be moved safely aside during removal of the engine. Be sure to secure the power steering pump out of the way, and take care not to kink the lines.

Fuel System

I recommend photographing the routing of your fuel lines so you know exactly how to route and place your fuel lines during reassembly. Once you disconnect the throttle linkage, fuel lines, and bolts, remove the carb. Along with the carburetor, remove the hard line to the fuel filter and pump and any linkages, such as the automatic transmission kickdown lever if applicable.

Remember that the carburetor also contains some residual fuel so you need to properly drain it. Remove it from the engine, and turn the carb upside down over a drain pan in a ventilated area to drain off the remaining fuel. At the same time, if you have fuel in the tank, siphon it into a can and dispose of it. It's easy to complete the rebuild, install the engine, connect all the hoses and lines, and then forget there's old gas in the tank. You don't want to ruin your rebuild by running old gas through your engine.

Wiring

Again, you should carefully tag and mark each of the electrical wires so you know exactly where they are routed, connected, and terminated. I also recommend you photograph the connections and routing of these wires so you have a visual record of them before you start removing them.

Distributor and Ignition

Remove the spark plug caps from the spark plugs. Unscrew the clamp that secures the distributor to the block. Then carefully pull the

PULLING THE ENGINE

distributor shaft through the engine and manifold. Put it in a safe place for later testing. Place a lint-free rag in the distributor hole in the manifold so no contaminants fall into the engine.

The spark plug wires can be removed from the plugs and then removed intact with the distributor cap. This avoids damaging the cap or wires during engine removal. I found that the engine bay clearance in a 1957 Ford does not require you to remove the cap and wires, but it still might not be a bad idea.

At this point, I make it a habit to remove any fragile components from the engine such as the ignition coil, ballast resistor, valve covers, and carburetor.

Belts

Take the tension off the belts by loosening the bolts that hold tension against the belts via the grooved brackets. If these belts are on a well-worn or never-rebuilt engine, you can rest assured that they are junk and need to be replaced. If the belts are relatively new, you can set them aside and inspect them later.

Lines and Hoses

If you must remove the A/C compressor from the vehicle, you need to properly evacuate the system first so you don't release contaminants into the atmosphere. The line to the fuel pump also has to be removed before removing the engine. This may consist of a hard line, flex line, rubber hose, or a combination. Be aware that some quantity of fuel can leak when the line is disconnected; be prepared to capture the fluid so that you can safely dispose of it.

Turn your attention to the top of the engine: the engine feed harness and vacuum and water hoses. These need to be identified and tagged. You should also perform digital photo documentation of the disassembly process to note their location, before being removed.

Hoist and Lift Brackets

Now is a good time to set up the engine hoist and get ready to lift the engine from the car.

If you are fortunate enough to have the factory-installed lift brackets on your engine, attach your lift chain(s) to them. Use only high-grade hardware, such as grade-8 bolts, when attaching the lifting chain to the engine. If your engine does not have lifting brackets (most don't) you can attach the lift chain(s) to intake manifold bolt holes in the cylinder heads.

Once you have attached the lift chain, use the hoist to take up any slack. This provides additional safety when the motor mounts have been disconnected. Now you can jack the car up and get it on jack stands. Do not work with the jack alone. Jack stands are a must. Cement or wood blocks should never be used. Getting the car into the air allows access to components that cannot be reached from the top, such as exhaust pipe flanges, and draining the oil from the engine.

Driveshaft

When you remove the driveshaft from the back of the transmission, plug the tailshaft to prevent fluid from leaking. Use a specialized plastic plug for this task or use an old driveshaft yoke inserted in the back of the transmission, if you happen to have one. In a pinch, I have used a freezer bag and duct tape to slow any fluid loss, although this is far from a perfect solution.

On vehicles equipped with an automatic transmission, you also have to deal with the cooling lines that run forward to the radiator. Check the lines for any brackets, securing them to the engine or chassis, or if their routing takes them behind the motor mount. The lines are fragile, and you must take care when removing them in order to prevent damage. Use the specialized line wrenches to make the work easier and help prevent any damage.

If your car is equipped with a standard transmission, remove the shift linkage as well as the clutch linkage (clutch equalizer or Z-bar) connecting the car's frame with the engine at the bellhousing.

Transmission

You may remove the transmission mount bolts at this time, but do not remove the transmission crossmember bolts until you have positioned a jack under the transmission to hold it in place. If you plan to remove the engine and leave the transmission in place, start by removing the starter from the bellhousing. In the case of a car equipped with an automatic transmission, remove the inspection cover from the lower front portion of the bellhousing, and remove the nuts holding the torque converter to the flywheel or flexplate by manually rotating the engine to gain access to the nuts. If you have a standard transmission vehicle, remove the clutch linkage and return spring.

At this stage, remove the bolts holding the bellhousing to the back of the engine block; this leaves the engine supported on its mounts and the engine hoist.

Engine Stand

After first checking to ensure that you have no slack in the chains connecting the engine to the hoist, you can now unbolt the motor mounts from the frame brackets to begin the lift. I prefer to roll the car out from under the engine as I have found that being able to roll the car forward or backward as the engine is lifted is easier and safer than trying to move the hoist.

At this point, I lower the car from the jacks and back onto the ground, if possible. I recommend a second set of hands and eyes to assist with lifting the engine from the car. Lift the engine with slow strokes, being careful to check for any wires, brackets, etc., that may be interfering with the engine. Continue lifting, and move the vehicle as necessary, until the lowest point of the engine clears the core support.

Once the engine is clear of the car, get it securely attached to an engine stand before releasing the remaining pressure on the hoist and removing the lift chain(s). With the engine out of the car and secured to the stand, it can be moved to a suitable location for disassembly.

Engine Removal

1 Mark Hinge Locations

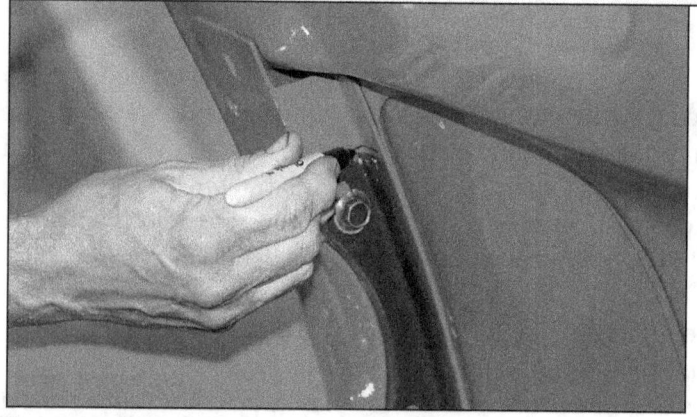

To make the work easier, remove the hood from the car before you pull the engine. You have much clearer access to the engine and engine bay components without the hood. Heck, it has to come off eventually anyway. Removing the hood now provides additional room to work and allows more light into the engine compartment. Mark the hood hinge locations with an indelible marker.

These marks designate the placement of the hinges on the hood and aid greatly when the car is reassembled at a later date. Be sure to store your hood where it will not be damaged. I often use an old quilt to cover the painted surface and Styrofoam blocks to protect the corners of the hood during storage.

2 Protect Fenders

Make sure that your fenders are protected. These Ford Racing fender covers work well and protect both paint and sheet metal during the engine removal process. You don't want to fix body damage that could have been avoided. Old blankets and soft towels also provide good protection.

3 Tag Wires and Connectors

Taking the time now to tag wires and connectors with identifiers helps the task of getting everything back in the right place after your newly rebuilt engine has been reinstalled in the car. Once wires have been tagged and disconnected, be sure to secure them out of the way before lifting the engine out of the car.

4 Inspect Wiring

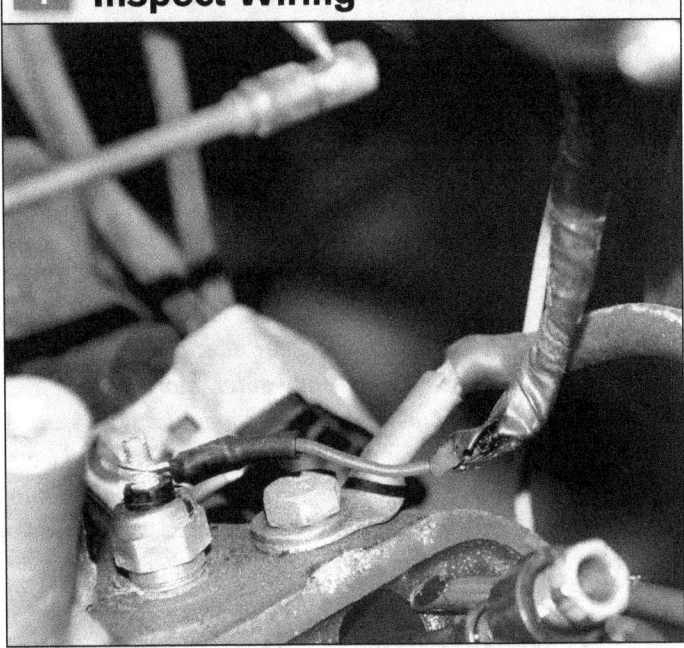

If the wire leading to the water temperature sending unit is in poor condition (this one has the wrong connector), cut off the connector, strip off 1 inch of the insulator sleeve, and crimp on the appropriate new connector. This problem is remedied while the engine is out of the car. With the engine removed from the chassis, you should tidy up the engine compartment. Don't forget to disconnect the engine ground wire before lifting the engine out. Also, don't forget to disconnect the cable running from the solenoid to the starter.

5 Drain Coolant

Starting from the front of the engine, drain the coolant and then begin removing accessories. These include the upper and lower radiator hoses, fan belts, generator/alternator, power-steering pump (if applicable), and radiator.

CHAPTER 2

Professional Mechanic Tip

6 Remove Carburetor, Coil and Intake Manifold

To start the process of removing the carburetor, disconnect the fuel line, distributor vacuum line, choke heat tube (if applicable), throttle return spring, and the linkage.

Don't forget to secure the carburetor linkage so it does not interfere with the lifting of the engine. The linkage connects to the carburetor via a spring clip, which is easily removed by hand. Once the linkage arm is removed, use a tie wrap or piece of tag wire to secure the throttle arm out of the way.

Four nuts on studs secure the carburetor to the intake. With these nuts removed, the carburetor can be lifted off the intake, drained of residual fuel, and safely stored out of the way. Use painters' or masking tape and a Sharpie to label the wires leading to the ignition coil. Remove and put it aside. Also remove the bracket holding the coil and ballast resistor to the intake. (I also chose to remove the intake manifold from the engine before lifting the engine from the car.) Take off the coolant bypass hose between the front of the intake manifold and water pump. Remove the intake manifold bolts/nuts, and then use gentle pressure to break the seal on the gaskets sealing the intake manifold to the cylinder heads. The more external components removed before lifting the engine from the car, the lighter the load on your hoist during the lift.

7 Remove Fuel Line

Remove the fuel line between the chassis and the fuel pump. The fuel pump must also be removed before lifting the engine. The fuel line is typically either a rubber hose secured with clamps or a flexible line with brass fittings. Use a flat-blade screwdriver to remove the clamps, but if your car is equipped with brass fittings, use line wrenches to detach it to avoid damage.

8 Prepare Hoist

Assemble and position the hoist in front of the car; it's almost time to lift out the engine. Secure the lift chains to the engine. You should perform a last-minute visual inspection to make sure all hoses, wires, and linkages have been disconnected from the engine. You don't want to strip wires or unnecessarily damage any components because you were not thorough and did not disconnect something. Nothing should remain connected so there are no impediments for removal.

9 Attach Hoist Chains to Engine

Attach the lifting chains to the engine via intake manifold bolt holes in the cylinder heads, which are diagonal from each other (front to back). Use only high-quality hardware to secure the lifting chains. Use grade-8 bolts threaded into the cylinder heads as far as possible. You can remove the engine and transmission as one unit, but you need to be careful and steady with the engine so you do not bang up the firewall or the core support. Otherwise, you can unbolt the transmission from the engine and pull the engine only. Although pulling an engine can be a solo project, it's easier with the help of a friend.

PULLING THE ENGINE

10 Attach Hoist Chains to Hoist

With the lifting chains secured to the engine, you can attach the chains to the hoist for the lift. As you begin to lift the engine, pay careful attention to the angle of the engine. You may have to lower the engine back onto its mounts so you can reposition the hoist's chain and hook.

11 Lift Engine

As you begin to lift the engine, have someone help you. An extra set of hands and eyes is invaluable in ensuring that the way is clear for the engine to come out of the car. That extra set of hands can steady the engine and keep it from swinging on the hoist once it is clear of the mounts. The secret here is to take your time, raise the engine slowly, and be careful. Keep in mind that the engine weighs more than 600 pounds.

12 Remove Car from under Hoist

The engine has now been lifted off its mounts and is high enough to clear the core support. Rather than attempting to roll the hoist with its 600-pound payload swinging free, I prefer to roll the car back and out from under the engine while an assistant holds the engine steady. To roll the car back, jack it up, remove the jack stands, lower it, and carefully roll the car back. Once the car is out from under the engine hoist, don't forget to chock the wheels to prevent it from rolling farther.

13 Secure Engine on Stand

Once the engine has been removed from the car, prepare to secure it to the engine stand. Remove the flywheel or flex plate, and then bolt the mounting arms of the stand to the back of the engine. The arms of the engine stand are slotted, which allows for adjustment. Use a socket and ratchet to firmly tighten the bolts that hold the engine to the arm. The flywheel mount on the back of the crankshaft is asymmetrical, so be sure to place corresponding marks on the flywheel and crankshaft flange to assist with reinstallation after the engine has been rebuilt.

Once the mounting arms have been secured to the bellhousing bolt holes at the back of the cylinder block, use the hoist to lower the engine to a point where the receiver of the engine stand aligns with the mounting arms. Keep some tension on the lifting chains until you are certain all components are secured. With the engine stand frame and mounting arms secured together, you can release the tension on the lifting chain and remove it from the engine.

CHAPTER 3

PREPARING TO REBUILD AN ENGINE

With the age of a Y-block engine, many are in need of a rebuild. Many have been rebuilt and some have been rebuilt several times. You need to be sure that your Y-block doesn't hide critical flaws and it's worth rebuilding.

Proper documentation is an essential part of any rebuilding project. If you want professional results, and, therefore, a reliable, strong-running engine, you need to take notes and photograph each important step of the process. Otherwise, you may end up guessing what's been done or how to reassemble a component. Take the time to write down complete and thorough notes when it's a complex procedure, and stop to take a photograph during an important step. You actually save time referring to notes and photos rather than trying to figure out how some parts or components go back together.

Facilities

Scenarios such as rebuilding an engine using a tree limb for a hoist and using the dirt floor of an old chicken coop for an assembly room should be avoided. The cleanliness of a shop is paramount; dirt, grit, and debris are enemies of any engine. If contaminants enter the engine during the rebuilding, at the least, engine life is much shorter and, at the worst, catastrophic engine failure results.

You need to keep your tools, workbench, and work area as clean as possible, and your workshop must be well-lit. In fact, many fine running engines, including some used in competitions, have been assembled in home shops. The degree to which you choose to outfit your home shop directly affects the ease with which the task at hand is accomplished.

Be sure you have adequate space to work on the engine, with proper and adequate storage for the parts as they come off the engine. Also, your new parts must be properly organized and stored, so you can find them when you need them and they aren't damaged. Heavy-duty shelving supports heavy parts, such as intakes,

While this home shop might not be up to television show standards, it has proved to be sufficient for quite a number of automotive projects, including several engine rebuilds. Keeping your work area clean, properly illuminated, and organized is the key to having a successful home shop. Set up your work area for the task at hand ahead of time, and things will go much smoother.

heads, and cast-iron exhaust manifolds. Have a shelving unit ready for the rebuild.

In addition, have plenty of blue painters' tape, baggies, tags, and a Sharpie. These are great for properly identifying fasteners, bolts, and parts that come off the engine so you can conveniently reassemble the engine with the correct parts.

Safety is Crucial

You never want to risk your health or well being during the engine-rebuilding journey. If you're uncomfortable performing any task, don't do it. Unless you're a trained ASE with all the training and tools available, some tasks may be beyond your skill, experience, or comfort level. There's no shame in asking for help or having a qualified professional do it, but there may be some shame in explaining to friends and family how you were hurt.

In all seriousness, many people are injured and killed every year while unsafely and unwisely performing mechanical procedures on cars. Always use common sense and your best judgment.

Organization and Planning

You need to properly plan and budget your project so you invest the resources in the right parts and machine services and attain your ultimate performance goal for your engine. You need to be patient and not just blindly dive into the project. If you methodically and carefully plan, prepare, and budget for your rebuild, it yields dividends: You complete a professional-caliber engine rebuild in a timely and efficient manner.

You need to carefully and accurately assess your skill set and available time. How much of the disassembly, parts inspection, and assembly will you do yourself? If you have the expertise and access to the specialized tools necessary to complete every operation of these processes and the time to do it, you save yourself money.

On the other hand, if you do not possess these tools and do not have the expertise to do all the service work, you need to hire a shop to do it, and you need to account for the cost. On the other hand, you may be able to do some of the service work, such as assembling the short-block, but you do not feel comfortable assembling the top end and particularly the heads. You likely are not a machinist so all the machine work will be performed by a qualified shop, and you need to budget for it and all other aspects of the project.

You need to define the type of engine build you're performing because that also dictates the time, cost, and complexity of the project. A Y-block rebuild can range from bone stock to full race, and in-between you have high-performance street. Each has its own set of requirements, cost of parts, and machining charges. If you're performing a stock rebuild, the machine operations are simpler, straightforward, and less expensive. You are not investing in high-performance heads, cam, intake, and other parts. On the other hand, if you build a high-performance street build, you buy high-performance heads, aggressive cam, aluminum intake, cam, and headers. The cost of all these parts adds up, and it also takes more machine work to properly modify them.

I recommend creating a project file in a spread-sheet program, such as Excel, to define budget, project costs, allot time for services, and schedule all the services that need to be performed. To form a budget, you can organize the project engine requirements in columns. These columns can include component name, such as heads, block, cam, and so forth. Then you should have a column to define existing or replacement part, replacement part cost, machine shop service required, and machine shop service cost. This basic plan allows you to calculate specific item costs and a total project cost.

To estimate the time required for your project, you can formulate a schedule for your particular engine build. This can include project name, start time, finish time, and duration of project. This allows you to prioritize and organize the particular services or tasks for completing the engine build, but it also allows you to project when it will be finished. Like all plans, it is subject to change. If you're honest with yourself and accurate in your assessments, your schedule should be close to the reality of building your particular engine.

I want to finish by saying that this has real value: "plan your work, and work your plan." It will make this rebuild or any other automotive job an easier, more pleasant, and rewarding undertaking.

When deciding your degree of involvement in your engine rebuild, you must consider three things. First, consider the time and expense of having someone else perform all the work. Second, consider the satisfaction of being directly responsible for a job well done. Third, consider your budget.

Before undertaking an engine rebuild you should do some research to determine the approximate cost of replacement parts and machine work. Although parts and machine work can be somewhat expensive based upon several factors, including whether you're using stock replacement or aftermarket performance parts, and the amount of machine work required to restore your engine to factory specifications. You can save considerably on labor costs by performing some tasks yourself, such as removing, disassembling, assembling, and installing the engine.

Although I'm as entertained as the next red-blooded American male by Hollywood's rendition of engine rebuilding and automotive restoration, there is little resemblance between what you see on the flat screen and what actually awaits you out in the garage. In the real world, the task of removing, rebuilding, and replacing the engine in your car or truck cannot be accomplished in an hour. You get a tad dirtier and are a bit more challenged than the guys and gals on your favorite automotive show.

Rationale for Rebuilding

Engines are rebuilt for various reasons. Worn rings, loose bearings, and many other ailments are common causes, as is the quest for more power. In a worst-case scenario, a failure of internal components makes a rebuild necessary. Regardless of the reason, you have decided to proceed with removing and rebuilding your engine. However, before the first wrench is turned or the first knuckle skinned, some questions must be answered and logistics arranged.

First, you need to determine the level of rebuild. Keep in mind that there are various types, or levels, of rebuild from just freshening up the engine with new pistons, rings, bearings, and gaskets to the modifications required for all-out competition. This may include a billet crankshaft, forged rods and pistons, high-performance aluminum cylinder heads, aluminum intake manifold, and the list goes on and on.

This book covers all aspects of a stock rebuild, which refers to restoring the engine to factory specifications using new, original, or correct replacement parts. In order to restore power and efficiency, the engine's internal clearances need to be returned to factory specifications through machining and replacement of worn parts.

The next level on the rebuild continuum consists of internal modifications that allow the engine to retain a factory appearance while providing improvements in performance and reliability.

Last but not least is the dedicated performance buildup that includes aftermarket internal parts and modifications, as well as external changes from oil pan to air cleaner.

In order to accomplish these types of rebuild for this book, I take you step-by-step through two separate engines: a stock 292 and a 322-ci performance version.

Tools and Equipment

By reading this book before beginning your rebuild, you gain insight into the task at hand, know what steps to follow, and recognize the differences and idiosyncrasies within the engine family known as the Ford Y-block V-8. Most of the tools and equipment you need are standard to any enthusiast's workshop.

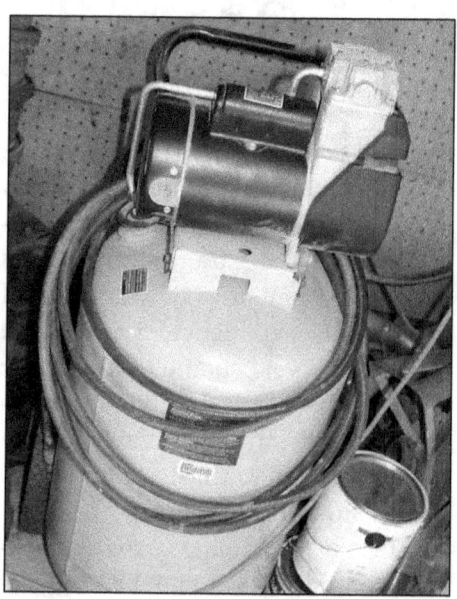

If you have air tools and a compressor in your home shop you will be able to accomplish tasks that would be otherwise impossible. Air tools often provide the extra punch needed to free the stubborn, rusted fasteners commonly encountered on older vehicles.

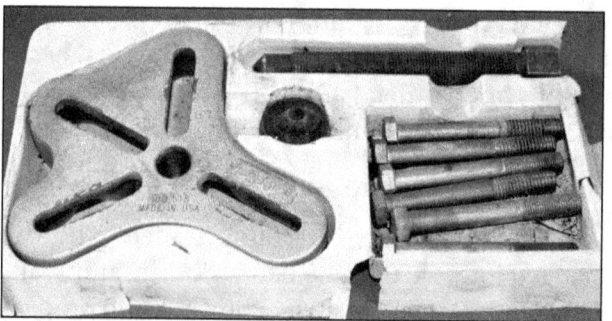

A puller of the type shown here is necessary to remove the vibration dampener from your engine. The force exerted by the puller draws the dampener straight off the snout of the crankshaft without damaging the key or keyway. Do not attempt to force the dampener off by other means; serious damage to the snout of the crankshaft and/or dampener may occur. Craftsman makes a sturdy puller set that is adaptable to various dampeners.

PREPARING TO REBUILD AN ENGINE

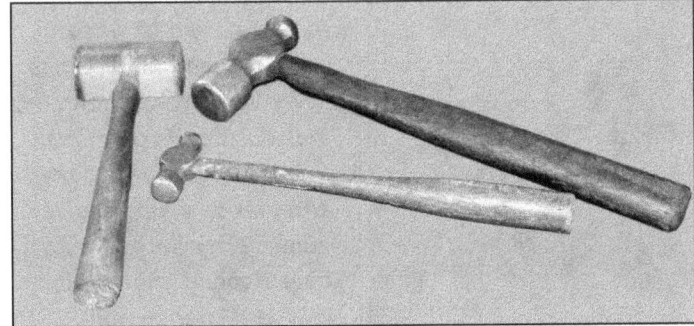

Several types and sizes of hammers are handy when coaxing loose parts that have been in place for many years and exposed to the elements. However, don't fall into the trap of "if it doesn't come loose, use a bigger hammer." Think through tasks, use common sense, and follow proper procedures.

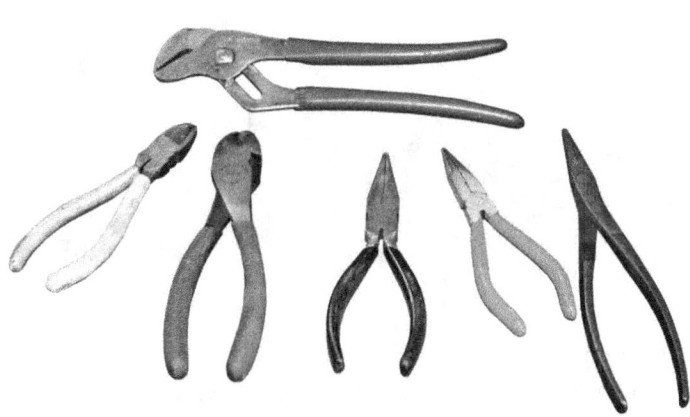

A good assortment of pliers and side cutters prove useful with this and many other auto projects undertaken in your home shop. Hose clamp and water pump pliers are a must for automotive projects. Duckbill and needle-nose pliers are also handy items to keep in your toolbox. Remember that pliers are not designed to remove nuts and bolts. Use the proper tool for the job.

Here's a tip: Some of the most important products to purchase before undertaking an engine rebuild come in the form of parts cleaners and rust-penetrating sprays. Rusted bolts and nuts to be removed during your rebuild should be soaked liberally, and well in advance, of applying a wrench to them. Products, such as PB Blaster and Liquid Wrench penetrating catalyst aerosols, have worked well for me over the years. For cleaning accumulations of grease and dirt from nuts and bolts before I put a wrench to them, I use Brakleen by CRC. This pressurized aerosol cleans without causing damage to surrounding wires and hoses.

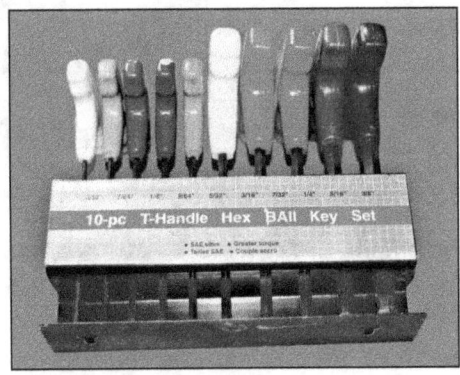

Specialized tools, such as this hex set, are not always necessary but can come in handy for many automotive projects in the home shop.

You will find many uses for a good set of drifts, punches, and chisels on your rebuild project. Remember to use these types of tools as designed and do not to force parts. Craftsman makes drifts, punches, and chisels in various sizes and lengths that are adaptable to many tasks.

With old, rusted, rounded-off bolts and nuts, this Bolt-Out set by Craftsman has helped me out on more than one occasion. You often need a tool like this only once but it's certainly worth the investment. If you must resort to using this type of tool to remove a damaged nut or bolt, remember to discard and replace the damaged fastener with one of appropriate size and design. Bolt-Out nut and bolt extractors are designed to grab even the most rusted and rounded-off hardware. Once you have encountered a nut or bolt that has been rounded off because someone used the wrong wrench, socket, or other tool in the past, the need for quality tools in your home shop becomes very clear. The time and effort saved is worth the investment.

CHAPTER 3

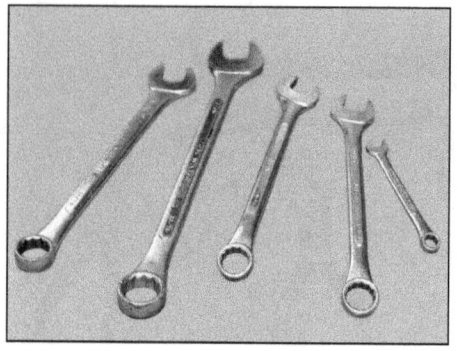

A set of combination wrenches in graduated sizes between 1/4 and 1¼ inches is necessary and guaranteed to get a workout on your engine rebuild project. Again, the quality of the tool is paramount in doing the job correctly. Combination wrenches are available in various lengths as well as angles for specific tasks.

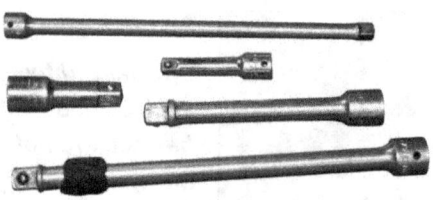

Extensions of varying lengths, in 1/4-, 3/8- and 1/2-inch drives provide reach and leverage, thus making your ratchet or breaker bar more effective. Also available are "wobble" extensions that allow you to access fasteners from different angles.

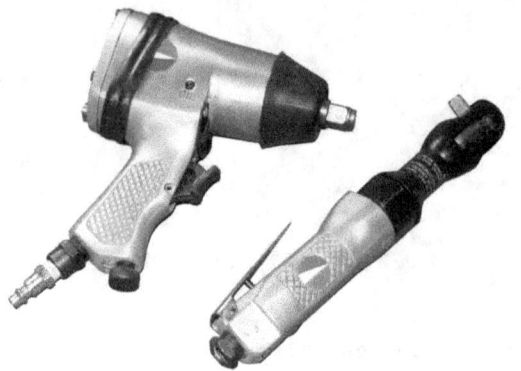

Air tools are a bit pricey and not the right choice for every home shop. However, they do speed up the task at hand while saving wear and tear on your arms and hands. Over the years I have depended on air tools only infrequently while working on an engine; one exception was the removal of an engine from the car and portions of the engine disassembly. I make it a practice not to use air tools when assembling an engine. Remember, it is difficult to control the amount of force an air tool exerts on a nut or bolt, and the time saved by using these tools may result in time added to your project in the form of broken or rounded-off hardware.

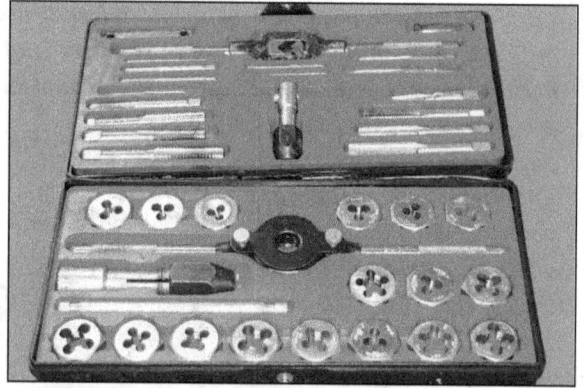

Craftsman sells inexpensive tap and die sets, such as this one. It has saved me time and money countless times on automotive projects. They are a good investment, particularly when working with old hardware. A cleanup chasing of threads on engine fasteners before assembly provides a more accurate torque application where required and eases the assembly of other components. Do not buy cheap off-brand tap and die sets. They are often made from inferior materials and not built to exacting standards of size. Believe me, nothing is more frustrating than breaking off a tap in a bolt hole.

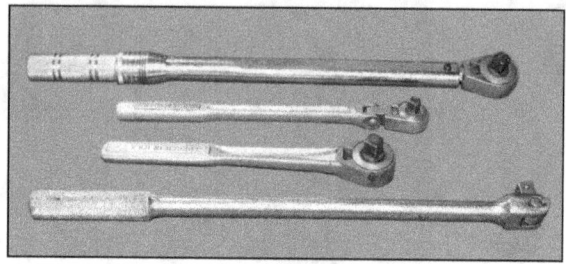

A Craftsman click-type torque wrench (top) is one item you cannot do without when assembling an engine. The swivel head, 3/8-inch drive ratchet (upper middle) assists you in removing nuts and bolts located in tight places. The 1/2-inch breaker bar and ratchet (lower middle and bottom) are used to deal with larger, tighter fasteners.

Use a Sharpie and masking tape to label containers for temporarily storing fluids drained from your project. By doing so you may avoid costly mishaps, such as pouring oil into the radiator from an old coolant bottle. Any motor oil that has been drained from the crankcase or antifreeze that is not going to be reused must be disposed of properly.

PREPARING TO REBUILD AN ENGINE

Machine Shop Services

You're probably not a professional machinist who has access to hundreds of thousands of dollars of commercial machining equipment. Therefore, you need to take your Y-block engine to the most qualified shop to do these critical machining procedures. They include (but are not limited to) overboring the block, milling the deck surfaces, line honing the main bearing caps, and turning down and truing the crankshaft. You are investing hundreds of dollars in a typical machining process for a rebuild, so you need to choose the machine shop that works on your parts wisely and methodically.

When it comes to choosing a machine shop for my Ford engine rebuilds, I have three hard-and-fast rules. Although some may not agree with my rationale, these rules should help you achieve your goals so your engine is strong and reliable.

Rule number one: I look around the shop for engine rebuilds with front-mounted distributors. If I don't see any other Ford engines, I usually pass on the shop. I also look around the shop to see what machines they have: mills, lathes, etc.

At the same time, I also inspect the shop for cleanliness. If the benches, floors, and other areas are greasy and dirty, it's unlikely they perform clean builds. A top-caliber shop is clean because the owners and management recognize the value of having a clean shop and providing a top-quality rebuild. If it's not clean, move on and seek another shop.

Ford engines are different than GM or Chrysler engines, and you should use a shop that has expertise rebuilding Ford engines. Better yet, they have rebuilt Y-block engines, because these engines carry some unusual design features. Certain Ford engines, and the Y-block among them, have some idiosyncrasies, and the machinist needs experience in these areas to get things just right.

For example, I once purchased an FE-series cylinder block. While examining the work the previous owner had performed by "his" machine shop, I noticed that the core plug at the back of the camshaft galley had been improperly installed. Had the engine been assembled this way it would have allowed the camshaft to "walk" in the block, possibly leading to catastrophic failure.

Now I arrive at rule number two: When working with older Ford engines, such as the Y-block and the FE, I prefer to see a little gray hair in the shop. In my mind this increases the possibility of the machinist having been born while these engine series were still in production, which means he may have actually seen one of these beasts in person in his lifetime.

And rule number three: When considering a performance buildup I insist on contracting with a shop that has an established reputation for building Ford engines. These shops have the necessary experience for performing the best rebuilds. They use established Ford engine rebuilding practices and many accepted procedures for wringing more power out of the engine. Some of the practices for rebuilding a Chevy engine are totally different than those applied to Fords and, in some cases, would actually be detrimental to a Ford engine.

A common practice among machinists attempting to gain additional compression, and thus performance, from a Chevy engine is to machine the deck surfaces of the cylinder block. In Ford circles, this is considered the kiss of death and to be avoided. Ford engines also benefit from the use of split lift and duration camshaft profiles (different lift and duration specifications between the intake and exhaust valves).

Specialized Ford engine building shops are found in most large cities, so take the time to search them out. In the end the quality of the machine shop work determines the quality of the engine build.

Years ago I chose, and continue to rely on, Jordan Automotive Machine in Hainesport, New Jersey. Proprietor and master machinist Gil Jordan is intimately familiar with Ford engines, including the Y-block, flathead, and FE series, which makes him an invaluable resource in my book. Ted Eaton from Texas is widely regarded as one of the top builders of Y-block Ford performance engines in the country.

CHAPTER 4

ENGINE DISASSEMBLY

Once the engine has been safely lifted out of the car, it's time to perform a methodical and professional disassembly of the engine. Once again, proper planning and preparation makes this task go much smoother. As always, safety is first. Securely bolt your engine to a good-quality engine stand in a clean, well-lit area of your workspace. This is of the utmost importance before disassembly begins. Remember, even a small-block V-8 engine weighs several hundred pounds, and members of the Y-block engine family tip the scales at more than 600 pounds.

Set up your work area to accommodate the numerous parts that make up your engine. Make sure that you have ample containers, bags, tags, etc., to store and keep track of the hardware for each component. Keeping your fasteners in order pays dividends in saving time when you put the engine back together. This is also a good time to replace any damaged, stripped, or overly rusted nuts and bolts, taking care to obtain fasteners with the exact thread pitch, dimensions, and hardness ratings. If your bolts are damaged or stretched, you are not achieving the proper clamping force and your entire rebuild is in jeopardy.

Companies such as AMK Products and the Gardner-Wescott Company are excellent sources of high-quality engine hardware that matches OEM nuts and bolts exactly.

Have your still or video camera handy to provide a record of how things come apart, and you will have a much easier time during reassembly. Note: If there are any indications that your engine has previously been apart (one of ours was, while the other was delivered from the factory), do not automatically assume that it was correctly reassembled. Someone who was unfamiliar with these engines may have previously worked on it. Carefully examine your engine and refer to the photos in this book that describe how to properly install certain components. This is vital to the success of your rebuild.

Once the main bearing caps have been removed, you can lift the crankshaft out of the block. V-8 crankshafts are typically 50 pounds or more, so be sure you can lift it out yourself or get someone else to help. If you drop it, you can damage it beyond repair.

ENGINE DISASSEMBLY

Valvetrain Disassembly

1 Remove Carburetor

If you chose not to remove the carburetor and distributor before lifting the engine from the car, keep in mind that the carburetor likely contains some residual fuel. Take the carburetor to a ventilated area away from any source of ignition. Turn it upside down, and drain the fuel into a container. Dispose of, or store, the container properly. Once the carb has been removed, place a lint-free rag in the intake. Even though you're going to rebuild the entire engine, avoid letting grit, grease, and debris fall into the engine. A simple clamp holds down the distributor but some prying force may be required to remove it from the block. Do not pry against the vacuum advance unit. Soak the area around the base of the distributor with a penetrant before attempting to remove it.

2 Remove Intake Manifold

Removing the intake manifold from a Y-block is fairly straightforward. The bypass hose is the biggest impediment between the water outlet and water pump. In this case, the hose still has its OEM spring clamps. Replace the hose unless you are undertaking an exact restoration to OEM specifications and your existing hose is in good condition. It is easier to simply cut the hose rather than deal with the clamps.

3 Remove Lifter Valley Cover

With the intake manifold out of the way, you have access to the lifter valley cover, which is secured by two bolts. Use a hammer handle or a piece of hardwood and insert it into the runner. Exert some prying force to remove the cover. Some find it easier to remove the cylinder heads before removing the lifter valley cover. Either way, care must be taken not to bend the cover during removal or oil leaks may occur later.

4 Inspect for Sludge

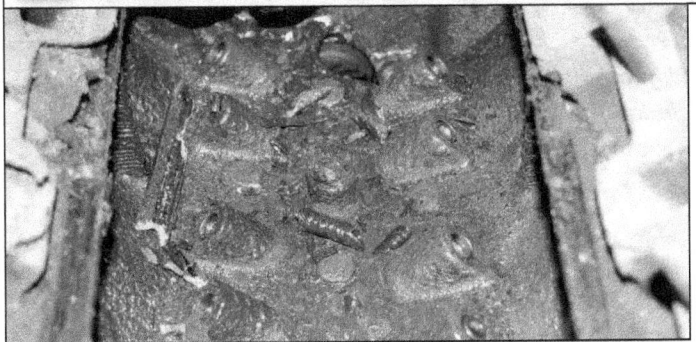

When you remove the lifter valley cover, you will likely be confronted with sludge buildup on the underside of the cover and in the lifter gallery. The sludge buildup is evidence of years of using improper motor oils or lack of maintenance.

5 Remove Valve Covers

Two studs hold the Y-block valve covers to the heads; they also anchor the rocker arm end stands. After removing the two nuts that hold the valve covers in place, some force may be required to remove the covers. Rather than using a prying tool, I prefer to strike the cover in several places with a rubber mallet to avoid damaging the cover.

6 Remove Drain-Back Tubes

Documentation Required

You now have access to the rocker arm assemblies and pushrods. Take note of the location of the oil drain-back tubes on the rocker assemblies. The passenger-side tube is located toward the front of the engine, while the driver-side tube is located toward the rear. The purpose of the location of the oil drain-back tubes is to provide lubrication for the distributor shaft and timing chain and gears. When it's time for reassembly, you will have to refer back to your notes so you install the oil drain-back tubes in the correct locations.

Camshaft Removal

1 Remove Rocker Arm Stands

A stud/nut combination and a bolt hold the rocker arm end stands in place. Use an open-end or box wrench to remove the nut from the stud. Secure the remaining rocker arm stands with two bolts each.

2 Remove Pushrods

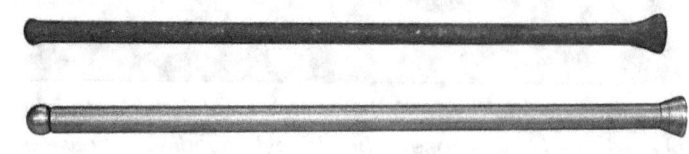

Remove all the pushrods and examine them. You may discover that your engine is equipped with the less-than-desirable one-piece pushrods (top). Replace them with tubular pushrods of the same length (bottom) as part of your rebuild.

3 Inspect for Sludge

With the rocker arm assemblies removed, you can see any sludge that has accumulated on the top of the cylinder heads over the engine's lifetime.

ENGINE DISASSEMBLY

4 Remove Accessories

I recommend removing as many accessories as possible from the front of the engine before lifting the engine from the car. It's easier to attach the lifting chain and clear the core support and other components in the engine compartment during the lift with accessories out of the way. Working from front to rear, remove the generator and attach brackets, water pump, and accessory drive pulley. Removing these parts provides access to the crankshaft dampener and timing cover. If the fuel pump has been left in place, remember that it may also contain some residual fuel (when you do remove it).

5 Remove Timing Pointer

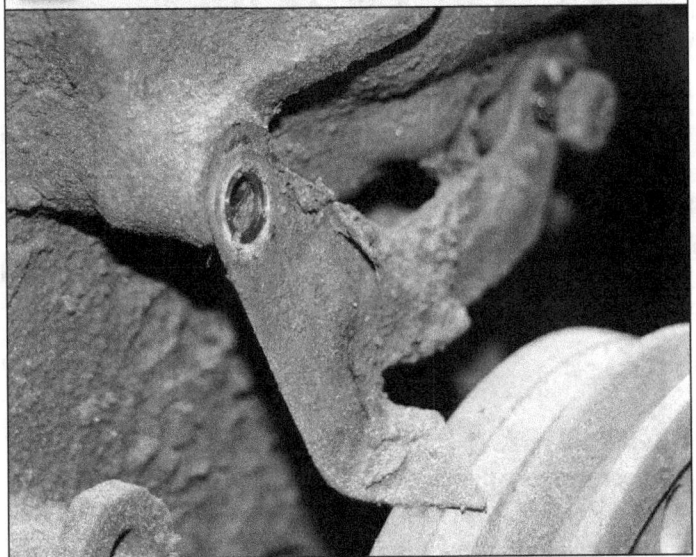

The ignition-timing pointer is bolted to the front of the timing cover. During removal be careful not to bend it because that could make it difficult to tune the engine at a later date.

6 Remove Motor Mounts

Before removing the motor mounts, note their orientation on the block so they align properly to the frame when the engine is reinstalled. It's a good idea to carefully examine the condition of the rubber portion of the motor mounts and replace them if their condition is suspect in any way. If the motor mounts are original, or very old, they should be replaced. Anchor-Doan is an inexpensive source for quality motor mounts for early vehicles.

7 Remove Canister

Removal of the canister that holds the road crankcase breather filter on the engine may reveal even more sludge buildup. This adds to the evidence that this engine was not properly maintained and could not have run very well. The canister is held in place by a bolt through its center.

CHAPTER 4

Cylinder Head Disassembly

1 Remove Crankcase Breather

Professional Mechanic Tip

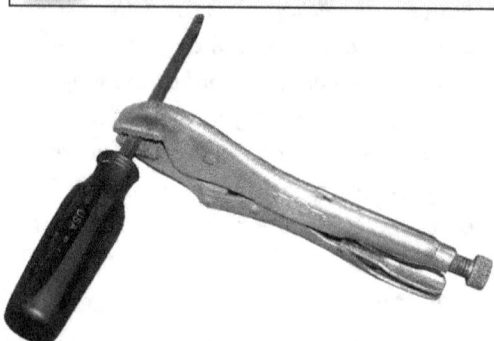

Two large Phillips-head screws attach the crankcase breather to the side of the block. It can be difficult to remove these screws, so be careful not to strip the heads. Be sure to choose the proper Phillips-head screwdriver, and before attempting to loosen the screws, give the screwdriver handle a good tap with a hammer. I have found that an impact driver is too large to access these screws. I use a Craftsman professional-grade screwdriver, which has a hexagonal shaft. I insert it onto the head and attach an adjustable wrench or Vise-Grips to the screwdriver shaft so it provides extra turning power on the screws.

2 Remove Heads

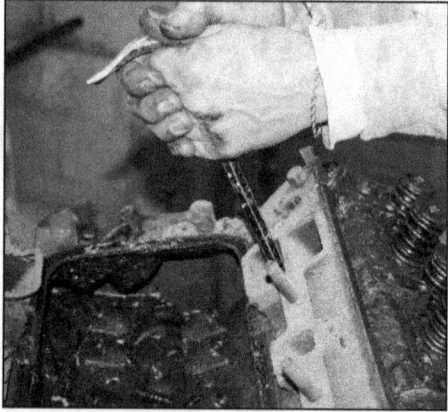

Use a breaker bar to remove the head bolts from the engine. Be sure to note that there are differences between the length of the upper and lower head bolts. The bolts used on the upper end of each cylinder head are also slightly longer than the others. With the cylinder head bolts removed, place the wooden handle of a hammer or a crowbar (shown) in the intake ports of the cylinder heads. Pry the heads away from the block and off the head dowels in the block. Take care when removing the cylinder heads from the block. They are heavy!

3 Inspect Cylinder Heads

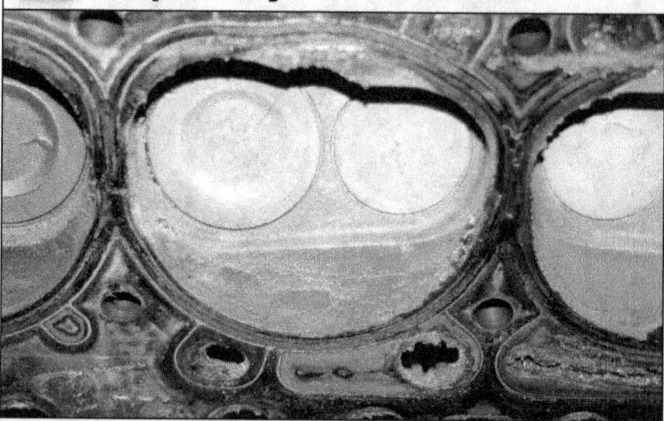

These cylinder heads show the signs of many years on the road. No visible problems, such as indications of blown head gaskets, cracks, or other damage are apparent at first glance. The heads will be thoroughly cleaned, disassembled, and inspected to determine any problems before machining.

4 Inspect for Damage

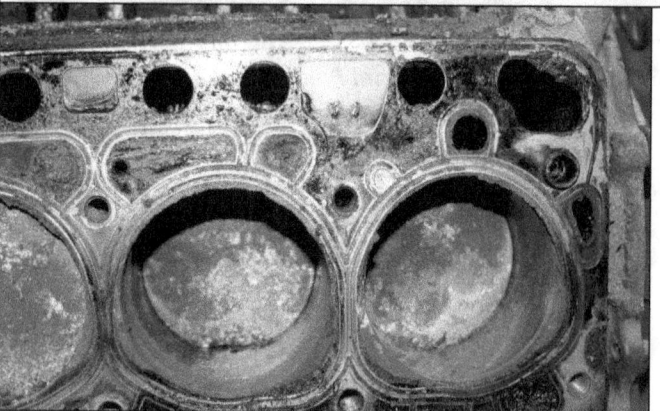

This is also a good time to do a visual inspection of the cylinder bores and piston tops for signs of obvious damage caused by excessive wear or component failure. Are the cylinder walls gouged because of a broken piston ring? Is there a ridge at the top of the cylinder bore? Does pitting appear on the tops of the pistons?

ENGINE DISASSEMBLY

5 Remove Vibration Dampener

Special Tool

Remove the vibration dampener from the crankshaft before you remove the timing cover; then you can access the timing chain and camshaft. A specialized puller, such as this one by Craftsman tools, is required. Do not attempt backyard methods for removing the dampener, such as beating it with a hammer or attempting to pry against it. You can damage both the dampener and the snout of the crankshaft and you may render them useless in the future.

Remove the bolt securing the dampener to the snout of the crankshaft. You may have to hold the crankshaft to keep it from rotating while you remove the bolt. This can be accomplished by reinstalling two flywheel/flexplate bolts into the crank flange and using a pry bar or large screwdriver to hold the crankshaft in place. With the bolt out of the way, attach the puller to the dampener by threading the bolts supplied with the tool into the holes spaced around the dampener.

Turn the threaded center of the tool in a clockwise direction, pulling the dampener from the crankshaft. Once the dampener is removed from the crankshaft, be sure to retain the woodruff key that secures it.

6 Remove Timing Cover

Once the timing cover has been removed, the timing gears and chain are exposed for removal. A few bolts hold the timing cover to the block. Remove the bolt that retains the top gear and fuel pump eccentric to the camshaft using a ratchet and 9/16 socket. The lower timing gear and the oil slinger in front of it are keyed to the crankshaft and slide off by hand.

7 Note Order of Cam Components

With the fuel pump eccentric out of the way, it's imperative to carefully note the order in which the other components are attached to the front of the camshaft. In this case, you see a keyed counterweight, while in others a keyed spacer may be found. One may be replaced with the other, but one or the other must be used. It would be a good idea to take a photo of the arrangement of components here.

8 Remove Top and Bottom Gears

After the camshaft retaining bolt, washers, fuel pump eccentric, and counterweight have been removed, use a pry bar or large flathead screwdriver to pry against the back of the top gear. The top gear separates from the cam, and the bottom gear slides off the keyway on the crankshaft.

9 Remove Cam Retaining Plate

Two bolts attach the camshaft retaining plate to the cylinder block. Once it has been removed, check the back side of the camshaft for any signs of excessive wear. Wear is indicated by grooves worn into the retaining plate.

CHAPTER 4

Critical Inspection

10 Inspect Thrust Washer

A thrust washer is behind the camshaft retaining plate. It is imperative to note that the beveled side of this washer faces the camshaft when it is reinstalled. Photograph the orientation of the camshaft hardware and, particularly, make a note regarding the thrust washer in order to facilitate correct reassembly.

11 Remove Oil Feed Tube

In order to remove the oil pan and pump, you must first remove the feed tube that connects the pump to the pickup. A large threaded nut fastens the pickup to the oil pump. I find that a large adjustable wrench works well for removing this nut.

Block Disassembly

1 Remove Oil Pump

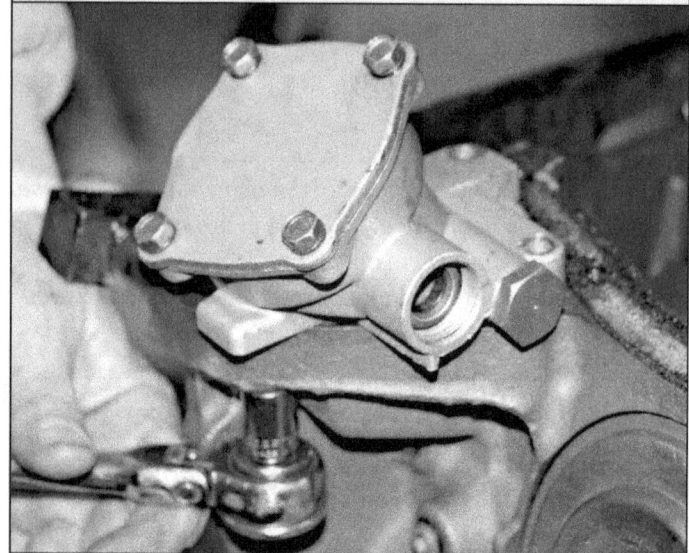

Three bolts fasten the oil pump to the cylinder block. One of the three bolts extends from the top and through the block casting. Use a ratchet and socket or box wrench to remove these bolts. The oil pump drive should remain in place at this time unless it is stuck in the distributor. If it is stuck, drop the pump straight down during removal. All that's left in this process is to remove the oil pan and pickup from the block.

2 Inspect Piston Bores

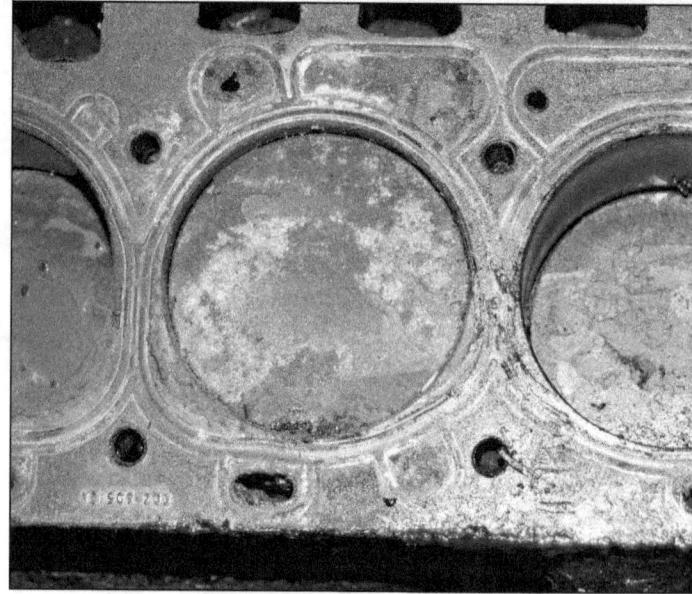

With the external components out of the way, the final step is to remove the rotating assembly, camshaft, and lifters from the cylinder block. Before attempting to remove the pistons from their respective cylinders, check each bore to ensure that it hasn't developed a ridge that interferes with the piston rings that could possibly damage the pistons as they are removed.

ENGINE DISASSEMBLY

3 Remove Ridge from Cylinder Bores

Special Tool

The cylinder bores in your block may have a ridge near the top. During the engine's service life, the piston wears down the cylinder sleeve, pushes the worn material to the top of the bore, and creates a ridge. It is composed of a combination of carbon, dirt, and oil that has accumulated because of poor tuning or excessive wear of components, such as piston rings, valveguides, etc. Use an old-school tool known as a ridge reamer to remove the ridge, which then makes it far easier to get the piston and rod assemblies out of the cylinder bores without causing damage.

The ridge reamer has a set of mildly abrasive stones that are mounted to the expandable tool. Once the tool has been placed in the cylinder bore and fitted to size, rotate it manually until the ridge has been removed from the top of the cylinder, which clears the path for piston and rod removal.

4 Check Connecting Rod Bolts

Once the bores have been checked or any ridge removed, roll the engine over on the stand to gain access to the pistons, rods, and crankshaft. In doing so, you may note that the OEM connecting rod bolts are fitted with Pal or jam nuts over the standard nuts. These archaic pieces cannot be installed in a new engine build, and they should be discarded, even if using connecting rod bolts and nuts.

5 Remove Piston and Rod Assemblies

Rotate the crankshaft so the throws line up with the cylinders or cylinders' rod and piston, so you can properly remove the piston and connecting rod assemblies from the block. I use two old flywheel bolts threaded into the flange at the back of the crankshaft and a pry bar to rotate the crank into the desired position.

FORD Y-BLOCK ENGINES: HOW TO REBUILD AND MODIFY

CHAPTER 4

6 Remove Piston and Rod Assemblies (continued)

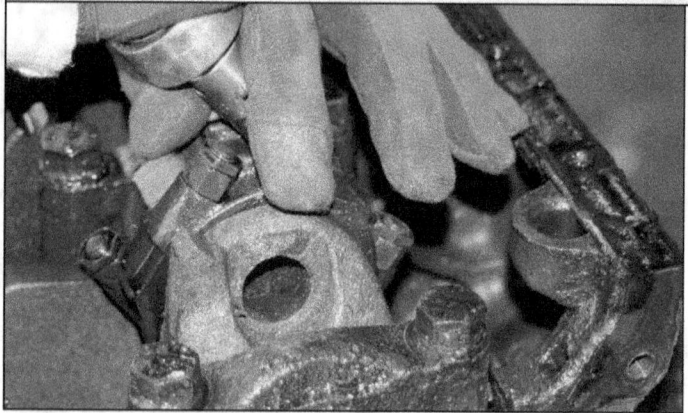

This crankshaft has been rotated in the correct position so the piston and connecting rod assembly can slide straight out of the cylinder. Be sure that the connecting rod and cap are each stamped with a number that corresponds with the respective cylinder. The numerals should be stamped on the portion of the rod and cap that face outward, or toward the oil pan rail of the cylinder block. After ensuring that the connecting rods are numerically marked, remove the nuts that hold the cap in place.

7 Number Connecting Rods

If you find that the connecting rods and caps in an engine are not numerically marked, most machine shops have number stamps, such as these, available. If your connecting rods are not numbered, it is best to stamp the numbers on them before they are removed from the block to avoid any mix-ups. When numbering the connecting rods in a Y-block, remember to consult the cylinder numbering chart on page 141 before proceeding.

8 Remove Connecting Rod Cap

If you find it difficult to remove the connecting rod cap after taking off the nuts, a simple brass drift punch and hammer usually solves the problem. A brass drift is a softer metal, which helps to avoid any damage to the connecting rod cap. Use a drift punch to tap against the surface where the cap joins the connecting rod. This typically separates them so that the cap can be removed.

Professional Mechanic Tip

9 Separate Rod Assembly from Crankshaft Throw

Examine the crankshaft throws before separating the connecting rod assembly from the crankshaft throw. During the removal process be careful not to damage the polished area of the crankshaft when disconnecting rod bolts. These simple rubber boots, available in most auto parts stores, slide over the threads and protect the crankshaft as the rod is removed. You can also use a piece of vacuum line hose of the proper diameter and length.

To remove the piston and rod assembly, push against the connecting rod with a hammer handle until the piston clears the cylinder bore. Once the piston and rod assembly have been removed from the bore, place the connecting rod cap back on the rod with the numbers in proper orientation. This way there is no confusion when your parts arrive at the machine shop.

ENGINE DISASSEMBLY

10 Check for Cap Identificaton

To ensure that they are replaced in the proper position during the reassembly phase of your engine rebuild, use a hammer and sharp punch to stamp dots in the main bearing caps for identification. The main bearing caps can also be stamped with numbers (shown).

11 Remove Main Seal Retainer

You must first remove the retainer that holds the lower portion of the rear main seal so you can access the bolts holding the rear main bearing cap. Two bolts with 12-point heads hold this retainer in place. A 7/16 12-point deep-well socket works best here.

12 Loosen Caps

After the bolts securing the main bearing caps have been removed, use a plastic mallet to tap the caps (as shown) to loosen them. Tap on them firmly enough to break them free, but be careful; you don't need to take a full swing. Once the cap is loose, you should be able to "walk" it from its register by hand.

13 Remove Camshaft and Lifters

The camshaft and lifters are the last components to be removed from the cylinder block. The unique mushroom-style valve lifters in a Y-block must be installed and removed from the bottom. Remove the camshaft from the cylinder block when it's positioned upside down on the engine stand.

To remove the camshaft, gently and carefully use a large screwdriver to pry against the side of one of the cam lobes. Clear the rear cam bearing extending from the front of the block. From this point, remove the cam by hand and feed each journal first through the cam bearings until it is out and then through each of the lifters.

If, for any reason, you intend to reuse the valve lifters, they must be kept in the order in which they contacted the lobes of the camshaft. Keeping them in order can be easily accomplished by marking a piece of cardboard with numbers and an arrow for front to back orientation. Never put used valve lifters on a new camshaft.

FORD Y-BLOCK ENGINES: HOW TO REBUILD AND MODIFY

CHAPTER 5

INSPECTION AND CLEANING

At this point your Ford Y-block engine should be completely disassembled. If you did it the right way, all of the parts and components are tagged, bagged, and organized. In addition, you should have documented the disassembly process so you can reassemble the engine without great difficulty. The various components of your engine rebuild project now need a thorough inspection and cleaning to reveal any damage, determine which parts need to be replaced, and decide which may be returned to within manufacturer's specification during the machining process.

For the disassembly phase, the engine can be separated into four major component groups:

- Carburetor, intake manifold, and cylinder heads
- Valvetrain (camshaft, lifters, pushrods, and rocker arm assemblies)
- Rotating assembly (crankshaft, connecting rods, pistons, dampener, and flywheel)
- Cylinder block

Professional Inspection

Although the average backyard mechanic is fully capable of visually inspecting and cleaning the rocker arm assemblies, pushrods, and camshaft, I recommend you place the other major engine components into the hands of a professional who is better equipped for it. A professional shop achieves professional results, in part, by being better equipped. After all, you want your engine to be as clean as possible. You don't want contaminants or debris to ruin an otherwise professional-caliber rebuild job. In my opinion, you cannot achieve the same results with a rented power washer or steam cleaner as a machine shop that is equipped with a baking oven and hot tank.

Media blasting is an effective means of cleaning engine components other than the cylinder block. A session in the blasting cabinet usually removes almost all traces of rust,

You need to carefully inspect every component of the engine before you start the rebuild process. If the block has cracked main bearing saddles or there is excessive damage in other areas, the block may need to be scrapped. In this case, no significant damage was found and the block is suitable for rebuilding.

INSPECTION AND CLEANING

corrosion, and old paint from your parts. However, the media used to blast the parts consists of aluminum oxide, or glass beads, propelled by high-pressure air, so parts that have been media blasted require additional cleaning with a liquid solvent to remove any residual media residue that may have collected in out-of-the-way places. (Failure to give your media-blasted parts a secondary cleaning could result in media particles being introduced into your newly rebuilt engine. The results are catastrophic.)

I use a two-pronged approach to inspecting components to identify flaws and determine if they remain within manufacturer's specifications. First I clean and visually inspect all components (the accuracy of the Mark I eyeball is not to be underestimated). If they pass this test, then I entrust them to an experienced machinist who possesses the proper equipment, such as micrometers, dial indicators, a dial bore gauge, and Magnafluxing capability.

Rocker Arm Assemblies

As mentioned earlier, the Y-block Ford V-8 suffered from oiling woes that were not entirely the fault of the engine's design. One of the areas affected first by sludge-blocked oil galleries was the rocker arm assembly. Sludge and lack of proper lubrication wreaks havoc on internal engine parts so don't be surprised if at the very least your rocker arm shafts need replacing during the rebuild.

The good news is that rocker shafts and rocker arms are still available through various parts sources. But this is not so for the stands that support the rocker assemblies, unless you wish to purchase aftermarket high-performance units. Be careful in handling the supports, and make sure they are adequately cleaned before reassembling your rocker arm assemblies.

Rocker Arm Assembly Installation

1 Inspect for Sludge

The rocker arm assemblies have been removed from the engine. Years worth of sludge buildup has likely been caused by paraffin-based motor oils and/or lack of regular maintenance. This amount of buildup should be a red flag and an obvious indicator of neglect. Sludge typically prevents proper lubrication and the resulting wear on parts. On a brighter note, if your rocker arms check out okay (no excessive wear or damage), they are fine to use. Longtime Y-block racer Jerry Christenson praises the strength and durability of the OEM rocker arms even under the most extreme use, such as drag racing.

2 Inspect and Clean Rocker Arm Assembly

After removing the cotter pin from one end of the rocker arm shaft, begin disassembly. A soft-headed or plastic mallet is often required to help separate the stands from the shafts. (Keep components in order as they are removed. Do not reuse cotter pins.) This is another good place to take a photo or two for reference before reassembling these components. This rocker arm assembly is now completely disassembled and ready for inspection and cleaning to determine if it can be reused. The rocker arm assemblies are a critical engine part, and any evidence of wear or damage in this area should result in the replacement of the part. I have seen people use abrasives, such as emery cloth, to smooth scored rocker arm shafts and then reuse the shafts in a rebuilt engine. Keep in mind that your rocker arm shafts have a hardened surface, and once this surface has been compromised, it continues to wear at an accelerated rate, whether or not it has been smoothed.

CHAPTER 5

3 Inspect Rocker Arm Shaft

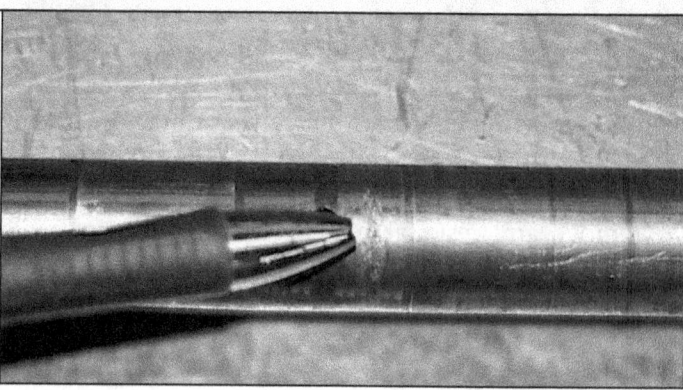

Visual inspection of this rocker arm shaft reveals baked-on sludge in an area not contacted by the rocker arms. Although this looks bad, it should clean up sufficiently to allow the shaft to be reused.

A combination of dirt and inadequate oil supply has caused obvious galling on this rocker arm shaft, and now it is reduced to the status of scrap metal. Rocker arms and shafts are available for the Y-block V-8 through aftermarket sources such as Sealed Power.

Critical Inspection

4 Inspect Rocker Arm Tip

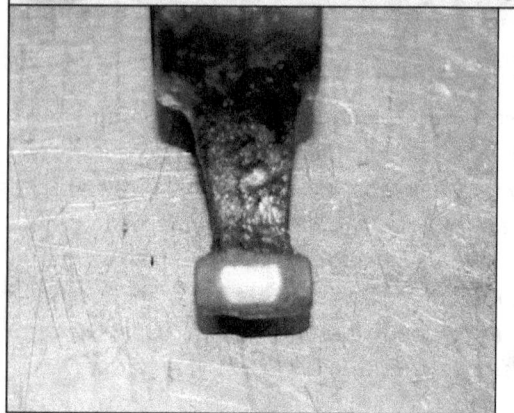

Carefully examine the tip of each rocker arm where it contacts the valvestem for signs of wear. The surface face of the rocker tip should be flat and smooth, and there should be no signs of pitting or cupping, which are signs of excessive wear. If only slightly worn, the rocker arm tip may be refaced using a grinding stone, allowing the rocker arm to be reused. Also critical is the inside radius of the rocker arm where it rides on the shaft. The inside radius is examined visually and tactilely. If there's any wear here, the rocker arm should be replaced. Do not take shortcuts with critical valvetrain components as they have a direct impact on how your engine runs and how long it lasts.

Camshaft and Lifters

If you have any intention of reusing the cam and lifters you remove from the engine, the lifters must be kept in the order they were removed from the block, so that when reinstalled they ride on the same camshaft lobe. Another important point is *never* install used lifters with a new camshaft. This is a recipe for disaster. When visually examining the camshaft and lifters, the most obvious signs of a problem are a pitting or wear pattern. Also look for any camshaft lobes that appear rounder than others (indicative of a wiped cam) or cupping in the face of the lifters.

With the advances in camshaft design made over the past five

Carefully examine the face of each valve lifter for any signs of pitting or cupping as these conditions indicate wear. A straightedge is helpful in determining if a lifter face is worn. A worn camshaft and lifters should not be reused under any circumstances. In addition, never use old lifters on a new camshaft.

FORD Y-BLOCK ENGINES: HOW TO REBUILD AND MODIFY

INSPECTION AND CLEANING

decades, it makes perfect sense to retire that old cam and lifters for a less worn and more efficient design. If you are rebuilding a high-mileage engine, give plenty of consideration to replacing the camshaft and lifters.

Cylinder Heads

With the cylinder heads off the engine, it's time to clean, inspect, and refurbish them. Begin by checking the overall condition of the heads using several simple, unsophisticated, but effective tests. The only tools required to perform this initial assessment of the cylinder heads are a valvespring compressor, a straightedge, some feeler gauges, your hands, and your eyes.

If you plan to reuse your original camshaft and lifters, keep these components and pushrods in the order in which they were installed in the engine. Cut holes in a piece of heavy cardboard, number the holes, and mark the components from each cylinder. This is an inexpensive way to keep your lifters and pushrods organized. (Crane Cams, Summit Racing, Jegs, or aftermarket performance camshaft manufacturers offer professional valvetrain organizers.)

I also make a habit of keeping an old lifter box or two in my home shop as a simple means of keeping lifters organized as I remove them from an engine. Be sure to note the orientation of the lifters to the cylinders on the box, that is, front right, front left, etc.

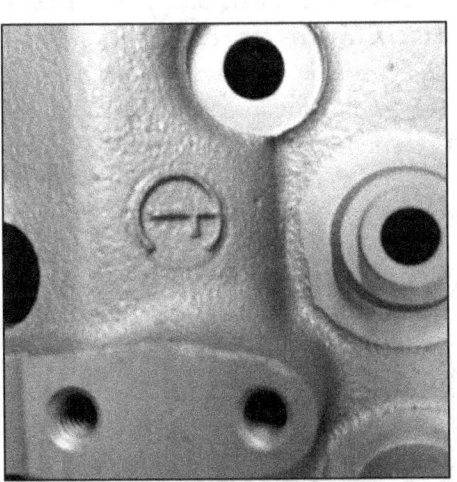

The "CF" casting on this cylinder head stands for the Cleveland Foundry. Unfortunately, Ford closed the Cleveland Foundry in 2012 after many decades of manufacturing engines. Engines took their name from this foundry. Legendary among Ford performance engines is the 351, which is now in short supply. However, more-efficient modern alternatives are available for the performance-minded Y-block owner. Be particularly careful when purchasing used Y-block cylinder head castings.

Along with the face of the valve lifters, the lobes of the camshaft must be examined for wear. Camshaft wear can have several causes, including incorrect valve lash adjustment and lack of scheduled oil changes. With any sign of wear, the camshaft should not be reused under any circumstances. If the cam is original to the engine and the engine has 80,000 miles or more, it's a pretty safe bet that you need to replace the cam, pushrods, lifters, and rocker arms. Perform a thorough and detailed inspection and evaluation of each. If you're performing a complete engine rebuild, these components should be replaced.

The large letter ECZ-G casting on this cylinder head identifies it as one of the very desirable "big valve" heads with 1.92-inch intake valves. Two cylinder head castings bear ECZ-G lettering. Interestingly the small-block Chevy cylinder heads have intake valves that are only slightly larger than the ECZ-G heads at 1.94 inch, and it has been proven that the Y-block Ford heads flow better than the Chevy small-block heads in stock configuration.

CHAPTER 5

Cylinder Head Inspection and Disassembly

1 Inspect Heads

With the cylinder heads off the engine, examine the combustion side of each head. As expected, the passage that feeds oil from the cylinder block to the rocker arm assemblies is thoroughly blocked with sludge. Thanks to modern lubricants, this common problem in the Y-block Ford V-8 of the 1950s and early 1960s is no longer a concern.

2 Inspect Heads (continued)

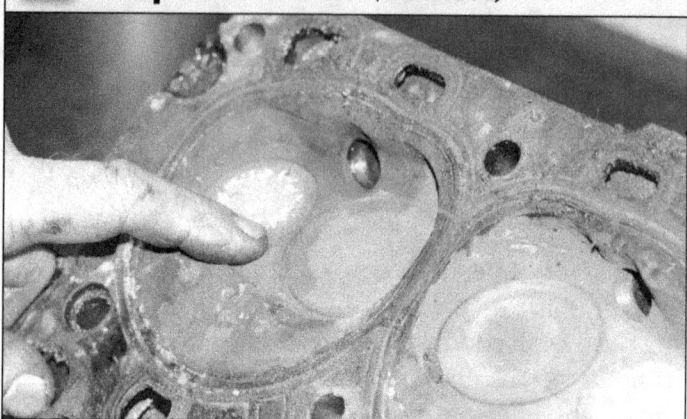

Conduct a visual inspection of the gasket surface, combustion chambers, and valves on any set of cylinder heads. In this case, my heads and parts reveal no obvious problems. A simple tactile test, in which you run your fingertips over the surface of the valves in each chamber, helps to determine if any of the valves have sunk in their seats because of excessive wear. The face of the valves, as they appear in each of the combustion chambers, speaks volumes. The exhaust valves typically bear the brunt of the wear and tear in an engine, and therefore, damage often reveals itself here first. The valves should be flush with the combustion chamber. If not, chances are they have sunk due to wear on the seats.

3 Inspect Heads (continued)

Apart from being very dirty, these cylinder heads appear to be in pretty good shape. This set has no obvious discoloration from burning on the heads of the valves or pits in the combustion chambers. Once disassembled and cleaned, further determination of their overall condition can be made. When dealing with five-decades-old high-mileage engine parts, it may be prudent to attempt to find suitable replacements before breaking your rebuild budget with costly repairs. In other words, take your time, do your homework, and be prepared.

4 Inspect Valvestem Tips

A visual inspection of the valvestem tips reveals signs of damage or wear. The tips of the valves may show galling or mushrooming if badly worn. A micrometer will later be used to determine if the valvestems have worn excessively. If this is the case, the valve should be replaced as with any damaged or worn critical engine component. Again, you are dealing with engine parts that are decades old and have gone through thousands of operating cycles. Here, I replaced the valves with Sealed Power units.

INSPECTION AND CLEANING

5. Disassemble Heads

Here, a pneumatic valvespring compressor is being used in the disassembly of the cylinder heads. Most home shops don't have the luxury of air tools like this one, but apart from slowing the process, a mechanical compressor works equally well. Over the years, I have seen many poor procedural techniques in engine building. Some mechanics have placed a large socket over the valvespring retainer and struck it with a hammer to disassemble a cylinder head. Never do this because costly damage may result. You could crack the head and/or damage the rockers. Always use the correct tool for the job at hand.

Once pressure is applied to the valvespring compressor, the tip of the valve is exposed above the valvespring retainer. Remove and set aside the two split locks that fit into a groove near the tip of the valvestem to hold the retainer and spring in place. When you release pressure on the compressor tool, the valvespring and retainer can be removed from the top and the valve pushed down through the guide and out of the combustion chamber.

6. Check Valveguide Wear

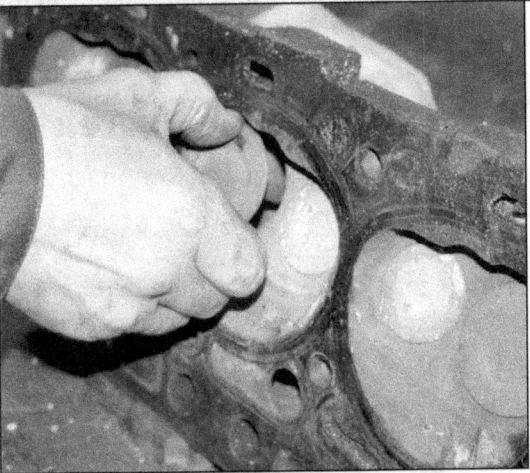

To check the valve, machinist Gil Jordan performs what he refers to as "the wobble test." He pushes the valve off its seat slightly, grasps the head of the valve firmly, and attempts to move it side to side. Obvious movement indicates guide wear that must be addressed. If the guides pass the wobble test, the machining process progresses.

TECH TIP: Two-Piece Valvespring Retainers

Most Y-block V-8s came from the factory with a two-piece valvespring retainer, which acted as a rudimentary rotator. For the sake of strength and durability, I highly recommend replacing the two-piece retainers with an aftermarket, high-strength, one-piece unit. I also make it a habit to replace the valvespring keepers when refurbishing the cylinder heads on any older or high-mileage vehicle. ■

Valves, Valveseats and Combustion Chamber Inspection

1. Inspect Valvestem

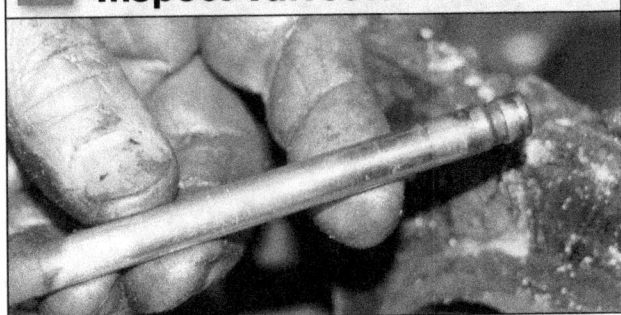

Conduct a visual inspection of each valvestem, and look for signs of galling or excessive wear. Shiny areas are indicative of wear and need to be checked further. Each valve should be examined thoroughly.

2. Measure Valvestem Wear

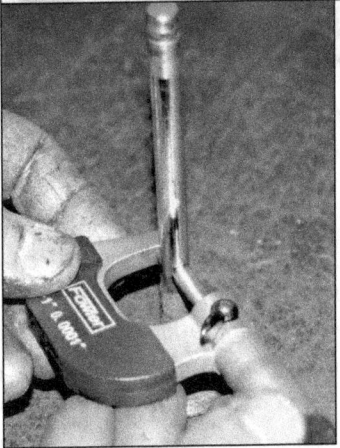

Use a micrometer to measure several areas of the valve-stem to accurately determine the amount of wear on each. Several checks should be made to each valve to determine if it may be reused. The area closest to the tip of the valve is normally the least worn; evidence of wear increases closer to the head of the valve. Compare the measurements to determine the amount of wear on the stem.

CHAPTER 5

3 Inspect Valveseats

With the valves removed from the cylinder head, examining the valveseats in the combustion chamber reveals rust. The moisture that caused the rust came from a leaking head gasket or an external source while the engine was sitting. However, there are no cracks, pitting, or immediate signs of damage or excessive wear. A valveseat that is obviously no longer concentric is also an indicator of significant wear.

4 Examine Cylinder Heads for Flatness

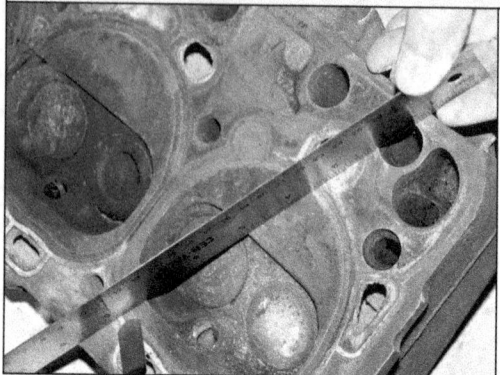

Use a simple straightedge and some feeler gauges to determine the condition or flatness of the cylinder heads. Although cast-iron cylinder heads typically do not warp as frequently as aluminum heads, it can happen, particularly with cases in which the engine has been overheated. Even if your feeler-gauge check reveals some irregularities in the surface of the head, a cleanup cut of a few thousandths at the machine shop often corrects the situation.

Cylinder Head Cleaning

With the initial inspection of the cylinder heads complete, you need to clean them in preparation for more thorough checks that are performed before machining and reassembly.

1 Check Head Passages for Sludge

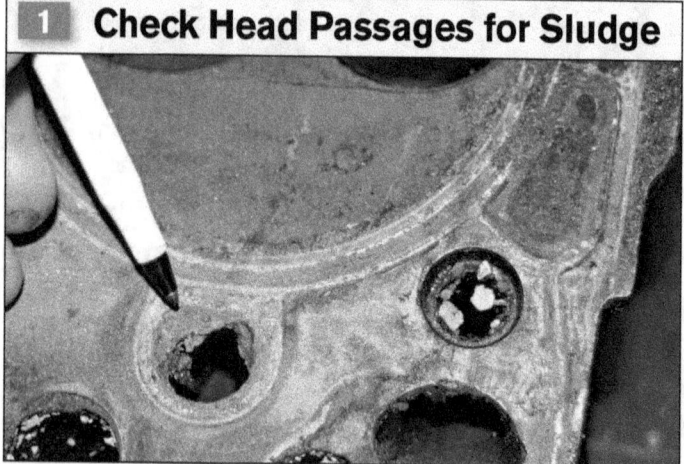

An accumulation of rust and scale has clogged the water passages in this cylinder head. This is common in older engines, particularly the Y-block Ford series. Failure to deal with this during the rebuild process may later cause overheating and premature engine failure. The cylinder heads go through cycles in a Bayco oven and high-temperature parts washer to remove this engine-killing buildup. Using modern coolants and proper maintenance keeps your rebuilt Y-block V-8 running cool for many years to come.

2 Remove Freeze Plugs

You can use a head bolt from a small-block Chevy engine to drive the freeze plugs out of a Y-block head. Strike the freeze plug off-center to cause it to rotate in its bore, and then pull it out using a set of pliers. Discard old freeze plugs and never reuse them.

INSPECTION AND CLEANING

3   Clean and Examine Cylinder Heads

After a cycle in the parts washer, dry the cylinder heads with compressed air and treat them to a thorough sandblasting. Carefully examine each cylinder head casting. Damage, excessive wear, and potential problem areas are much easier to identify now that the castings are clean and free of buildup.

Cylinder Head Repair

It is most important to check cast-iron components, such as the engine block and cylinder heads, for cracks or damage before proceeding with the rebuilding process. Failure to properly check these parts for cracks may lead to future damage and/or failure of your engine. The standard machine shop method of checking cast-iron parts for cracks is called Magnafluxing. This process reveals cracks that are not visible to the naked eye and is a relatively simple and inexpensive means of detecting potentially catastrophic cracks.

After disassembling my cylinder heads and performing a visual inspection, the heads were degreased by way of an overnight stay in the Bayco oven, a thorough bath in the hot tank, and bead blasting. Further visual inspection of the now-clean head castings revealed no apparent problems but, in very short order, a small crack was discovered in one combustion chamber during the Magnaflux process. The size and location of the crack led master machinist Gil Jordan to determine that the best course of action was to perform a cold-fusion crack repair. This type of crack repair is relatively simple but somewhat time-consuming.

Drill a series of overlapping holes along the length of the crack. Thread tapered plugs into the holes and tighten so the head of the plug breaks off. Flatten the protruding portions of the plugs with a peening tool and grind smooth.

The product's manufacturer states that the plugs expand and contract at the same rate as the parent metal, making this type of repair more effective and stronger than welding or other methods. ■

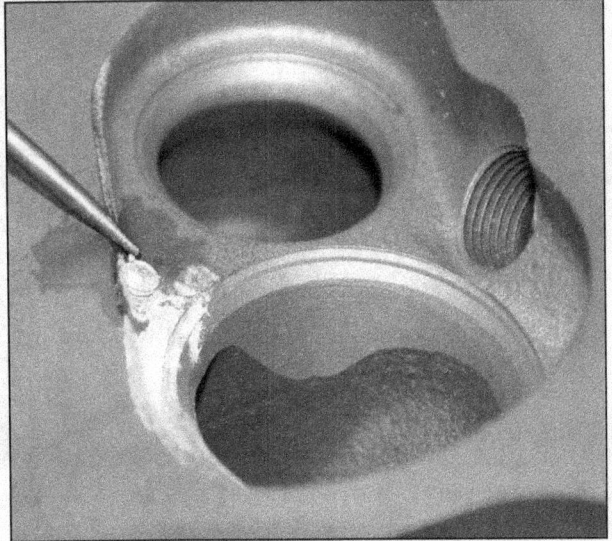
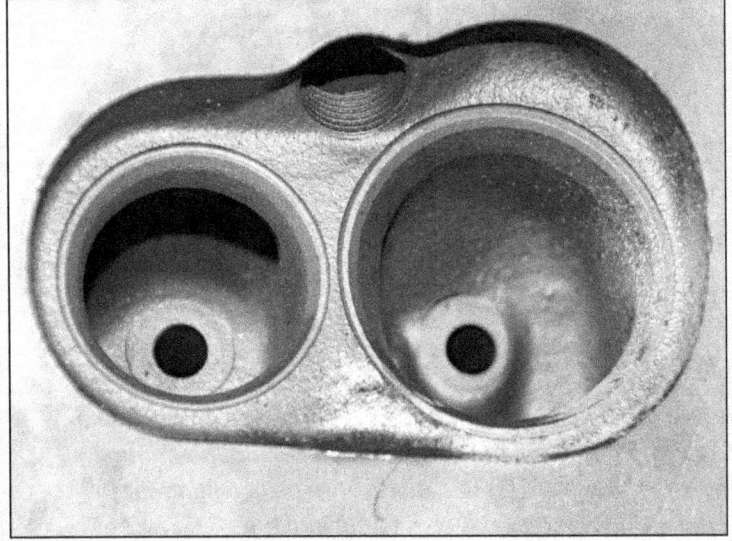

CHAPTER 5

Accurately Identify Engine Parts

Here is one to file under the title "Let the buyer beware." At a recent swap meet a seller was offering a set of well-rusted Y-block cylinder heads at a high price, which suggested that they must be something quite rare. When questioned regarding the pedigree of his parts, the seller indicated that the S cast in the head indicated they were the rare and desirable 312 supercharger castings. They were, in fact, nothing more than regular service heads. I'm certain that no amount of reasoning would have convinced this man that the heads were not for a supercharged engine. ■

You have now reached a critical point in the refurbishing process of the cylinder heads. It is time to search for cracks and other unseen damage. Magnaflux the heads before you perform any machining on the heads. You may waste a lot of money if you skip this step and machine your heads; if you find a serious crack or damage in the heads, your investment in machining will have been wasted.

Magnafluxing is an electromagnetic process that's used to reveal cracks that may be invisible to the naked eye. The areas around the exhaust valves are of particular importance; they are subject to the greatest amount of heat and more prone to crack. Cracks may also appear around bolt holes.

Cylinder Block

To begin an inspection of a block, check each cylinder bore visually and then with a dial bore gauge. You are looking for obvious signs of wear, tapering of the cylinder bores, scuffing, etc.

Block Cleaning

Before sending the block to the Bayco oven for the first step in the cleaning process, remove all freeze plugs, cam bearings, dowel pins, and galley plugs. Be sure to make note of the location from which each galley plug is removed, and store the plugs in a secure location because they will be reused.

1 Remove Freeze Plugs

Before the block is cleaned remove all freeze plugs. Use a discarded head bolt or a blunt-ended punch and hammer and strike it off-center to dislodge the plug. Hitting the plug straight-on may cause it to fall into the water jacket and become lodged, adding unnecessary time to the job.

2 Remove Freeze Plugs (continued)

Once the freeze plug has been rotated sideways, use Vise-Grips to complete its removal. Freeze plugs should never be reused (discard them).

INSPECTION AND CLEANING

3 Inspect Water Jackets

Once the freeze plugs have been removed from the water jackets you see years of accumulated rust and scale. This is a common problem in older cylinder blocks. Baking the block in a specialized oven is the most effective way to remove this buildup. This reduces the material to ash; the follow-up is a trip through the high-pressure parts washer.

4 Remove Oil Filter Adapter

Use an impact wrench to remove the threaded oil filter adapter. It allows removal of the plate, which is a major source of sludge accumulation in the Y-block family of engines. If you don't have an impact wrench, use a 1/2-inch-drive breaker bar and extension, along with the appropriate socket. Some muscle power is required to break the bolt loose.

5 Loosen Mounting Plate

Once the threaded adapter has been removed, use a hammer and brass punch to gently tap the oil filter mounting plate loose. Fasteners do not hold the plate to the block, but sludge likely has it stuck to the block. Caution: Do not use too much force. If the plate is bent during removal, it will leak when reassembled.

6 Remove Mounting Plate

Sludge has accumulated behind the oil filter adapter plate. Remove the plate before cleaning the cylinder block on your freshly rebuilt engine. It is critical to clean this area completely and properly. Sludge buildup here is a common condition in the Y-block V-8.

7 Remove Galley Plugs

Also remove all the threaded galley plugs from the block before cleaning. Apply a penetrating product, such as PB Blaster, and strike the plugs with a hammer and brass punch before attempting to loosen them.

Professional Mechanic Tip

8 Remove Galley Plugs (continued)

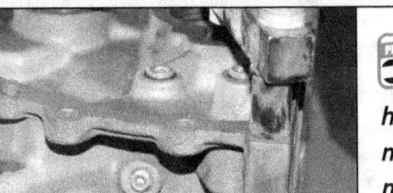

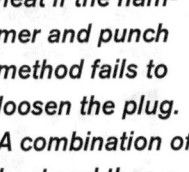

Use a torch to apply heat if the hammer and punch method fails to loosen the plug. A combination of heat and then a sharp blow with a hammer and punch may do the trick. Be careful whenever you work with an open flame.

CHAPTER 5

9 Remove Block Plugs

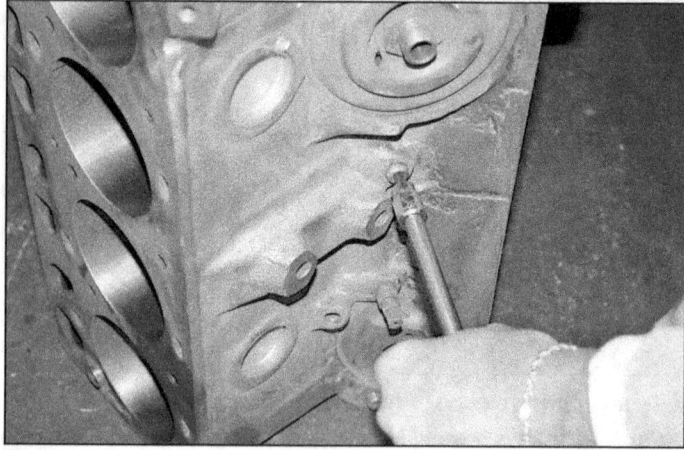

Use an Allen or hex-head socket, extension, and breaker bar or ratchet to remove threaded plugs from the block. The old-fashioned Allen/hex key does not provide adequate torque to get the job done, and you may end up with a rounded-off plug that must be drilled out.

If you've heated the plug and worked at it with a hammer and punch but it still won't come out, you may have to drill it out. Caution: Do not give up and leave the plug in place because dirt may remain behind and that could cause damage to your newly rebuilt engine. When drilling out the plug, be sure to take your time and use a drill bit that is smaller in diameter than the plug so you do not damage the threads.

Special Tool

10 Remove Cam Bearings

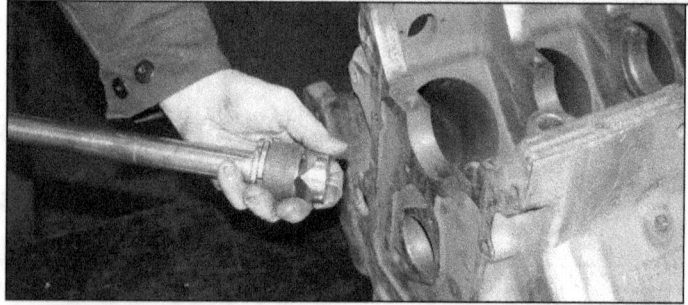

Use this specialized cam bearing removal tool to extract cam bearings from the block before cleaning. Cam bearings should not be left in the block during the cleaning process and never reuse them.

Slide the tool into the cam tunnel and expand it to fit the inside diameter of the bearing by turning in a clockwise direction. When the tool has been expanded and is firmly seated against the bearing, strike the end of the bearing tool to drive the bearing out of the journal.

Special Tool

11 Remove Cam Bearings (continued)

Once a cam bearing has been removed from its bore, the tool and the bearing slips off the fixture. Repeat this process until all the cam bearings have been removed.

INSPECTION AND CLEANING

12 Place Block and Heads in Bayco Oven

The disassembled cylinder heads join the block for an overnight 750-degree bake in the Bayco oven. This is the first step to looking like new for these parts.

An overnight stay in the Bayco oven has converted the five decades of grease and grime into ash.

Block Magnafluxing

Next up is the Magnaflux process, which reveals any cracks not visible to the naked eye. Satisfied that the block is sound, you need to remove any rust and scale that may have been left during the previous steps.

Thoroughly inspect the block for any cracks, flaws, or serious damage. You don't want to machine and spend money on a block that's fatally flawed and should be scrapped. Use a Magnaflux test to locate any cracks or other damage.

To perform the test, the block must first be clean. If the block is not clean the magnetic material does not cling to the cracked area. Use the Magnaflux tool to apply the electromagnetic field. An electromagnetic field is introduced through the cast iron and then an iron powder of contrasting color is applied. The powder accumulates around and reveals imperfections in the casting and, in particular, along the length of a crack. Critical areas to check, particularly on the 312-ci cylinder blocks, are the main bearing supports.

Deck Area Inspection

The deck surface of the cylinder block is first examined visually and tactilely; you're looking for signs that you can see or feel with your hand such as pitting, gouging, or cracking. This is followed by a simple, but effective, means of determining warping by using a straightedge and feeler gauge applied across the surface from different angles. Finally, the deck surface is Magnafluxed to reveal any crack that cannot be seen with the naked eye.

CHAPTER 5

Critical Inspection

1 Inspect for Block Cracks

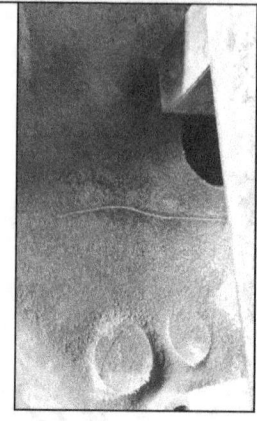

The cylinder block deck surface is another area that's prone to cracks. The bolt holes closest to the perimeter of the block and nearest the water jackets are particularly prone to cracking. Typically, you see spider-web cracks emanating outward from the bolt holes. Although cracks are not good news, cracks may not reduce the status of your cylinder block to scrap iron. The location and size of the crack and cost of repair are the determining factors as to whether a repair can, or should, be attempted.

If a crack is present, the magnetic material used in the Magnaflux test accumulates and adheres to the cracked area so you can easily see the crack.

2 Check for Casting Flash

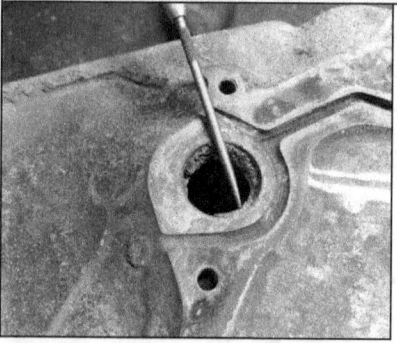

This block has received a thorough baking and washing to remove the accumulated grease, rust, and scale, but casting flash still remains at the opening to a water jacket in the front of the block. This flashing, a thin layer of metal left over from the foundry's casting of the block, can cause stress risers, and cracks in the block may develop. It also impedes coolant flow and could cause your rebuilt engine to run hot.

Professional Mechanic Tip

3 Remove Casting Flash

Use a die grinder to remove the casting flash from the water jacket. Removal of this material allows for maximum coolant flow within the block and ensures proper operating temperatures in the engine. Remove only the flashing material from water jackets. Do not attempt to increase the size of any openings.

Professional Mechanic Tip

4 Remove Casting Flash (continued)

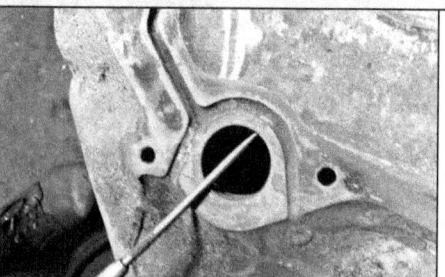

After several minutes of grinding, the water jacket opening is now the proper diameter and without any obstructions. Grind down the parting line. By doing this you have helped eliminate the potential for overheating your newly rebuilt engine. Use a bimetal grinding bit, suitable for use on cast iron, on the rotary tool to remove flashing material.

5 Inspect Water Jackets

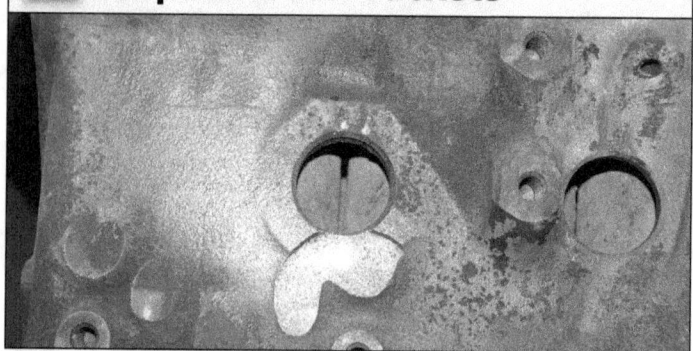

The water jackets surrounding the cylinders are a critical area for cooling the engine. Even after a thorough cleaning, some leftover rust and scale may remain. Carefully inspect these areas and use an inspection light if necessary to make sure all rust and scale have been removed from the water jackets.

INSPECTION AND CLEANING

6 Remove Water Jacket Rust and Scale

You can feed a coat hanger or a welding rod into the water passages to remove leftover rust from the water jackets in the cylinder block. Every piece of unwanted rust removed from the cylinder block improves cooling and increases engine longevity.

Just a short time scraping loose metal from the water jackets of the cleaned block resulted in this pile of rust. Allowing rust to remain in the block adversely affects the engine's cooling and creates hot spots that decrease combustion efficiency.

Main Bearing Saddle Inspection

Verify the alignment of the main bearing saddles and caps in relation to factory specification and one another. Any discrepancies noted here are corrected by line honing the block during the machining process.

You can lightly use a Mill Bastard file to remove sharp edges from the main bearing saddles in the block in preparation for checking the line bore to verify that the main bearing bores are within specification. The main bearing caps receive this treatment also. You must remove sharp edges or burrs to ease bearing installation during reassembly.

The gasket mounting surfaces of the block are dressed with a sander using fine-grit paper, which smooths but does not gouge. The purpose here is not to remove a lot of material but merely smooth out any rough spots or burrs and help prevent future leaks when the engine is reassembled. You may also find that even after a thorough cleaning, stubborn gasket material remains on some surfaces.

Make sure the threads of the main bearing bolts are clean and not damaged. Examine the spiral pattern of the threads, and if it is wavy or malformed, throw away the bolts. The 312 blocks are prone to cracks in this area because of their enlarged main bearing saddles and inaccurate torque specifications initially listed by the factory.

Some engines in the Y-block family use two different-length main bearing cap bolts. The longer ones (shown) are used in the number-5 cap located at the rear of the block. During disassembly, these bolts and main bearing caps need to be labeled, organized, and stored.

FORD Y-BLOCK ENGINES: HOW TO REBUILD AND MODIFY

CHAPTER 5

1. Apply Motor Oil

Apply a light coating of 30-weight motor oil to the threads on each of the main bearing cap bolts before assembly. This ensures a proper torque reading when the bolts are tightened.

Coat the underside of the head on each main bearing cap bolt with oil. Failure to do so could result in a false torque reading. I prefer to use a squirt can to do this, but you can brush it on or work the oil into the surface with your fingers.

2. Snug Main Bearing Cap Bolts

Use a speed wrench to snug up the main bolts. This method allows you to feel for any problems in the threads, such as burrs. Do the same when you're assembling the engine. As you tighten the main bolts, feel for any binding or excessive resistance. If you feel some, chase the threads again to make sure they are clean. If that doesn't resolve the problem, tap the bolt hole, but that should only be required in severe circumstances. Remember, air tools should never be used for this process or other delicate assembly processes.

Torque Fasteners

3. Tighten Main Bearing Cap Bolts

Tighten the main bearing cap bolts in three increments and alternate from side to side until you reach 95 ft-lbs. The correct torque spec for OEM hardware is 95 ft-lbs, but torque specs vary between aftermarket and OEM hardware.

In addition, the assembly oil or lube also affects the final torque spec. Follow the hardware manufacturer's torque spec and assembly lube recommendations and correctly follow the torquing process. If you arrive at the wrong spec, you could break bolts or engine failure could result at start-up.

For these bolts, first torque to 32, then 64, and finally 95 ft-lbs. Be warned that incorrect torque values for Y-block main bearing bolts have previously been published. Overtightening of these bolts could result in cracks developing in the block's main bearing webs. If you use aftermarket hardware and/or assembly paste (such as ARP provides) be sure to follow the bolt manufacturer's torque recommendations.

Critical Inspection

4. Measure Bores

With the main bearing caps torqued into place, use a dial bore gauge to measure each main bearing bore. You must ensure that the main bearing bores are concentric and in alignment to one another; this is critical to engine longevity.

INSPECTION AND CLEANING

Pistons and Connecting Rods

Consider the number of rotations as well as heating and cooling cycles experienced by these critical parts before an engine rebuild is necessary. A visual inspection of the pistons can provide a wealth of information about the condition of the engine. Beginning with the combustion surface (top) of the piston, evidence of excessive carbon buildup reveals the use of poor-grade fuels or an improperly tuned engine. Pitting or burning on the surface of the piston indicates a lean condition in the cylinder, and wet, oily deposits are indicative of valveguide or piston ring wear. Scuffing (shiny areas) on the skirts of the pistons also indicates excessive wear. At the machine shop a micrometer is used to accurately determine the amount of wear by measuring several areas of each piston skirt.

In order to remove the pistons from the connecting rods, you can use a pair of snap ring pliers to remove the wrist pin retainer from one side. Since Y-block engines have full-floating wrist pins, the pin can be easily tapped out, disconnecting the piston from the rod. The wrist pin retainer has a small hole in the end of each of its loops. Insert the tip of the snap ring plier into these holes, so you can compress the retainer enough to allow removal from the groove in the piston.

Place the connecting rod securely in a soft-jawed vise, and use a brass mallet to tap out the connecting rod bolts. Knurl the connecting rod bolts where they fit into the rod to keep them from spinning.

Connecting rods should be reconditioned for almost all rebuilds. The bearing ends that ride on the crankshaft are resized (brought back to a concentric shape within recommended specification by machining) and the piston pin bushings in the small ends are replaced. I make it a habit to replace the connecting rod bolts and nuts with new hardware.

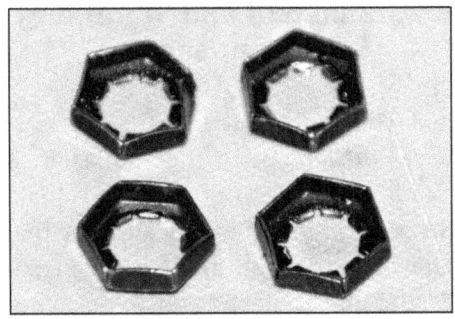

Ford installed Pal nuts in the Y-block V-8 engines at the factory, and they helped secure the connecting rod hardware. With the advent of modern bolts and nuts, such as the type supplied by ARP, they are no longer necessary and should be discarded along with the old nuts and bolts.

Discard the OEM connecting rod bolts and never reuse them. Bolts have a memory; if they have been stretched, they do not have the correct clamping force, so don't cut corners by reusing them. Use modern, high-performance replacement fasteners, such as these from ARP. I seldom reuse connecting rod bolts, especially in older engines. Take a moment to consider how many heating and cooling cycles as well as rotational forces these bolts have endured over the life of the engine, and the argument for replacement becomes crystal clear.

Pistons can be read to determine what has been happening in individual cylinders in an engine when it was running. The top of this piston shows an accumulation of carbon buildup that is indicative of the engine's mileage. If I had observed pitting on the top of the piston, it would have been a sign of detonation because of an overly lean fuel mixture or incorrect ignition timing.

From the side, this piston shows a buildup of sludge in and around the piston rings and ring lands, along with scuffing on the piston skirt, which is the shiny area. Both are indicative of excessive clearance that's caused from wear because of high mileage. In a running engine, this condition manifests itself through an internal noise referred to as "piston slap."

FORD Y-BLOCK ENGINES: HOW TO REBUILD AND MODIFY

CHAPTER 5

Crankshaft and Vibration Dampener

The first step to identify excessive wear or damage to the crankshaft is reading connecting rod and main bearing inserts. Bearing surfaces that are worn through to the copper coating are an indication of wear. Excessively worn bearings show signs of thinning in portions of their material; this is a result of severe pounding caused by a combination of wear and/or lack of proper lubrication. When reading a connecting rod bearing insert be aware that the top portion of the insert bears most of the load in an engine and shows the most wear.

Problems with the crankshaft that can be detected upon initial inspection are in the area of the snout and keyway, where the vibration dampener mounts, and, of course, the machined areas of the main and rod journals. Running a fingernail across the polished surfaces of the crank journals may reveal small grooves caused by wear. Even if no obvious signs of wear are present the crankshaft journals should be checked with a micrometer to determine if they remain within factory specifications or have been previously machined. After a thorough cleaning, the crankshaft should be Magnafluxed to reveal any hidden cracks.

The vibration dampener is often overlooked during an engine rebuild, and failure to identify problems with this critical component in the rotating assembly may lead to later problems. In conducting a visual inspection of the vibration dampener, look for obvious signs of wear, such as cracking or separation in the rubber between the inner and outer portions of the dampener. You also need to check the machined inner and outer surface of the dampener and its keyway (where it mounts on the snout of the crankshaft and contacts the timing cover seal).

Crankshaft and Vibration Dampener Inspection

1 Inspect Machined Areas

Visually inspect the machined areas of the throws where the connecting rod and main bearings ride. If they can be felt, they can be seen. Initially look for obvious cracks, grooves, burrs, or evidence of heat (a bluing of the metal on the journal). Inspect the main bearings to see if any signs that the crank might be bent. If the crank is bent, you see an uneven wear pattern on the bearing surfaces. Typically, a qualified machinist performs the run-out procedure. In this case the machinist, taking all the above factors into consideration, chose not to go to the additional expense.

You can check run-out by installing the main bearings in the block, lubricating them with oil, setting the crank in the block, and then install the number-1 and number-5 main caps. Set up a dial indicator with magnetic base to contact the number-3 (thrust) journal of the crankshaft. Slowly turn the crank and note any deviation.

2 Check Specs — Documentation Required

Use a micrometer to determine if the crankshaft is still within factory spec and if its journals have been previously machined undersize. Check each journal in turn, and record the results. Rod journal specifications for both the 292 and 312 should be 2.1880 to 2.1888 inches. The 292 main bearing journals should measure 2.4980 to 2.4988 inches. The 312's larger main bearing journal specifications are 2.6235 to 2.6243 inches.

INSPECTION AND CLEANING

3 Test for Cracks

The crankshaft is also treated to a Magnaflux test for cracks as was done with the cylinder heads and block. A magnetic powder is applied to areas of the crankshaft prone to cracks, such as oil supply holes, after which a magnetic field is introduced. The magnetic powder collects in any cracks. For the most part, a crack in a crankshaft may not spell doom. In the case of a crankshaft, the location, length, and depth of the crack are the determining factors. I have seen crankshafts used in racing engines that have detectable cracks.

4 Chamfer Oil Holes

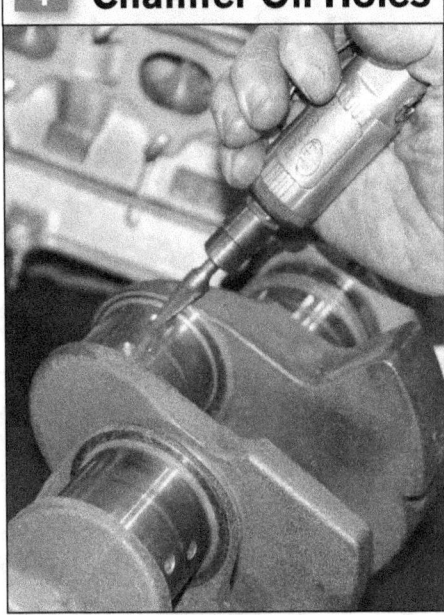

This particular crankshaft passed all tests with flying colors. It is not cracked, and the journals are within factory spec and need only a polishing of the rod and main bearing journal surfaces to be serviceable.

The next step in the process of preparing the crankshaft is to carefully use a die grinder to chamfer the oil holes in the journals to improve lubrication. Chamfering refers to using a die grinder with a polishing stone to remove the sharp edges from openings. Doing so allows oil to flow more smoothly.

After this, the crankshaft will receive the first of several cleanings in preparation for polishing. Measuring crankshaft runout is typically a machine shop procedure. The at-home mechanic can check runout by installing the main bearings in the block, lubricating them with oil, setting the crank in the block, then installing the number-1 and number-5 main caps. A dial indicator with magnetic base is then setup to contact the number-3 thrust journal of the crankshaft. The crank is then slowly turned and any deflection is measured.

5 Polish Crankshaft

With the crankshaft cleaned and the oil holes chamfered, it is now ready for polishing, which is followed by a final cleaning with solvent. The crankshaft and most other critical engine components have been cleaned several times before assembly of the engine begins. Critical engine components cannot be too clean.

Polishing the crankshaft journals involves the crankshaft being set up in a lathe that spins at low speed during the polishing process.

6 Polish Crankshaft (continued) — Important!

Mount the crankshaft in the lathe for crankshaft polishing. Use two different grit-polishing belts to smooth the surface of the journals. One important note: During this process the crankshaft must be spun in the same direction in which it rotates in the engine. This is because of the microscopic peaks in the metal created during the machining process.

7 Remove Sharp Edges

After inspecting the crankshaft to identify any sharp edges or other stress risers, use a die grinder to remove them. Sharp edges can produce stress risers, and this can lead to outright failure of the crankshaft, so you need to identify these areas and grind them down. Using a die grinder and bit suitable for cast iron, carefully grind down these edges to prevent cracks from forming. The crankshaft receives yet another thorough cleaning before the engine assembly begins.

8 Verify Crankshaft Type

It is easy to differentiate between the 292 and 312 crankshafts and determine which crankshaft you have. The 312 crankshaft (right) has a button (raised round area) on the flywheel flange while the 292 crankshaft (left) does not. The stroke and main journal diameters are also different between the 292 and 312 engines.

9 Check Crankshaft Balance

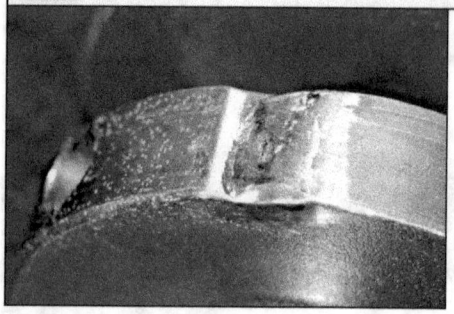

This is a crankshaft that has been dynamically balanced. During this process, Mallory metal was added to the crankshaft until proper balance was achieved. If you change components of the rotating assembly during your rebuild, check the balance to avoid the possibility of internal vibration, which can cause catastrophic damage to the engine.

10 Verify Fit

This 312 Y-block crankshaft's main bearing journals have been machined to a 2.498-inch diameter so the crank fits in a 292 block. The oil slinger at the rear of the crank is also turned down because most machine shops do not have a stone narrow enough to perform the task of machining this area separately. There are two schools of thought on this particular procedure. Some say that when using a neoprene rear main seal, which the 292 has, it causes no problems. Others say that turning down the slinger creates oil leaks.

INSPECTION AND CLEANING

11. Inspect Oil Slinger

This is a Y-block crankshaft with the oil slinger intact as delivered from the factory. The purpose of the slinger is to divert engine oil away from the rear main seal area and prevent leaks. This engineering feature was particularly critical in engines that used a rope-type rear main seal.

Professional Mechanic Tip

12. Inspect Dampener

More than 50 years have taken their toll on this dampener, and, as a result, the rubber ring between the inner and outer portions of the dampener is cracked. A crankshaft dampener has a reliable service life, and after 50 years, it's a good idea to replace the dampener. These cracks are a red flag, so this dampener should be replaced to avoid future catastrophic failure on any newly rebuilt engine.

Careful examination of this dampener reveals that the rubber insulator ring and the machined surfaces are sound. The timing marks are in excellent condition as well, so you are able to easily set timing using this dampener. This dampener is serviceable and will be used on the rebuilt engine.

Sonic Testing

The purpose of sonic testing a block is to measure the overall thickness of the cylinder walls to determine how far the block may be safely bored oversize. Sonic checking allows you to measure the thickness of a part, such as a cylinder wall, when you have access only to one side of the part.

The procedure consists of applying a jelly substance to the cylinder walls' after which a probe is used to send ultrasonic sound waves through the material. The length of time it takes for the sound waves to return to the machine indicates the thickness of the cylinder wall. Measurements are taken from top to bottom, front to rear, thrust, and opposite sides of the cylinder walls. The thickness on the thrust side is the most critical because this area is the most stressed when an engine is running.

Ford Y-block V-8 blocks were cast in the days before the process of thin-wall castings was perfected and became standard for Ford engines in 1962. Does this mean you should not go to the additional expense to have your block sonic checked? I say no if there are no immediate questions about the cylinder block.

From the perspective of a racer, Jerry Christenson recommends a sonic check for any Y-block that is to be bored more than .060. This is based on the fact that race engines are subjected to far more stresses in a short period than a stock rebuild sees in a lifetime of service.

If you decide to have your block sonic checked, the accepted minimum thickness for cylinder walls is .200 inch.

An engine block sonic tester costs approximately $300. If you're rebuilding several engines, you can probably justify the cost of buying one. However, if you only plan to rebuild one particular Y-block engine, you should take the engine to a machinist with a sonic tester and have it carefully inspected.

You need to verify that the cylinder wall has the minimum thickness for the necessary overbore. You don't want to have the block overbored and then find out the cylinder walls are too thin; this will cause you to break into the water jackets. The end result is a high likelihood of failure because the block isn't strong enough for typical operating demands.

CHAPTER 6

MACHINING AND PARTS SELECTION

This is the stage in the rebuilding process at which your Y-block gains a new lease on life. During the machining process, you're truing all surfaces and components, so it functions like a factory-new engine. Allow me to impart the mantra of master machinist Gil Jordan to begin this chapter on machine work. It is simple and to the point. "Flat is flat, straight is straight, and round is round." To rebuild an engine that provides years of service you have to pay careful attention to detail, clean and prepare properly, contract professional machine work, choose a combination of quality parts that work in concert with one another, and carefully follow proper assembly procedures.

Parts Sources

It has always been a little harder to find high-quality parts for Ford engines, perhaps with the exception of the modern small-block V-8. Therefore, before you start rebuilding, you must find a reliable source of the correct parts. The availability of parts for the Y-block V-8 has increased tenfold. With the increased demand for these engines comes a renewed aftermarket interest in the manufacture of dedicated performance parts.

I can almost guarantee that if you inquired about the most common replacement parts for your Y-block engine in your average chain auto parts store, you would be met with a blank stare from the eighteen-year-old behind the computer. I look for an old-time, established parts store, where I am more likely to encounter employees with years of experience, a willingness to help, and access to actual parts catalogs, not just a computerized inventory.

Connecting Rods

Connecting rod reconditioning consists of resizing the big ends (crankshaft end) to make them concentric, replacing the bushings in the small ends (piston end) to remove any play created by years of wear, and the replacement of hardware (rod bolts and nuts).

To maximize cylinder sealing and pressure, the head surfaces must be trued; the milling machine removes irregularities and warping. First .003 inch of material was removed from the surface of the cylinder head on the first cut. A second cut of .002 resulted in a clean, flat surface. A total of .005 was removed from the face of each cylinder head during this process.

Connecting Rod Installation

Here's a tip: I have chosen to replace the OEM five-decades-old connecting rod bolts with stronger, more modern hardware from ARP in both of the engines. Taking into account that these engines are more than 50 years old and have experienced the stresses of normal use and countless cycles of heating and cooling, replacing the connecting rod bolts in a Y-block rebuild falls into the category of inexpensive insurance.

1 Remove Burrs on Rods

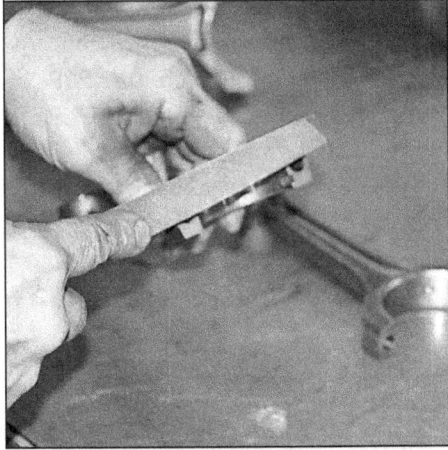

The original bolts have been removed in preparation for resizing. Use a flat file to go over the connecting rods and remove any burrs from the cap and rod. If the connecting rod has any burrs on its machined areas, there could be a mismatch between the rod cap and rod.

2 Grind Faces

Have a machine shop perform this procedure. A Sunnen cap-grinding machine corrects the faces of the mating surfaces of the connecting rods and caps. This process removes a couple of thousandths of material so that a flat surface between the rod and cap is attained.

3 Remove Burrs on Caps

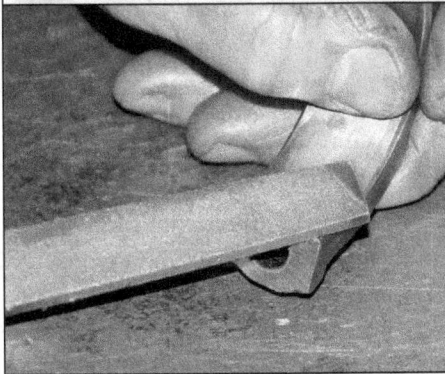

Use a flat file to remove any burrs or sharp edges after the caps and rods have been refaced. Be careful not to mar or damage any of the freshly machined surfaces. Install the bearing when the engine is reassembled.

4 Use Parts Washer

The connecting rods and caps take a trip through the parts washer between steps in the reconditioning process. Critical engine parts cannot be cleaned too frequently before assembly.

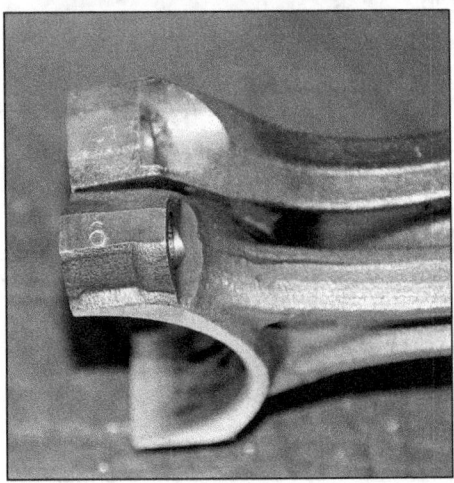

The small-block Chevy V-8 connecting rod (top) is compared to the Ford Y-block's connecting rod (bottom). The Chevy rod is broach-cut to accommodate its bolts while the Y-block rod is spot-faced, leaving more material for greater strength.

CHAPTER 6

5 Face Rods

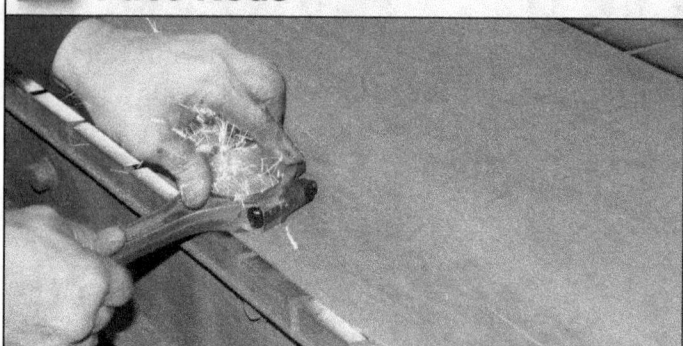

Face the sides of the connecting rods on a head-resurfacing machine. Once again, it is just to remove burrs and sharp edges. Very little material is removed during this process since the purpose is simply to smooth the surface of the rod.

6 Verify Rod Bolt Length

The 292 (EBU forging) and 312 (ECG forging) connecting rods are different lengths. The 292s measure 6.324 inches while the 312s are 6.252 inches and use different-length bolts. According to ARP, the correct bolt for the 239- to 292-ci engine is ARP PN 154-6005, while the correct bolt for the 312 is PN 154-6004. Some folks believe that the 292 truck connecting rod (C1TE forging) is stronger than the passenger car forging. If, for any reason, you are thinking of using the truck connecting rod, please note that they are the same length as the 312 rod at 6.252 inches.

7 Install Rod Bolts

Important!

Secure the connecting rods in this fixture in a press to install the rod bolts. Use a brass drift to install the ARP rod bolts. It is important to ensure that each bolt goes into the connecting rod straight and that it seats fully against the spot face. If, for any reason, the bolt does not fit tight in the connecting rod, the rod should be replaced.

8 Torque Bolts

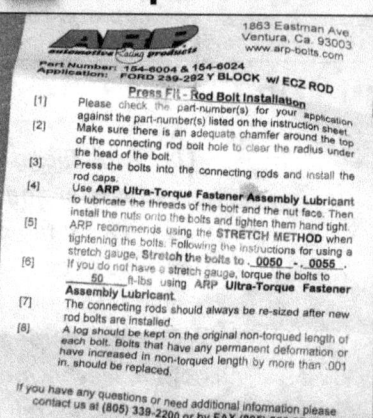

You absolutely must read the ARP instructions that come with rod bolts. If you have prior experience with this brand of bolt you know that three torque sequences are no longer required to prestretch the bolts. Torque the bolts one time for proper stretch. Also note that when using the included ARP lubricant, torque values other than OEM specification are listed.

9 Torque Bolts (continued)

Tighten the ARP connecting rod bolts to the recommended torque value to prestretch them. A stretch gauge is not required, and these particular ARP bolts require just one torque application on their bolts.

10 Inspect Connecting Rod

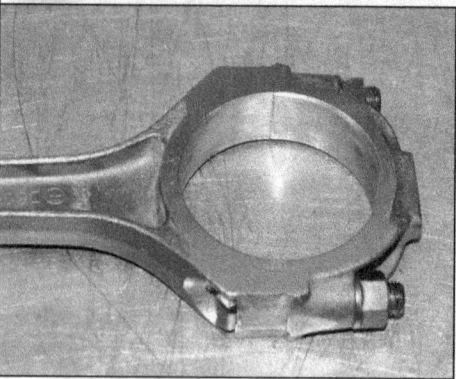

This finished connecting rod has new hardware installed. It's smooth, flat, and ready for the next step in the reconditioning process: resizing the big ends.

FORD Y-BLOCK ENGINES: HOW TO REBUILD AND MODIFY

Big End Preparation

1 Set Tolerance

Use a dial indicator affixed to the connecting rod machine to set the tolerance for resizing the big ends on each connecting rod.

2 Resize Ends

Resize the big ends of the connecting rods using various stones, graduating from coarse to fine. Once completed, each rod's big end is concentric and within specification.

Small End Preparation

1 Inspect Small Ends

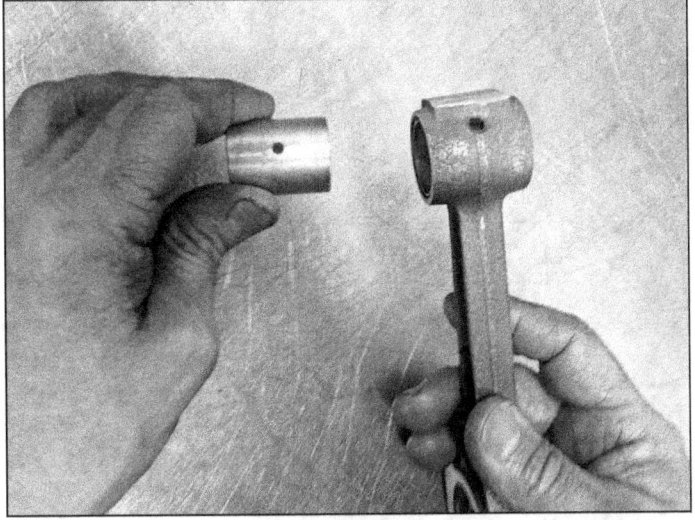

As part of the reconditioning of the connecting rods, the bushings in the small ends will be replaced. Note that the bushing and rod both have an oil hole drilled in them. These holes must line up. If they are not properly aligned, the wrist pin does not receive adequate lubrication, and catastrophic failure could result.

2 Insert in Vise

To remove and replace the bushing, secure the connecting rod in a soft-jawed vise. This prevents any movement of the rod, or damage, during the process.

CHAPTER 6

3 Remove Old Bushing

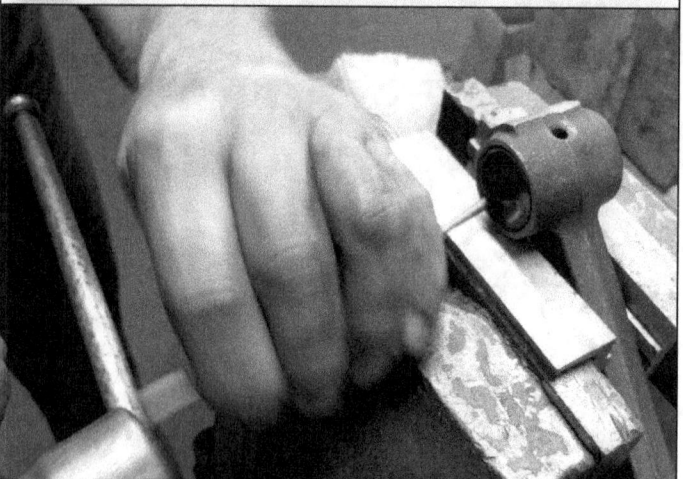

With the connecting rod secured in a vise, use a hammer and driver to carefully remove the old bushing. The technique is to place the pick as close to the joint in the bushing as possible and then drive against it with the hammer to force the bushing from the rod. Before proceeding, the connecting rod receives yet another close visual and tactile inspection for burrs.

5 Install New Bushing

Lubricate the bushings with 30-weight oil and align the bushing on the edge of the bores. Use the soft-jawed vise to press the new bushing into the rod. The chamfered side of the bushing then goes up against the chamfered side of the connecting rod. Pay careful attention to the alignment of the oil hole in the bushing relative to the oil hole in the connecting rod.

4 Choose New Bushing

Two replacement pin bushings are offered for the Y-block. One has the standard inside diameter and the other has a .020-inch-thicker inside diameter to allow for honing to "custom fit" the wrist pins.

6 Verify Oil Hole Alignment

With the new bushing installed, visually check the small end of the rod to ensure proper oil hole alignment. Ensuring that the oil holes in the bushing and connecting rod are properly aligned is critical for proper lubrication of the wrist pin.

7 Burnish Bushing

Burnish the outside edges of the newly installed bushings on both sides with a round tool.

MACHINING AND PARTS SELECTION

8 Resize Rod

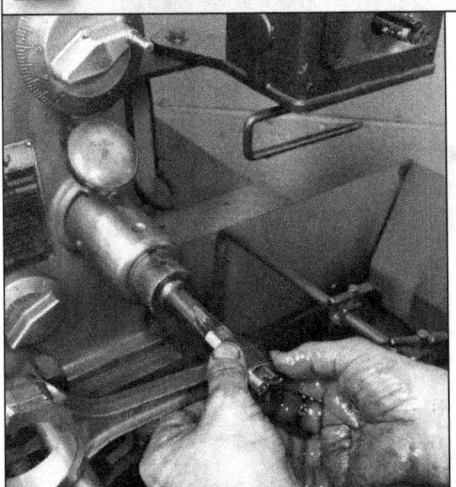

This fixture on the Sunnen connecting rod resizing machine is used to hone the inside diameter of the newly installed bushing to proper tolerance. The honing stones remove small amounts of material until the desired dimension has been achieved. When finished, there is a small clearance between the bushing and the wrist pin (which connects the piston to the rod) to allow for lubrication.

9 Verify Inside Diameter

As the honing process proceeds, frequently check the bushings with a dial indicator until the proper inside diameter has been achieved. Clearance should be .0003 to .0005 inch.

Rotating Assembly

It is time for balancing when the crankshaft is clean and has been checked for cracks, the rod and main bearing journals have been either machined undersize or polished, and all of them thoroughly cleaned again. As it relates to automotive applications, balancing refers to equalizing the weights of reciprocating and rotating components.

Reciprocating weight is the force each piston and connecting rod exerts on the crankshaft as they move up and down. To determine reciprocating weight the individual weight in grams of the pistons, wrist pins, wrist pin locks, piston rings, and small ends of the connecting rods are determined and added together. The big end of the connecting rods is not part of the sum of reciprocating weight. The big- and small-end weights of the connecting rods are determined separately.

This is achieved through the use of a special fixture. Placing each connecting rod in this fixture eliminates the small end of the rod from the indicated weight. Once the big ends of the connecting rods have been weighed each is machined by removing material from the pad on the bottom of the rod cap so that all match the weight of the lightest rod.

Next, small-end weight is determined and, again, each is matched to the lightest rod by machining material off the pad at the top of the small end of the rod. This weight is then added to the total reciprocating weight total.

Rotating weight refers to the centrifugal forces exerted on the crankshaft from the mass of the big ends of the connecting rods and rod bearings as it spins. To calculate the rotating weight (in grams) add the weight of the big ends of the connecting rods to the weight of the connecting rod. The reciprocating weight and rotating weight are used to create the bobweight.

To determine bobweight, 50 percent of the reciprocating mass is added to 100 percent of the rotating mass. The crankshaft, with its balancer attached, is then mounted in a balancing machine fitted with a magnetic probe attached to the balancer at the centerline of the crankshaft. Bobweights are then assembled and clamped to all four connecting rod journals of the crankshaft. The crankshaft is test spun by hand. Then the flywheel is fitted to the crankshaft, and the balancing machine is activated. A digital readout indicates where weight should be added or removed from the crankshaft to achieve balance.

TECH TIP: Sample Bobweight

Here is the bobweight formula for my 322-ci, high-performance Y-block. ■

Component	Weight (grams)
Piston	518
Pin	120
Locks	3
Piston rings	52
Small end of rod	173
Big end of rod	465 x 2
(two connecting rods for each crankshaft journal)	
Connecting rod bearings	50 x 2
Oil in rod	3
Total weight	**1,899**

Rotating Assembly Balancing
Documentation Required

1 Weigh Rotating Assembly

Use a gram scale to accurately weigh the components of the rotating assembly as part of the balancing process and then record the weights. The recorded component weights will be used to determine where material should be removed to achieve the closest possible balance between components.

2 Weigh Wrist Pin

Weigh the wrist pin from each piston and record the number.

3 Weigh Ring Set

Weigh the ring set for each piston individually and record. Next, weigh the upper and lower connecting rod and then the bearing inserts for each rod.

4 Weigh Pistons

Weigh the pistons (without wrist pins). The custom-made forged-aluminum pistons from Race-Tec for my high-performance engine build weighed exactly the same across the board. This is a testament to the quality of the product and attention to detail by the manufacturer.

These Sealed Power .040 oversize replacement pistons are for my stock engine rebuild. All pistons weighed within 2 grams of one another. Matching the heaviest pistons with the lightest of the 292 connecting rods easily compensates for the difference in weight. The decision to bore the 292 block .040 oversize was based on the machinist's evaluation of the cylinder walls. The advice of a professional machinist is invaluable and should be sought when making such decisions. Failure to do so may result in you buying unnecessary parts.

5 Weigh Big Ends

Use this fixture to weigh the big ends of the connecting rods separately from the entire rod. Then record the weight of each of the big ends to determine which rod is the lightest.

6 Grind Rod Cap

Once the rod with the lightest big-end weight has been determined, the other connecting rods must match that weight. To do that grind small amounts of material from the pad of each connecting rod cap until the weights are equal.

7 Record Total Weight

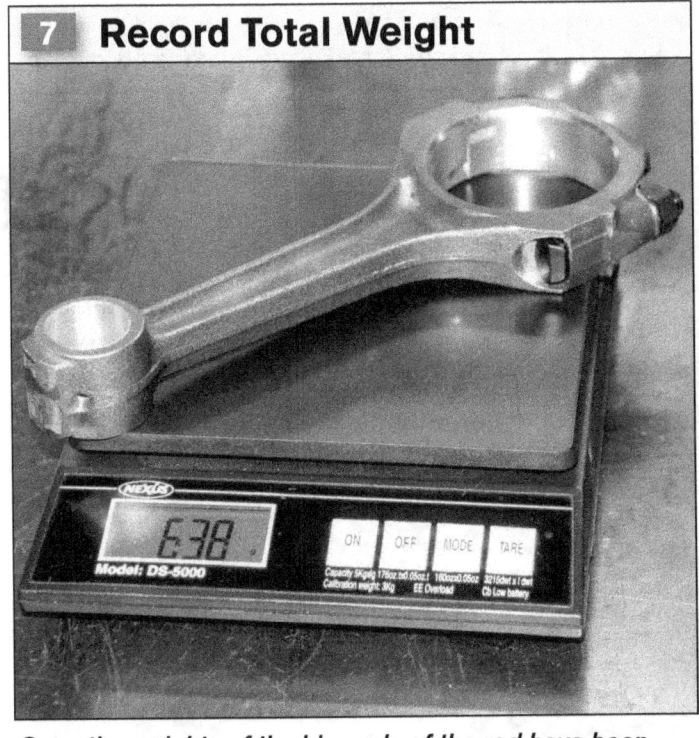

Once the weights of the big ends of the rod have been equaled on all eight rods, weigh them on a gram scale and record the total.

8 Make Weight Adjustments

Any discrepancies in the weight of the connecting rods after the big-end weights have been equaled is compensated for by removing small amounts of material from the end of each rod until all match in weight.

Dynamic Balancing

Dynamic balancing refers to a process in which the crankshaft is fitted into a specialized machine and spun to determine if the counterweights are in harmony with one another and within factory specification for balance. A crankshaft that is out of balance causes premature main bearing wear; in a worst-case scenario, it will cause a detectable vibration in a running engine.

1 Insert New Pilot Bushing

Before the dynamic balancing process begins for a manual-transmission car or truck, the crankshaft must have a new pilot bushing. In a pinch, I have used a large 1/2-inch-drive socket and a hammer as a pilot-bushing driver. The important thing here is to drive the bushing in straight and make sure it is fully seated in the crankshaft.

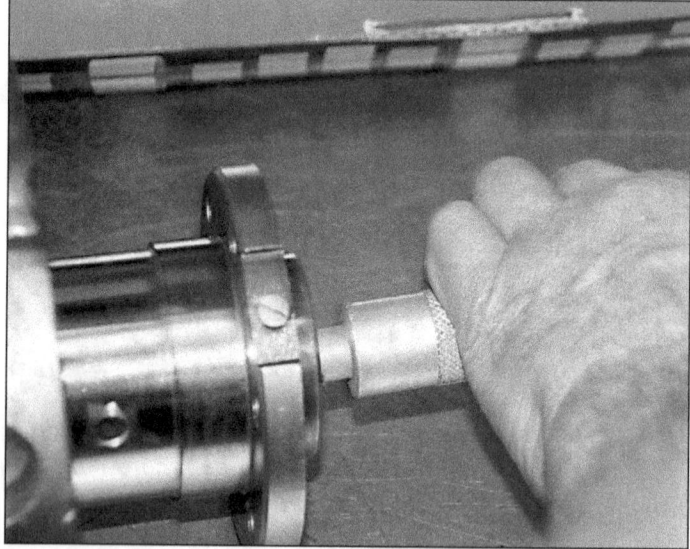

The driver must match the diameter of the pilot bushing. Use a substantial hammer to seat the pilot bushing into the back of the crankshaft. Make sure that the bushing is properly aligned with the opening in the crankshaft before driving it in.

2 Install Bobweight

Based on previous calculations, affix the bobweights to the crankshaft, which is mounted in a balancing machine so it can be spun. Properly balancing the rotating assembly eliminates annoying and potentially damaging vibrations when the engine is running.

MACHINING AND PARTS SELECTION

3 Install Flywheel

As part of the dynamic balancing of the crankshaft, install the flywheel as part of the assembly while the crankshaft is on the balancing machine.

4 Install Balancer

Also install the balancer/vibration dampener on the crankshaft during this process.

5 Install Rotating Assembly

Mount the rotating assembly (without the connecting rods and pistons) on the balancing machine. Put bobweights in place and they are ready to be spun.

6 Add or Remove Weight

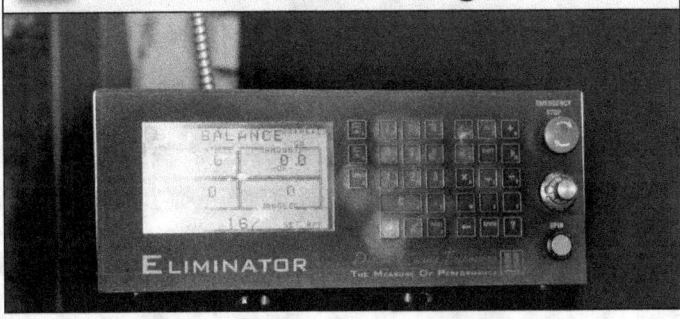

This digital readout on the crank balancing machine tells the operator where weight needs to be added or removed from the rotating assembly to bring it within balance. You add or remove weight from the large counterweights of the crankshaft until the ideal balance is achieved.

7 Add or Remove Weight (continued)

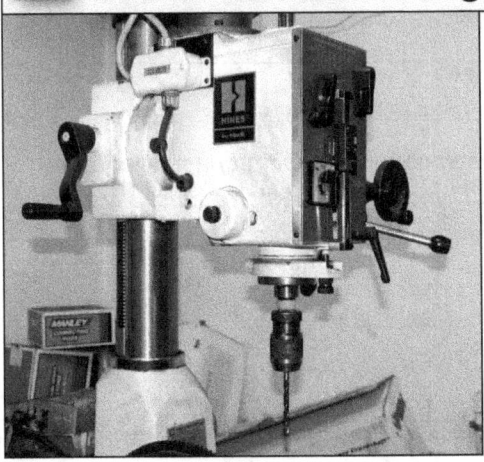

Use a drill press, mounted on the balancing machine, to remove material from the crankshaft counterweights as needed.

8 Inspect Balancer

You may remove small amounts of material from several spots on the balancer/vibration dampener during the dynamic balancing process.

FORD Y-BLOCK ENGINES: HOW TO REBUILD AND MODIFY

CHAPTER 6

Cylinder Block

You must measure the block's critical dimensions to determine if it is within the tolerances recommended by the manufacturer. Usually an old or worn Y-block needs machining to bring it back to prime operating condition. You should take detailed measurements of all of the block's critical areas before you start the machining process.

Deck Surface Squaring

You are performing a professional-caliber engine rebuild and, therefore, all deck surfaces need to be flat and square. If the deck surfaces are not square, the heads aren't effective against the block, cylinder pressure drops, and performance degrades. Most likely you will notice oil seeping between the heads and the deck surface, and it appears as if the engine has a blown gasket. At this stage, several important machining processes are required so that deck surfaces are square.

Critical Inspection

1 Inspect Block Surface

If you used the simple but effective straightedge method to determine that the deck surfaces of the block are not completely flat, set it up in a machine for resurfacing. This process ensures that the decks are level and also removes the slight rust and pitting to allow the head gaskets to seal more effectively.

2 Measure Deck Surface

The resurfacing machine has a dial indicator that accurately tracks the amount of material to be removed. You may need to remove only a few thousandths of an inch to true the deck surfaces. If more than a few thousandths of material is taken off, the head is closer to the centerline of the crank, the TDC of the piston is higher, the bore and the compression ratio increases, and valvetrain geometry (the angle between the pushrods, rocker arms, and valvestems) changes. All of these dimensions are interrelated, and when one changes, it changes another.

3 Check for High Spots

The resurfacing machine makes its first pass over the block, removing .001 inch of material. Now visually check the surface for evidence of high spots.

MACHINING AND PARTS SELECTION

4 Remove Material

You can easily see the high spots once the resurfacing machine has made its first pass over the deck surface of the block. An additional cut makes it level and provides the desired smooth surface for gasket sealing.

5 Inspect Level Surface

After removing .003 from the deck surface, it is now level and devoid of any pits or rust that might cause head gasket sealing problems. This provides a level surface for assembly.

Block Boring

If the cylinder bores remain concentric and show no excessive taper, you may be able to get away with just honing them. Keep in mind that during the honing process, material is being removed from the cylinder walls, and this may take the bore beyond tolerance. In other words, if in doubt, opt to bore the cylinders. Any high-mileage engine greatly benefits from boring, as this restores the cylinders to a concentric shape and improves their alignment relative to one another.

Once you have decided to bore the block, you must decide how much oversize you need to go. As a general rule you want to bore the cylinders as little oversize as possible. A big consideration when boring a Y-block Ford engine is the availability of oversize pistons and rings. Staying within the dimensions of available replacement parts saves a considerable amount of money in piston costs and hours of work required to hand-fit piston rings. It is also critical that the deck surfaces of the cylinder block are flat and without excessive rust or pitting. Machining the deck surfaces ensures that they are square relative to the crankshaft, and head gaskets seal better when the engine is reassembled.

1 Use Boring Machine

Level the block in the boring machine before the boring process begins. Having first cut the deck surfaces on the block ensures that it will be as level as possible while being bored.

2 Inspect Overbore

The boring bar overbores this 292 block to .040 oversize. When boring the cylinders, a few thousandths of material is left. You remove this during the honing process, which provides the desired finish for sealing the piston rings to the cylinder walls.

FORD Y-BLOCK ENGINES: HOW TO REBUILD AND MODIFY

CHAPTER 6

Block Line Honing

Line boring trues the main bearing saddles and main bearing caps and larger bearings must be installed. It must be carefully checked for any misalignment. You need to pay attention to the distance between the main saddles of the cylinder block and the main bearing journals of the crankshaft. If the line bore is out of specification excessive wear to the main bearings results. Should there be any discrepancy in the line bore of the cylinder block, it is easily corrected through the use of a specialized honing tool.

When using improved main hardware (studs or ARP main cap bolts, for example), it is imperative that the cylinder block be line honed even if the line bore had previously proved to be within specification. The reason for the line hone is based on the fact that the improved main cap hardware provides superior clamping forces when torque is applied, and this alters the bore diameters.

Before the honing process begins, chamfer the tops of each bore using the honing tool attached to a drill.

Use three different honing stones, ranging from 70 to 280 grit. You achieve the final finish by using a high-plateau hone that has abrasive, impregnated bristles that remove microscopic peaks and scuffs in the cylinder walls. This final finish allows piston rings to seat immediately, resulting in better compression, oil control, and lower emissions.

During the honing process, check each cylinder periodically, both visually and with a dial bore gauge, which ensures that it remains within specification.

I previously checked the alignment of the main bearing saddles in the cylinder block (with the main caps installed and torqued to spec) and determined that the relationship between the main bores was off. This is corrected through line honing. The cylinder block is leveled in the machine, and a boring bar is passed through the main bearing area, removing material, until the main bearing bores are in correct alignment. Line honing prevents premature wear to main bearing inserts, while allowing the crankshaft to spin with less friction. As a result, the engine produces more power and operates with greater efficiency.

Cam Bearing Installation

It is imperative that the cam bearings are properly installed in the cylinder block, and that the clearance between the bearings and the camshaft journals is sufficient to allow for smooth operation. A specialized tool is used to remove the old camshaft bearings and install new ones.

Because of the critical nature of the installation, I recommend leaving this process to a qualified machinist.

1. Choose Tool

Special Tool

Dura-Bond cam bearings are widely regarded as the best choice for the Y-block Ford V-8. Machinist Gil Jordan uses this specialized tool to install the cam bearings in the cylinder block. Great care must be taken to align the oil holes in the cam bearings with the oil passages in the block. Although cam bearing installation tools are commercially available, and it is possible to install cam bearings in your home shop, you should leave this critical procedure to a professional.

2 Align Oil Holes

Feed a thin metal rod through an oil passage in the block to ensure that the holes in the cam bearings have been properly aligned with the oil passages. Using a handheld light, check the proper alignment between the cam bearing holes and the oil passages in the block. You must be sure they are properly aligned, because any misalignment leads to oil starvation to the upper end of the engine. This would ultimately cause parts to wear and fail prematurely.

3 Test Fit Camshaft

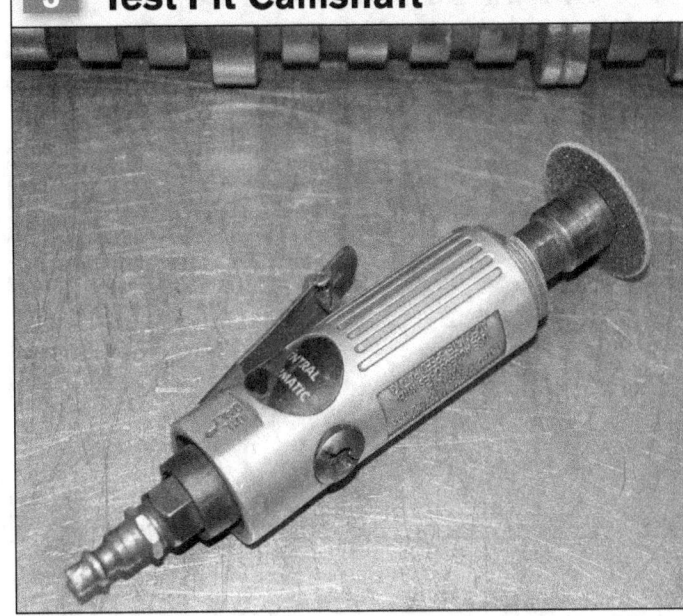

This die grinder and cut-off wheel constitute a specialized tool that may be required when fitting the camshaft to the cam bearings in the block. The cam bearing bores on Y-blocks typically have a slight misalignment. After the cam bearings have been installed, it is imperative to test-fit the camshaft into the block. If the camshaft does not turn easily upon installation, this homemade tool offers the solution and provides more camshaft-bearing clearance.

4 Remove Sharp Edges

Use an old camshaft as a tool to remove a small amount of material from the face of the cam bearings, so the new camshaft spins smoothly in its bores. Use a die grinder and cutting wheel to make diagonal cuts into the bearing journals of the old cam. The sharp edges of these cuts serve to hone material from the cam bearings when the improvised tool is placed in the block and rotated a number of times. Repeat the process until the new camshaft spins smoothly in its bores.

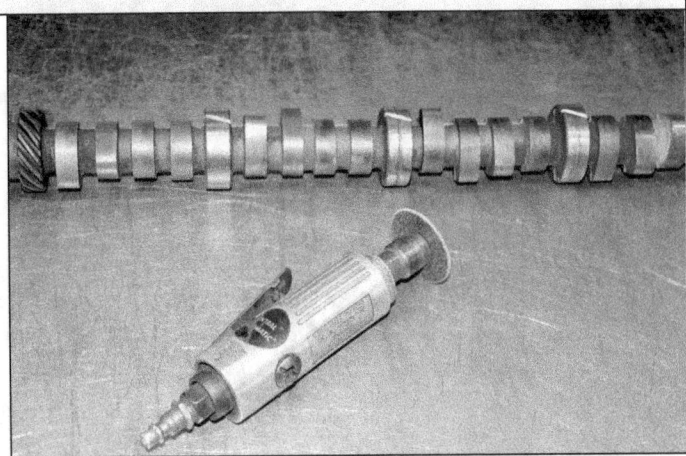

The modified camshaft now takes its place among specialized tools that may be needed to properly rebuild and assemble any future Y-block Ford V-8 engines.

CHAPTER 6

5 Install Cam Core Plug

Note the close proximity between the cam bearing and the opening for the cam core plug at the back of the block. Do not drive the cam plug in too far when installing it in the block. Cam installation tools are not available for the Y-block, so please follow this installation procedure.

With the cam bearings in the block, install a new core plug in the back of the camshaft bore. Apply Permatex sealer around the opening that retains the plug and then use a driver and hammer to install the cam plug in the block. It must align with the shoulder of the block; be careful not to drive the cam plug down in the block any farther than the surface of the shoulder. If the plug goes in too far it binds the camshaft and does not allow adequate endplay.

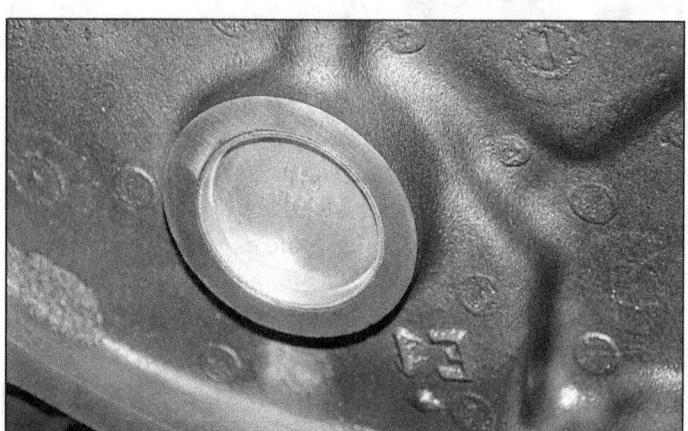

The cam plug is now installed. Again, it should be no deeper than flush with the shoulder of the opening. While at the back of the block, also install new threaded plugs into the oil galleries. Use thread sealer on all galley plugs.

Professional Mechanic Tip

6 Apply Sealer

Apply a thin coat of Permatex sealer around the freeze plug openings in the block. Although the interference fit between the plugs and the block is typically adequate to prevent leaks, the sealer provides extra insurance.

7 Install Freeze Plug

Use a proper size driver (as shown) to install freeze plugs. This ensures that they go in straight, seat properly, and don't develop leaks.

MACHINING AND PARTS SELECTION

8. Add Thread Sealer to Galley Plug

Use a thin coat of thread sealer on each of the galley plugs to be installed in the block. Use a hex-head socket, as opposed to a hex key, to install them. This ensures that the plugs are tight and don't leak.

TECH TIP: Hardened Valveseats

Do you need hardened valveseats? There are probably many viable arguments for installing hardened valveseats in cylinder heads, particularly since the abolition of leaded fuels and their lubricating properties. I have not found a need for hardened valveseats in any of the engines I have assembled since the advent of unleaded fuels, and I have not suffered any ill effects because of my choice. I have had far more trouble with the current ethanol-added fuels attacking the fuel system components in my classic cars; now I carefully examine parts on a regular basis and also add stabilizing products to my fuel tank. ■

Cylinder Heads

In this book I work with two engines as well as two distinctly different sets of cylinder head castings. The first set is OEM 1957-vintage cast-iron heads that adorn the engine I chose for my stock rebuild. The second set is current state-of-the-art high-performance aluminum castings from John Mummert. These were selected to provide maximum performance and efficiency to my 322-ci-performance Y-block engine.

The stock castings are thoroughly reconditioned; they received new valveguides, seals, valvesprings, keepers, and a three-angle valve job to ensure effective sealing. Although the aluminum cylinder heads are brand-new and ready to bolt on out of the box, they must also be checked to ensure that there are no unseen issues.

Cylinder Head Casting Numbers

Year	Casting Number	Engine	Application
1954	EBU	239	Ford passenger car
	EBY	256	Mercury passenger car
1955	ECL-A /ECG-A	272	Ford passenger car
	ECG-B ECG-C	272	Ford passenger car
	ECG-D	272	Ford passenger car
	ECK-A / ECL-A	292	Mercury passenger car
	ECK-B	292	Thunderbird
	ECK-C / ECL-B	292	Thunderbird and Mercury
	ECL-C	292	Thunderbird and Mercury
1956	ECG-H / ECG-R	272	Ford passenger car
	ECZ-B / EDB-B	292	Ford passenger car
	ECZ-C	292	Ford and T-Bird
	ECZ-B /ECZ-C	312	Ford, Mercury, Thunderbird
	ECZ-A	312	Mercury
1957	ECZ-G	292	Ford, Mercury, Thunderbird
	EDB-D / EDB-E	312	Ford supercharged
1958	ECZ-G	292	Ford passenger car
	ECZ-G	312	Mercury
1959	5752-113	292	Ford passenger car
	5750-471	312	Mercury
1960	C0AE	292	Ford passenger car
	C0AE	312	Mercury
1961–1962	C1AE	292	Ford passenger car

FORD Y-BLOCK ENGINES: HOW TO REBUILD AND MODIFY

CHAPTER 6

Cylinder Head and Block Preparation for Assembly

1 Inspect Cylinder Head Passages

Sludge buildup often clogs the oil-feed holes in the cylinder heads, and this has contributed to the Y-block engine series' bad reputation for reliability in some circles. Chamfering the oil holes helps to correct the problem.

2 Chamfer Oil Passages

Use a die grinder to chamfer the oil passages in each cylinder head. Chamfering removes the sharp edges and sharp turns from the opening; doing so eliminates areas where debris could collect and improves oil flow. It only took five minutes to perform this important upgrade to these cylinder heads, and it was well worth it.

3 Chamfer Oil Passages (continued)

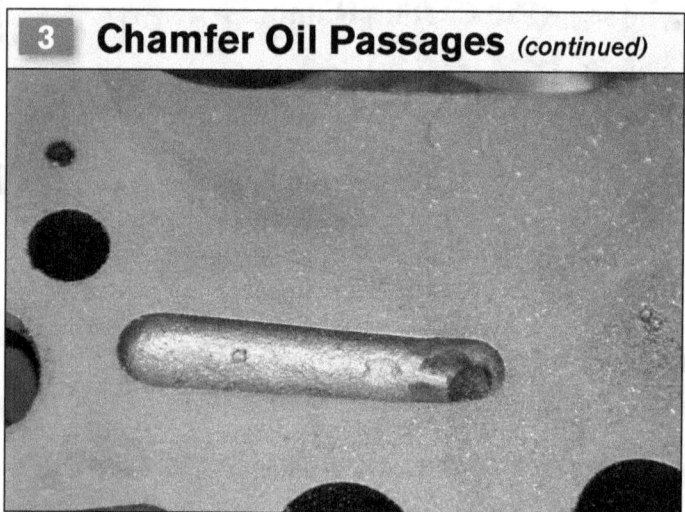

The oil feed hole has been chamfered. The finished product reveals that very little material had to be removed to make an improvement in the lubrication of the top end of the engine. This procedure will pay dividends in reliability and longevity.

4 Remove Bowl Area Rough Edges

It's a good time to make a few other improvements to the cylinder heads while the die grinder is out. Begin by gently blending the bowl area under the valves and removing rough edges and any casting flash. The purpose is to improve flow, which in turn aids power and efficiency. It also removes hot spots caused by flashing and sharp edges.

MACHINING AND PARTS SELECTION

5 Remove Bowl Area Rough Edges (continued)

Blend the bowl areas under each intake and exhaust valve. In doing so, you are not attempting to change the cylinder heads' original configuration, but merely seeking to improve efficiency for a better-running, longer-lasting engine.

6 Remove Intake and Exhaust Port Rough Edges

Give the intake and exhaust ports on the cylinder heads the same cleanup with a die grinder as the bowl areas under the valveseats. The goal is to create a smoother flow and fewer hot spots.

This lump of casting slag is in one of the intake ports of the cylinder heads. It's a perfect example of the type of imperfection you should take the time to remove. Slag, left over from the casting process, can cause hot spots and impede flow. In the worse-case scenario, slag can break off and damage vital engine parts.

7 Smooth Ports

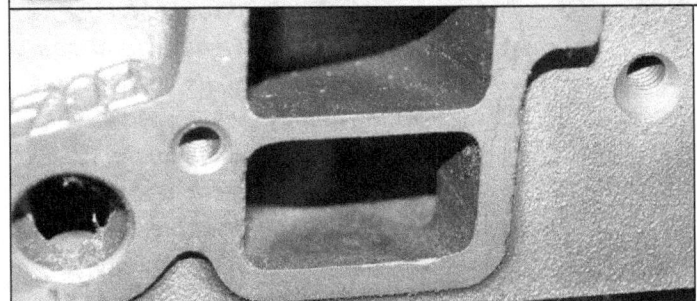

Just a few minutes of work with the die grinder removes the slag, and, by doing so, you eliminate potential problems that might have been created by leaving it in place. The addition of Viton positive valve seals is another modern improvement you can make to your engine. These seals replace the old Ford umbrella-type seals; they provide a better seal and are less prone to cracking because of heat.

FORD Y-BLOCK ENGINES: HOW TO REBUILD AND MODIFY

CHAPTER 6

8 Turn Down Valveguide Shoulders

The valveguide shoulders must be turned down to install the Viton positive seals. This is easily accomplished at the machine shop by using the tool shown here with the new seals.

9 Cut Casting

Special Tool

The installation tool for the Viton positive seals cuts the casting around the valveguide shoulders to the proper diameter to allow the installation of the seals. A machinist performs this procedure because improper use of this tool could ruin an otherwise good set of cylinder heads.

10 Cut Casting (continued)

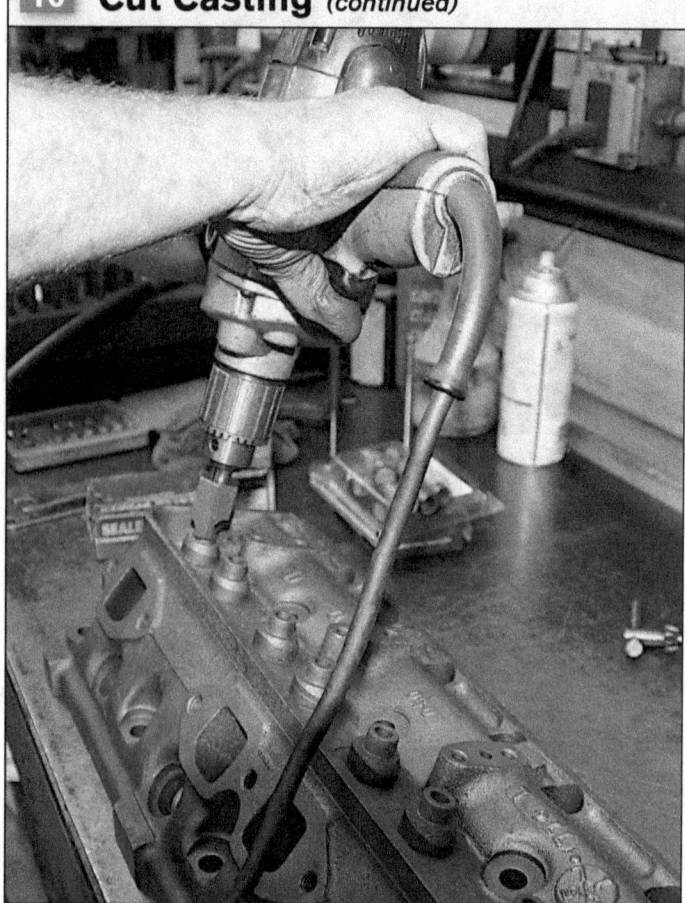

Mount the tool used for cutting the valveguide shoulders to size in a 1/2-inch drill. The teeth of the tool cut away just enough cast iron from the valveguide shoulders to allow fitting of the new seals.

11 Inspect Valveguide Shoulders

The finished product is a valveguide shoulder that is the proper size to accept the more efficient Viton positive valve seals.

12 Install Valve Seals

Use a special tool, provided by the manufacturer of the seals, to install the Viton positive valve seals on the valveguide shoulders after they have been cut to the proper size.

MACHINING AND PARTS SELECTION

13 Confirm Clearance

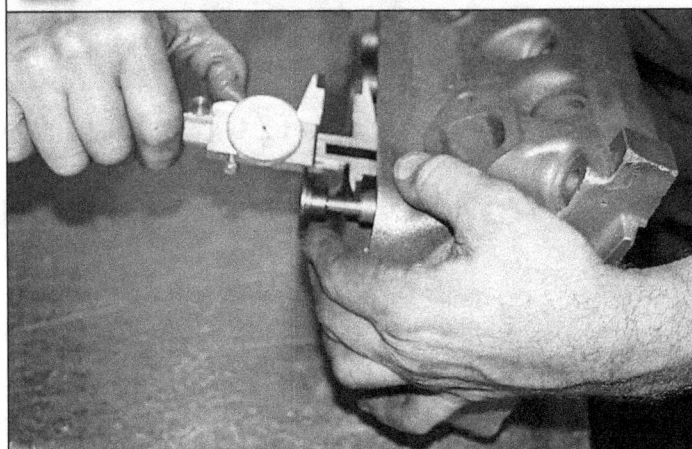

Take a measurement with the Viton positive seal now installed. With a valvespring retainer installed, take a measurement from the top edge of the seal to the lower edge of the retainer. This indicates whether there is enough clearance to allow for valvespring travel because of camshaft lift. Too little clearance here, combined with a high-lift camshaft, could cause valvespring bind.

Cylinder Head Resurfacing

Critical Inspection

1 Inspect Cylinder Head Surface

I discovered this slight imperfection in the surface of one of the cylinder heads, likely caused by moisture and the engine being unused for many years. I machined the faces of both cylinder heads several thousandths of an inch to remove these imperfections and any others. This process also trues up the faces of the cylinder heads, which provides for better sealing of the head gaskets.

2 Level Head in Machine

Before machining the surface of a cylinder head, ensure it is level and lock it down in the machine so you achieve an accurate cut. Once the head is leveled in the machine, adjust the cutting head for the first cut.

 **Posted Cylinder Heads**

In response to reported problems with cylinder head deck surface thickness, Ford made an engineering change to Y-block cylinder heads as of May 1957. Heads cast after May received two additional internal support structures. These are known as posts because of their shape and purpose; they added additional rigidity to the deck surface. Obviously, posted cylinder heads lend themselves to milling better than those that are not posted. ■

FORD Y-BLOCK ENGINES: HOW TO REBUILD AND MODIFY

CHAPTER 6

3 Measure Head Surface

Use a dial indicator to set the machine for the amount of material to be removed from the surface of the cylinder head on the first cut. In this case machinist Gil Jordan chose .003 inch.

4 Finish Milling

Slight irregularities were still evident after .003 inch of material was removed from the surface of the cylinder head on the first cut. A second cut of .002 inch resulted in a clean, flat surface that provides good sealing for the head gaskets when the engine is assembled. A total of .005 inch was removed from the face of each cylinder head during this process. This amount of milling does not have a significant impact on compression ratio or the angle of the mating surface between the intake manifold and cylinder heads.

Valve Job

1 Inspect Valveguides and Valveseats for Wear

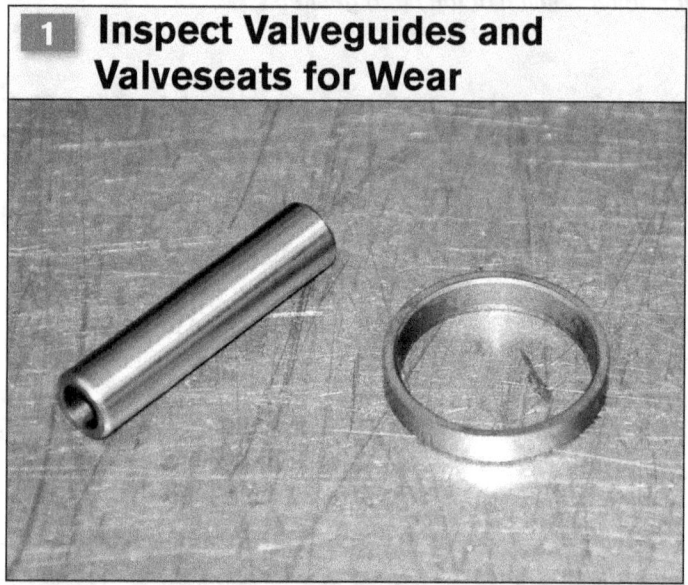

Replace valveguides and valveseats in cases of excessive wear or damage. If your Y-block has more than 50,000 miles, or has been sitting for an extended period of time where moisture exists, in most cases the guides and seats need to be replaced.

2 Remove Old Valveguide

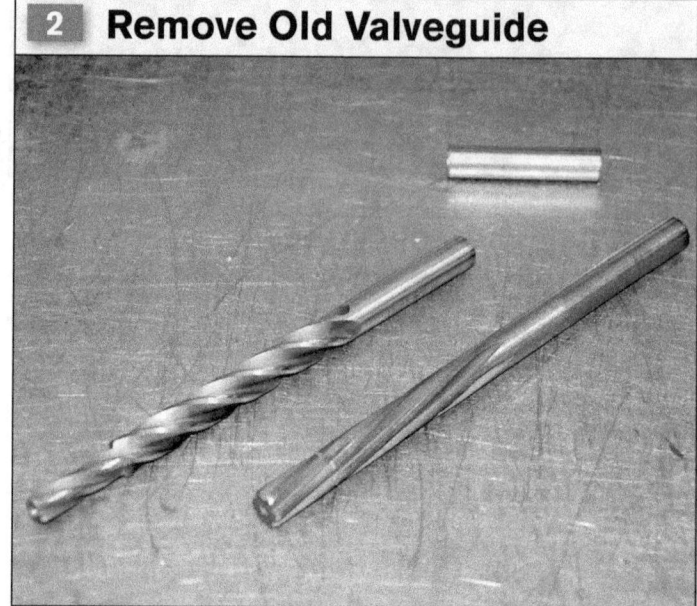

You install the valveguide (left) after you use the reamer (right) to remove the old guide from the cylinder head.

3 Remove Old Valveseat

You can use this specialized cutting tool, found in machine shops, to remove the old valveseat from the cylinder head, allowing for the installation of a fresh seat.

Here is the cutter in action removing the old valveseat from the cylinder head. Once the old seat has been cut away, press the new seat into place and then face it.

4 Install New Valveseat

With the cylinder head leveled and secured in the Kwik-Way Master Head Shop machine, insert an alignment tool into the valveguide to ensure that the seat goes in straight.

Use a driver and hammer to press the new valveseat into place in the cylinder head. The next step in the process is to face the seat with cutting stones.

5 Modify Valveseat Face Angles

Use these cutting tools and stones to achieve the face angles in the valveseats that provide the tight seal required to contain cylinder pressures. Give the cylinder heads a classic three-angle valve job.

Cut the face of the valve at 45 degrees and cut the seats at 30 degrees above the seat. Cut a 46-degree cut where the valve contacts the seat and is 60 degrees below the seat near the bowl area. The discrepancy of 1 degree on the valve provides for positive interference where it contacts the seat. The valve and the seat have more contact at the upper/outer machined surfaces of the two, and this contact gets better as the engine runs and breaks in.

CHAPTER 6

6 Make Valve Seat Cuts

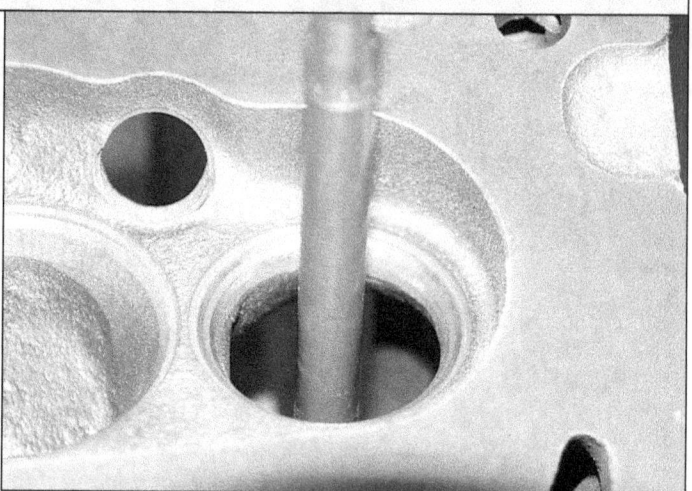

These are the first of three stones used in a three-angle valve job at 30, 46, and 60 degrees. Use the stones to cut each of the valves. It's a classic three-angle valve job.

This shiny area shows the first angle cut into the valveseat. There are two more angles to go before the seat is finished.

7 Inspect Valveseat

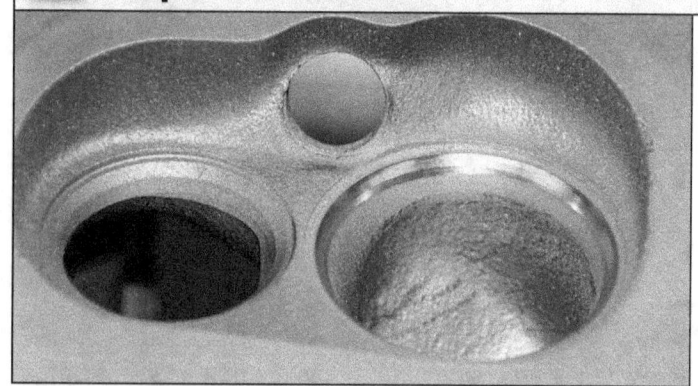

After being faced with the stones, the finished product is a valveseat that provides a positive seal between itself and the face of the valve. Gil Jordan does not believe in the old-school process of lapping-in the valves, which is smearing an abrasive valve-grinding compound between the valve and seat, and then using a tool to spin the valve. This process is messy, time-consuming, and forces the abrasive compound into the metal surfaces. He believes that two precision-machined surfaces do not need any further work.

8 Face Contact Seats

Face the surfaces of the valves that contact the seats with a valve-grinding machine. A stream of lubricating oil cools the work surface and allows for a smooth finish.

9 True Valve Ends

True the ends of the valves in another fixture of the valve-grinding machine. This provides a flat surface between the tip of the valve and the rocker arm that actuates it.

MACHINING AND PARTS SELECTION

10 Check Seat Pattern

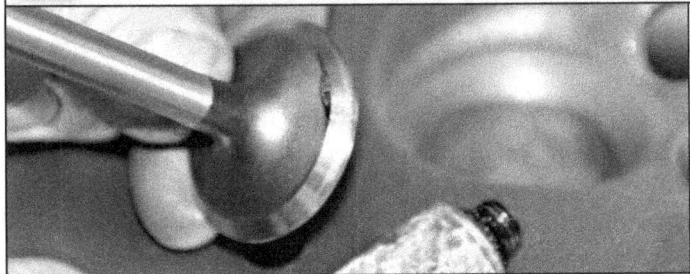

Use a dye, such as Prussian Blue, to coat the face of the valve and then insert it into its seat in the cylinder head to determine if a proper contact pattern exists between the valve and seat. The margin shown toward the top of the valve (upper edge) reveals that the desired pattern has been achieved.

11 Check Vacuum

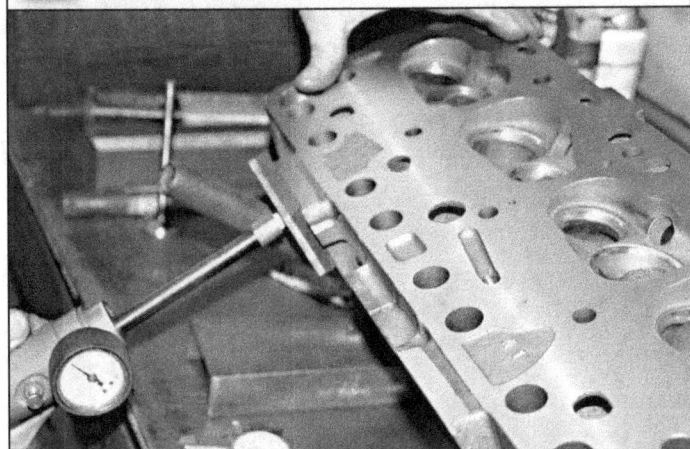

Leave nothing to chance. Drop each valve into its seat in the cylinder head and check the vacuum to ensure that a proper seal exists between valve and seat.

12 Clean Heads and Parts

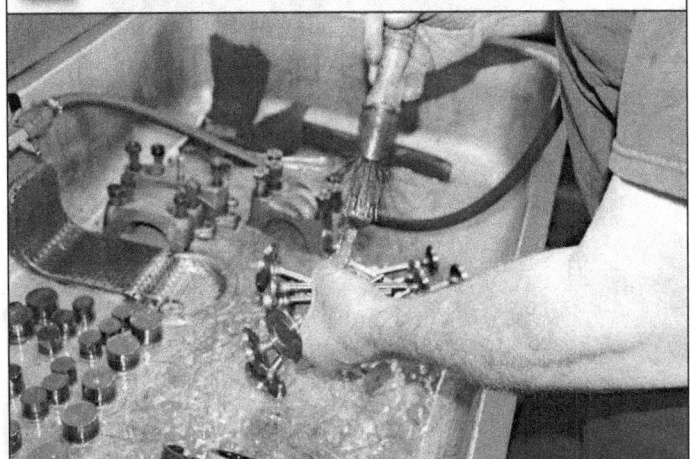

Thoroughly clean the cylinder heads in the parts washer to remove any foreign particles before you begin final assembly.

Cylinder Head Assembly

1 Check Valvespring Pressure

I installed valvesprings from a 1969 Ford 351 Windsor V-8 on the Y-block 292 heads. These 351 Windsor springs are the same size as the 292 spring, but are easier to buy and are offered in various spring pressures. These springs provide the engine builder with greater flexibility when aftermarket camshafts are used. Even if your valvesprings are new, check each one for pressure. These particular springs have 85 pounds of pressure on the seat at installed height, which is sufficient for this stock rebuild.

2 Verify Valvespring Height

Critical Inspection

Use a barrel micrometer or a dial caliper to determine valvespring height. Push the valve against its seat, then install the valvespring retainer and split locks. Measure the gap from the bottom of the retainer to the point on the cylinder head where the valvespring seats. In order to avoid spring bind on these heads I am shooting for a spring height of 1.82 inches.

FORD Y-BLOCK ENGINES: HOW TO REBUILD AND MODIFY

CHAPTER 6

3 Install Valvespring Retainer

Along with the selected 351W valvesprings, I chose one-piece valvespring retainers from Liberty Performance (PN LR-2500) to replace the antiquated two-piece OEM retainers. Place the retainer on top of the valvespring and use a valvespring compressor to compress the valvespring and retainer. Compress these components until the tip of the valvestem protrudes above the retainer and then align the split locks in the grooved area of the valvestem. Once the split locks are correctly installed, release the pressure on the compressor. You can use graduated shims under each valvespring to achieve the desired assembled height.

4 Coat Freeze Plug

Install the three 29/32-inch freeze plugs into the Y-block cylinder heads. The passenger-side head has a bung for the water temperature sender that takes the place of one freeze plug. Before installing the freeze plugs, apply a coat of Permatex sealer to the opening in the head.

5 Install Freeze Plug

Select a driver of the correct diameter to install the freeze plug in the cylinder head. If you don't have a set of drivers, a socket of the correct size may be substituted. The finished product is an evenly and fully seated freeze plug that does not leak under pressure.

6 Inspect Cylinder Head

This view from the top shows the result of careful attention to detail and the installation of correct, high-quality parts. It appears as delivered from the factory in 1957 but performs much better.

Here is the completely refurbished cylinder heads for the stock engine build shown from the bottom. They have been cleaned of five decades of dirt and corrosion, had new valveseats and guides installed, received a three-angle valve job, and have freshly machined head-gasket mating surfaces.

Piston and Connecting Rod Installation

1 Install First Snap Ring

To hang the pistons onto the connecting rods begin by installing a snap ring in one side of the wrist pin opening in the piston. Note: If the snap ring has a beveled or rounded side, that side goes toward the wrist pin. Thoroughly lubricate the wrist pins with 30-weight motor oil at this time.

2 Organize Connecting Rods

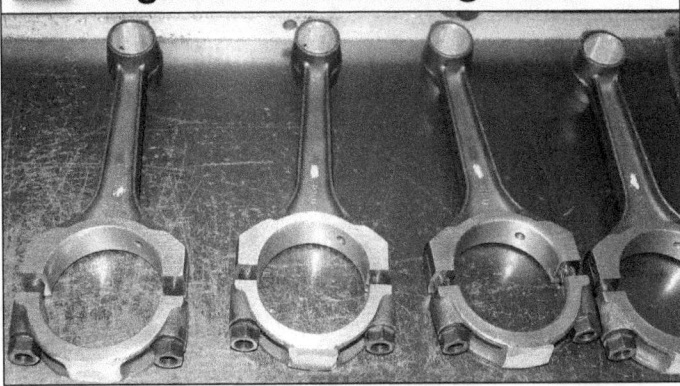

Lay out the connecting rods so that they are in proper orientation to the pistons. The stamped identifying numbers on the connecting rods face toward the outside, or oil pan rail, of the cylinder block.

3 Determine Orientation

Once the proper connecting rod–to-piston orientation has been determined and the rods are laid out, mark with a Sharpie on each rod to specify the direction in which it mounts. Laying out your work in the correct order, on a clean, well-lit work surface, is the correct way to approach it.

A notch (as shown) or an arrow on the top of the piston often indicates piston orientation relative to the cylinder bore. The orientation mark faces forward in the block.

4 Install Second Snap Ring

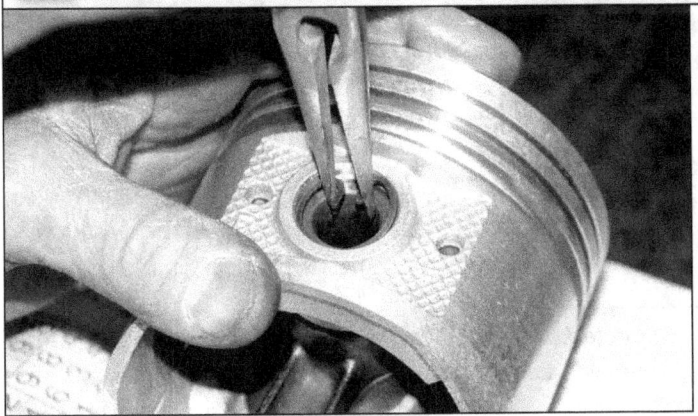

Once the pistons have been mounted on the connecting rods in the proper orientation, install the second snap ring using snap-ring pliers. Note the open end of the snap ring goes toward the bottom of the piston. This particular piston manufacturer's explanation for orienting the snap rings this way is: "To take advantage of the largest bearing area to withstand the greater upward inertia forces." Read the manufacturer's instructions for their recommendations.

CHAPTER 7

ASSEMBLY

The actual nuts-and-bolts of your engine rebuild is about to commence. By this stage, all the cleaning, machining, parts selection, and painting should be complete. This critical portion of your project has great bearing on whether all your time, effort, and money result in success or failure. Consequently, this is the most detailed chapter in this book. I cover the processes step by step, and subassembly by subassembly, to help you get everything right the first time.

Proper engine assembly takes place in phases; assemblies and subassemblies must be dealt with in a certain order. I set up my work area with only the tools and parts that are required during that phase of assembly. This reduces clutter while keeping parts in order and away from possible contamination.

If you take the time to make your work area safe, clean, and organized, your project goes smoother, and you achieve better results.

Remember to *take your time* and double-check your work as you proceed for best results.

Safety and Cleanliness

Take the time to keep your work area safe during engine assembly. You are working with heavy parts, potentially harmful or combustible chemicals, and tools with sharp edges or points. This is not the time to set aside the fire extinguisher, safety glasses, and dust mask or disregard the need for proper ventilation of your workspace.

Make sure the work area, workbenches, and parts storage shelves are clean and stay that way before you begin to assemble the engine. I often use clean cardboard or newspaper to cover surfaces during this phase. Don't forget to clean your tools before you use them to avoid contaminating clean parts. The old adage "cleanliness is next to godliness" really does apply when it comes to assembling your engine, because the smallest contaminants can cause

Now that all of its components have been thoroughly cleaned, inspected, replaced as necessary, and machined back to acceptable tolerances you can begin the assembly of your engine.

ASSEMBLY

major damage later. Although it may sound somewhat excessive, I take the time to clean my hands as often as possible during engine assembly.

The shops of professional racing engine builders often have a "clean room" or area that is separated from other shop activities or where engines are assembled. The clean rooms are for the sole purpose of preventing the contamination of engines.

You must thoroughly clean the block before beginning the assembly process. You should do this even though the block is fresh from the machine shop. It fairly sparkles and even came home sealed in a plastic bag. The following few simple, yet critical, steps quickly show why your cylinder block needs a thorough scrubbing before assembly begins.

Wash Block

Give the cylinder block a hot bath with proper products and implements. I use a bucket of hot water, Tide-brand laundry detergent (racing engine builders have used it for decades), various brushes, a garden hose, and compressed air. I start using the hot, soapy water to thoroughly scrub down all the interior and exterior surfaces of the cylinder block. Although a standard scrub brush works well for most of the job, specialized brushes are required to access the oil galleries and smaller areas.

Dry Block

Use a lint-free towel to thoroughly dry the engine block. Remember that the exposed cast iron is wet and starts rusting immediately. Some owners paint their blocks; if you want to keep the surface of the block from rusting, you must coat it with a lubricant, such as WD-40.

Clean Cylinder Walls

With all the soap and scrubbing the block must be clean enough to assemble now, right? Wrong! The cylinder walls have proven this. Take a clean paper towel, and soak it with a small amount of automatic transmission fluid (ATF). Now wipe the surface of one of your freshly machined and thoroughly washed, cylinder walls. The machining process leaves microscopic lines in the cylinder bores. The dark material

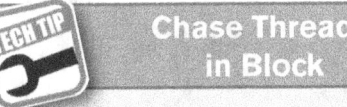

Chase Threads in Block

Here is one more helpful hint before you begin to assemble your engine. Chase all the bolt holes in the cylinder block with taps. This cleans up any suspect threads, removes any leftover dirt or corrosion, and in the case of the threads for the cylinder head bolts, it ensures even clamping pressure across the block surface, which helps to avoid head gasket sealing problems. ∎

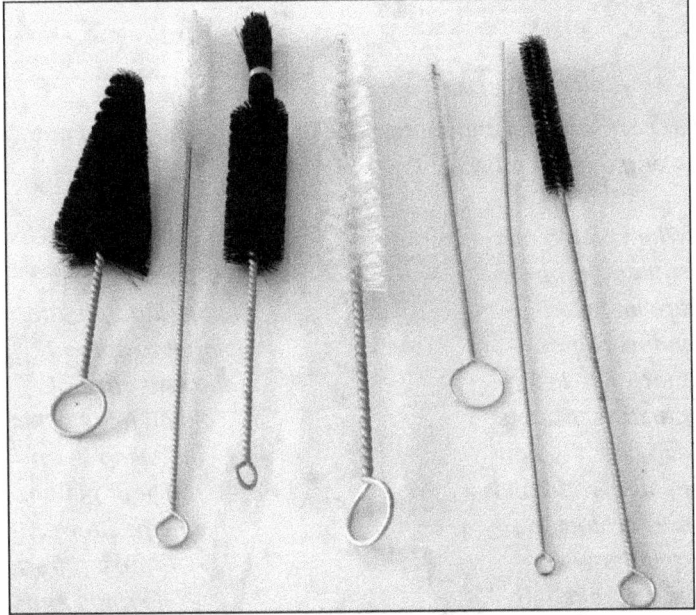

This set of specialized brushes, purchased from Harbor Freight, has proved to be most useful in cleaning the hard-to-get-at, out-of-the-way places in the cylinder block. You can also use firearms-cleaning brushes.

Once the block has been scrubbed clean and rinsed with clean water, use compressed air to blow all the surfaces dry. Coat all these wet surfaces with lubricant because it takes very little time for rust to form. Once dry, coat all machined surfaces of the block, with the exception of the cylinder bores, with either oil or WD-40. Pay particular attention to machined surfaces and bolt holes when drying.

CHAPTER 7

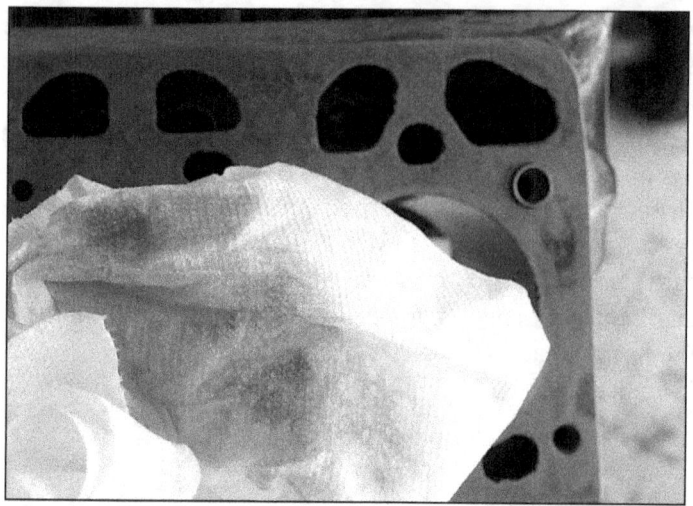

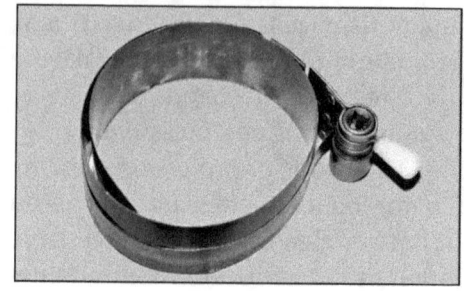

This photo shows the results of wiping the cylinder walls of the block with automatic transmission fluid (ATF). In spite of previous cleaning procedures, a small amount of dirt remains in the machined areas of the cylinder walls. Failure to clean the cylinders properly could adversely affect the seating of the piston rings and also lead to premature wear in your rebuilt engine.

A piston ring compressor is a must-have tool when assembling an engine. Ring compressors are available in various styles. Some choices are an individual fixed tapered-style from ARP; pliers-style from K-D tool; and the spring-steel type, adjustable from 3½ to 7 inches by Lisle tool, which is the type I prefer.

appears on the paper towel as dirt. You need to wipe down the cylinder bores with paper towels and ATF so your block is clean and ready for assembly.

Specialized Tools and Products

A number of specialized tools and products ease the task of assembling your engine while ensuring the fit and longevity of critical components. First and foremost is a sturdy engine stand that allows the engine to be rotated, as well as stopped at various points, during the assembly process.

Although I don't use RTV (room temperature vulcanizing) in place of gaskets when assembling an engine as some builders do, I find gray RTV to be an excellent gasket sealer in areas where it cannot get into oil passages.

Anti-seize lubricant is a must when parts and fasteners are of two dissimilar metals, such as when a stainless-steel bolt is installed in a cast-iron part. Failure to use anti-seize in such cases results in galling of the threads in the part.

Indian Head gasket shellac is a time-honored product that I have depended on for sealing engine gaskets, particularly those relating to the cooling system, for many years. The fact that it is still available is a testament to the product's effectiveness.

In addition to your standard collection of hand tools, you need the following tools and products to aid you in your task.

Plastigauge is used to perform final clearance checks on connecting rod and main bearings during engine assembly.

When piston and rod assemblies are installed in the cylinder block, these simple rubber boots slip over the connecting rod bolts and protect the cylinder walls and crankshaft throws from being damaged. They are available from most auto parts stores.

This simple tool is a piston ring spreader. Using it to spread the end gaps of piston rings when installing them on your pistons helps prevent breaking fragile rings and damaging pistons. It will also save your fingers.

ASSEMBLY

Piston ring end gaps are critical to seal the cylinders in an engine properly. A ring filer, such as the one shown, assists you in getting the ring end gaps for your engine uniform and within specification. This tool is available through Summit Racing (PN SUM-906795).

This handy item is a crankshaft socket, which allows you rotate the crankshaft during engine assembly. It slides over the snout of the crank; its keyway engages the woodruff key that secures the vibration dampener. Several manufacturers offer this tool: Moroso, Pro-Form, and Milodon. All are available through Summit Racing or Jegs.

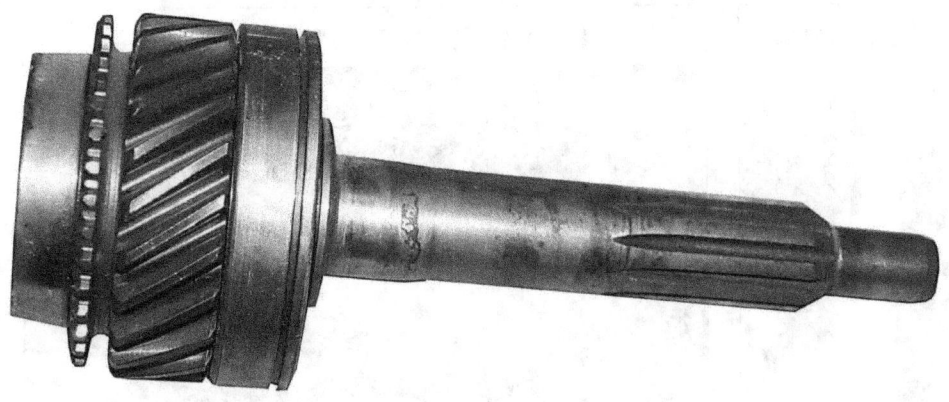

When installing the clutch disc and pressure plate on a flywheel, the input shaft from an old transmission (with a spline compatible with your clutch disc) is a handy item to have in your home shop.

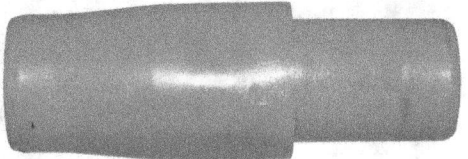

A tailshaft plug in the output shaft of a transmission prevents fluids from escaping past the tail shaft seal (and all over your garage floor) during the installation of the engine and transmission. They are available in various sizes to fit most applications from Powerhouse Products and Moroso. Both may be ordered through Summit Racing or Jegs.

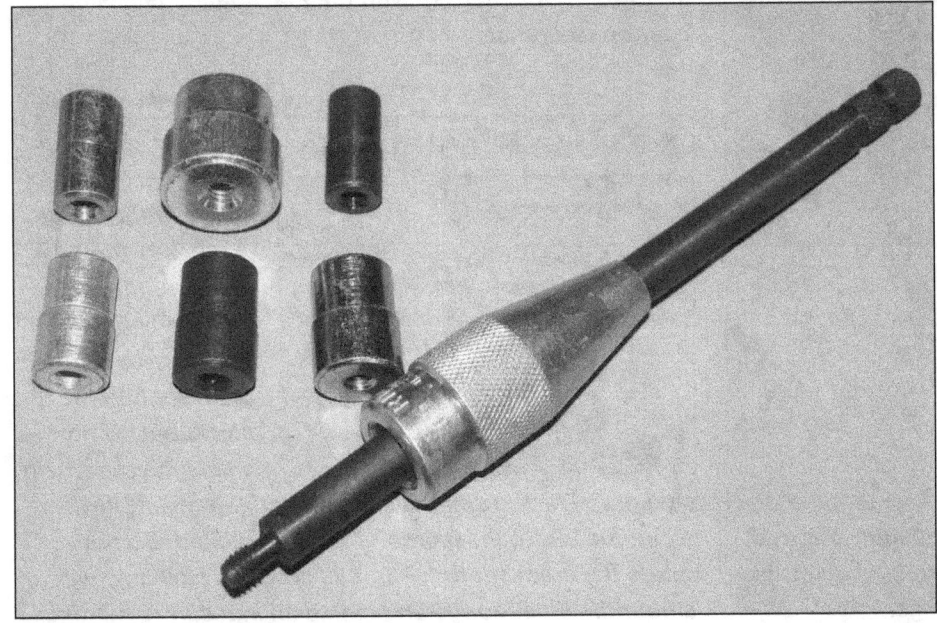

If you have no old transmission input shafts in your inventory, clutch alignment tools are commercially produced and available from auto parts stores. They run the gamut from a simple, inexpensive, one-size plastic tool by ACT to a professional-grade set by Lisle. This tool comes with various sized adapters to fit a multitude of clutch discs.

CHAPTER 7

Cam Installation Tip

One particular trick that should be noted any time you are replacing the camshaft in your Y-block relates to the oil groove in the center journal. Although your new cam surely has the groove right where it should be, it may not be of sufficient depth to provide proper lubrication. The oil groove should be .035 inch deep, and, if it is not, as was the case with both the aftermarket camshafts purchased for the engines in this project, you need to have a competent machine shop correct the situation. Failure to do so may result in too little oil reaching the top end of your new engine.

Something else to note is that early Y-blocks used cross-drilled oiling holes in the camshaft journals rather than the groove, and, in the case of the 1954 239 engine, you might find that the cam journals are a larger diameter than those used in all other Y-blocks. ■

Bottom End Assembly

1 Check Main Bearing Clearance

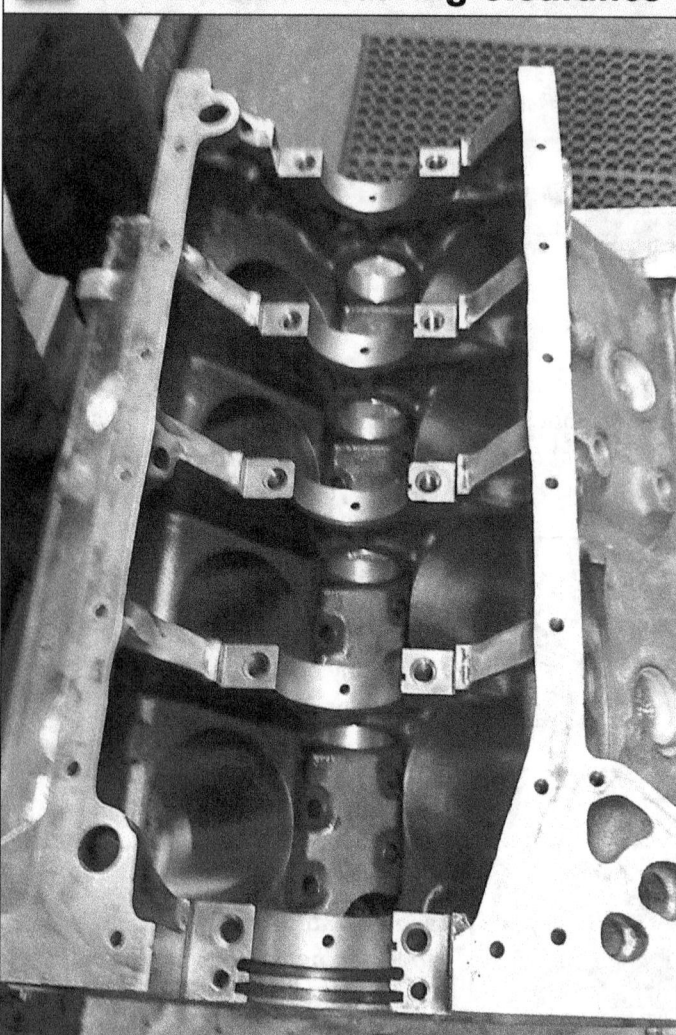

Now that the cylinder block has been thoroughly cleaned and dried, the next step, before final assembly begins, is to check the clearance on the main bearings.

2 Install Upper Inserts

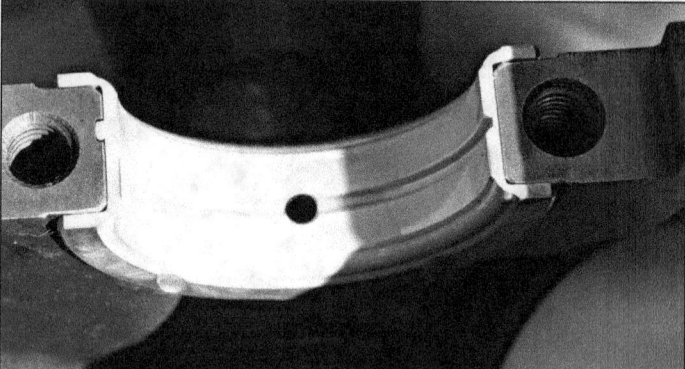

Install the upper portion of the main bearing inserts in their respective saddles in the cylinder block. No lubricant or assembly lube is applied to the bearings at this time; to do so would interfere with the Plastigauge checking bearing clearance.

Critical Inspection

3 Use Plastigauge

At this stage, you should measure the main bearing clearance. You have to set the crankshaft in the block, but do not install the rear main seal now. Place a small piece of Plastigauge lengthwise along the top of the journal(s) to be checked. Do not rotate the crankshaft during this process. Doing so will smear the Plastigauge and cause an inaccurate reading.

ASSEMBLY

4 Apply Oil

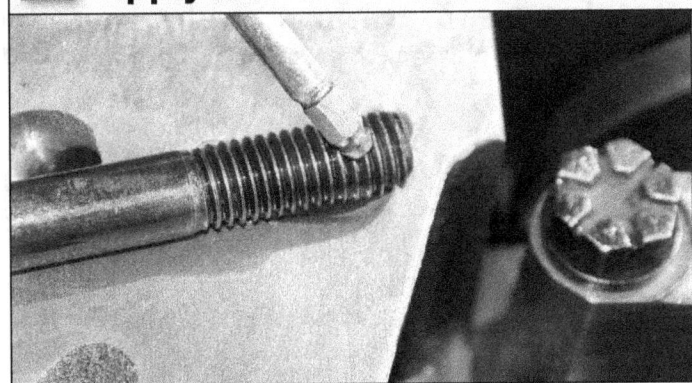

Before installing the main bearing caps in the block apply some oil to the threads and under the heads of the main bearing bolts to ensure a proper torque reading. Here, I am using ARP hardware that comes with hardened washers. Be sure that the beveled side of the washer faces toward the head of the bolt when using ARP hardware. The 312 blocks have taller main bearing caps than the 292; the exception is the rear main cap, which is the same height. As a result, the 312 has two different-length main bearing bolts, with the shorter ones used on the rear cap.

5 Install Lower Inserts

Torque Fasteners

Place the lower half of the main bearing inserts into the main caps (again without lubricant), and then install the main bearing caps in their respective registers in the block, taking care to ensure that they are properly seated and oriented. Torque the main bearing bolts in three steps: 45 to 65 to 95 ft-lbs (239 and 272 engines are 80 to 90 ft-lbs), alternating side to side and cap to cap.

Next, loosen the bolts, remove the main bearing caps, and using the scale on the packaging measure the now-compressed Plastigauge to determine if the clearance shown is within an acceptable range (.001 to .0250 inch). The crankshaft can now be removed from the block.

6 Install Lifters and Cam

Installing the valve lifters and camshaft in the block now (before the crankshaft) makes things much easier. Keep in mind that because the mushroom design of the valve lifters used in the Y-block, it is necessary to install them into the block first and from the bottom. Before installing the camshaft and lifters, be sure to liberally coat the faces of the lifters and the lobes of the camshaft with an assembly lube. Most aftermarket camshaft companies include their recommended product with the cam.

Do not use the camshaft lube on the journals of the cam that contact the camshaft bearings in the cylinder block. Use motor oil on the journals and bearings. Use great care when installing the camshaft into the block so as not to damage the cam bearings. Failure to properly lubricate the cam and lifters could result in the destruction of your cam and damage to your newly rebuilt engine upon initial start-up. With the camshaft and lifters in place, apply a liberal coating of oil or assembly lube to the main bearing inserts before installing the crankshaft and main bearing caps in the block.

Again, make sure the main caps are properly oriented. Snug the main bearing cap bolts but don't torque them at this point.

FORD Y-BLOCK ENGINES: HOW TO REBUILD AND MODIFY

CHAPTER 7

7 Use Hardened Lifters — *Important!*

While I am on the subject of Y-block valve lifters, it is important to use a hardened lifter. I was lucky to find these original replacements from NAPA instead of having to buy inferior-quality foreign-made parts.

8 Install Rear Main Seal

Early Y-blocks and all 312s used a rope-style rear main seal. Hand-fit one length of the seal into the groove machined in the block. Install the other in the separate lower seal retainer used in the Y-block series of engines.

9 Install Rear Main Seal *(continued)* — *Special Tool*

Although Ford dealer service departments had a special tool available for installing the rope-style rear main seal (Ford PN T52L-6701-AGD), over the years I have found that using a 1/2-inch-drive extension and a rolling motion gets the job done. Once the seal halves have been installed in the block and seal retainer, use a utility knife to cut them off flush with the surface.

10 Install Rear Main Seal *(continued)*

Later versions of the Y-block used a neoprene rear main seal. When installing this style of seal, follow the instructions on the package because they may have special requirements. Use motor oil to lightly lubricate the seal, and then install it in the block and retainer with the raised lip of the seal facing the front of the engine. You avoid oil leaks at the seal area if you install the halves with a corresponding offset to the machined surface of the seal grooves in the cylinder block and retainer.

You can also see here a simple means for rotating the crankshaft during assembly if you don't happen to have the rotator tool. You can thread two old flywheel bolts into the flange at the back of the crank and use a large screwdriver for the leverage needed to rotate the crank.

TECH TIP: Rear Main Seal Installation

NOTE: Do not proceed with rear main seal installation before reading this.

Because of the design of the separate rear main seal retainer in the Y-block you must first torque the main bearing cap bolts before installing the retainer. Torque all the main cap bolts, except for those in the number-3 cap (which holds the thrust bearing), in three steps: to 45, to 65, and to 95 ft-lbs. Skipping the bolts on the number-3 cap will allow you to set the thrust once the rear main seal installation is complete. ■

ASSEMBLY

11 Install Spacers

The rear main seal set includes two side spacers that fit into vertical grooves in the seal retainer. Apply a little RTV to the sides of the retainer as additional insurance against oil leaks.

Two nails are supplied with the rear main seal, which you drive into the spaces between the side spacers and the cylinder block. Use a soft mallet to tap the nails into place.

Torque Fasteners

12 Measure Crankshaft Endplay

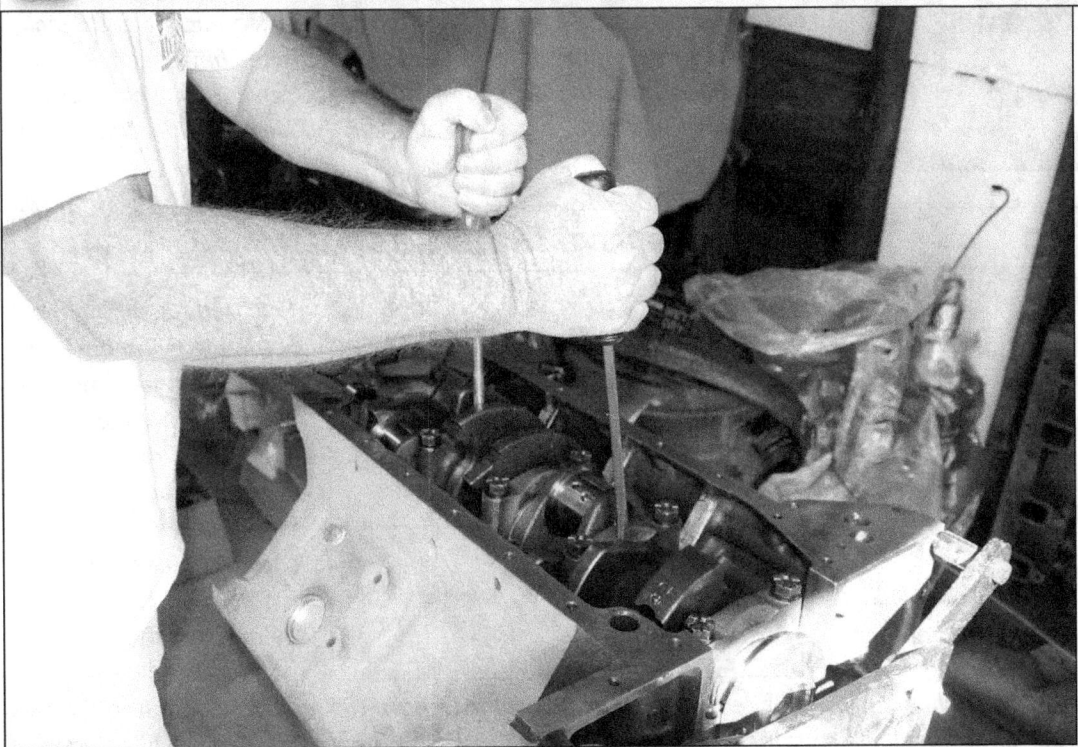

Once the other main bearing caps have been torqued to specification, insert a large screwdriver between the front of one of the front main bearing caps (not number-3) and a crankshaft counterweight. Pry the crankshaft forward in the block. Place forward pressure against this screwdriver, and insert another screwdriver between the crankshaft and the number-3 main cap. Pry the main cap toward the rear of the block. Now remove the screwdriver prying the main cap to the rear while maintaining forward pressure on the crank. Torque the bolts on the number-3 cap to specification.

Measure crankshaft endplay by attaching a dial indicator to the crankshaft and prying it forward and backward to attain a reading. Endplay should not exceed .010 inch; .002 to .006 is the acceptable range.

FORD Y-BLOCK ENGINES: HOW TO REBUILD AND MODIFY

Clearance Measurement

Clearance measurements are important when dealing with piston rings, connecting rod bearings, installing piston and rod assemblies, and checking rod bearing clearance. When installing replacement piston rings, the end gap between the top and second ring must be within specification and not too tight or loose. If the end gap of a piston ring is too large, oversize rings are required. If the ring end gap is too tight, the rings may be carefully filed until the proper gap has been achieved.

The clearances between the connecting rods and their respective bearings and the crankshaft main bearings are extremely critical for engine life and proper performance. A qualified machinist ensures that the parts associated with the bearings are machined to within acceptable tolerance, after which you should use Plastigauge to double-check the clearances during assembly.

1 Select Pistons

For this rebuild, I selected the .040 oversize Sealed Power cast-aluminum pistons (PN 1022P), which are a more modern direct replacement for the OEM pistons (PN 3798). Quality pistons stand up to years of typical service in a properly tuned, well-maintained engine. The minimum suggested piston-to-wall clearance is .0015 inch. The cylinder bores have been finish-honed to provide .002 clearance between the pistons and cylinder walls.

Critical Inspection

2 Choose Piston Rings

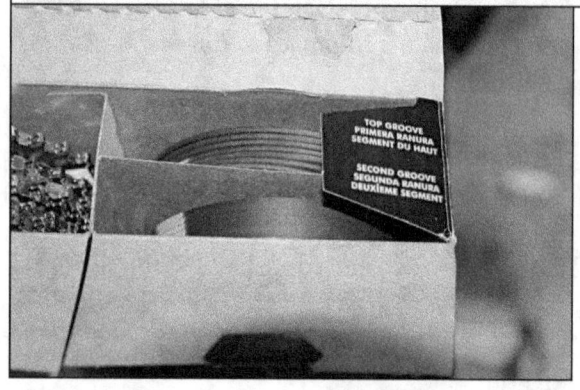

Replacement piston rings come in compartmentalized boxes that identify the location of the ring in relation to the piston. Piston rings are also marked (usually a dot on the ring) to indicate which side of the ring faces the top of the piston.

3 Check End Gap

Piston ring end gaps are critical in sealing the cylinders. To check end gap, insert a ring into the cylinder bore approximately 1½ inches down from the deck surface. Although specialized tools are available to ensure that the ring is square in the bore, using one of the piston-and-connecting-rod assemblies works well for this purpose.

4 Remove Material

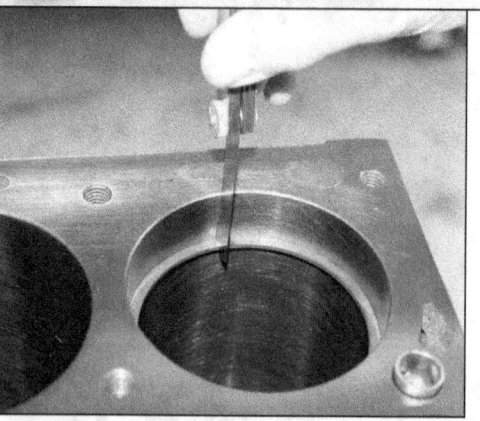

After squaring the ring in the bore, use a feeler gauge to measure the end gap of the ring. The general rule is .004 of gap for each inch of bore. If the ring end gap is too tight, use a piston ring filing tool to remove the amount of material required to achieve the desired gap. Be careful not to remove too much material from the rings at one time. Check end gaps frequently during the filing process.

Although this is tedious and time-consuming, it is a necessary step. If ring end gaps are too loose, rings of the next size are required. If you do file rings to fit, be sure to use a fine file to deburr the ends before installing the rings on the pistons.

ASSEMBLY

5 Install Oil Rings

Piston ring installation begins at the bottom of the piston, so it starts with the oil rings. Oil rings come in three pieces, which are an expander and two rails. Install the expander first, and then make sure that the end gaps butt together and do not overlap.

For reference, align the end gaps with the side of the piston pin that faces to the rear in the engine. Install the top rail next and offset the end gaps slightly to one side of the piston pin. Install the bottom rail next, with the end gaps offset to the other side of the piston pin. Check your work when completed to ensure that the expander end gaps have not overlapped.

6 Verify Ring Alignment

Use the ring spreader to install the second ring and then the top ring. The piston ring manufacturer often includes recommendations for ring alignment on the pistons in their instructions. The important point here is to ensure that the ring end gaps of the top and second rings are not in alignment with each other.

7 Install Bearings

Install the connecting rod bearings in the rods, making sure that the hole in the bearing insert aligns with the oil hole in the rod. Each bearing has a tang that fits into a slot machined in the connecting rod to keep it in place.

8 Prepare Rod Assembly

To install the piston connecting rod assemblies into the block, a few simple steps, which are repeated eight times, are required. Lubricate the connecting rod bearings with oil or assembly lube and install the protective boots on the connecting rod bolts to avoid damaging the crankshaft. You should also squirt a little oil onto the wrist pins for adequate lubrication during start-up. Then give the cylinder walls and piston rings a coat of oil to assist the installation process.

Rotate the engine stand so that the bank of the engine that contains the bore into which the piston is to go is set at an advantageous angle. Align the connecting rod journal of the crankshaft with the bottom of the cylinder bore. A piston ring compressor is required to fit the piston and rod with rings in place into the cylinder. Ascertain proper piston orientation as it relates to the block. Most pistons have an arrow or notch to indicate the front, and the identifying numbers stamped on each connecting rod should face outward, toward the oil pan rail of the block.

CHAPTER 7

9 Install Rod Assembly

Lower the piston and rod assembly into the cylinder bore until the piston ring compressor contacts the top of the bore. Tap around the edges of the ring compressor with a plastic mallet to seat it to the bore. With the heel of your hand against the head, use the handle of a hammer or mallet to push the piston-and-rod assembly down into the bore in one motion.

If the piston and rod assembly fails to slide smoothly into the cylinder, do not attempt to force it. Take it out and repeat the previous steps. Forcing the assembly into the bore may result in a broken piston ring.

Torque Fasteners

10 Verify Bearing Clearance

With the piston and rod assembly seated against the crankshaft journal, remove the protective boots from the rod bolts. Check the connecting rod bearing clearance to ensure that it is within specification.

As you did with the main journal, place a small piece of Plastigauge on the rod journal. Next, put the other half of the connecting rod bearing in the cap, leaving it without lubricant for this phase, and slide it onto the rod bolts, taking care that it seats properly against the connecting rod and that the numbers on the cap align with those on the rod.

In this rebuild I am using ARP connecting rod bolts and nuts, which come with a specially formulated assembly paste. They are torqued to 50 ft-lbs in increments of 20, 30, and 50 alternating between the bolts. Now loosen the nuts and remove the cap from the rod.

As you did with the main bearings, use the scale on the Plastigauge packaging to measure the compressed material on the rod journal. After ensuring that connecting rod bearing clearance is okay, coat the bearing insert with oil or assembly lube, reinstall the cap on the connecting rod, and torque the bolts.

11 Verify Rod Clearance

Use a feeler gauge to check the connecting rod side clearance. The gap between the rods on a Y-block should not exceed .019 inch.

12 Inspect Installation

With the rotating assembly, crankshaft, pistons, connecting rods, and camshaft installed, the 292 rebuild is coming together and the pile of parts on the workbench gets smaller; it's starting to look like an engine again.

100   FORD Y-BLOCK ENGINES: HOW TO REBUILD AND MODIFY

ASSEMBLY

Timing Chain and Gear Installation

If your Y-block has experienced oil starvation, your timing gears may be excessively worn or damaged and need replacement. Make sure the entire area is clean before you begin. You must follow these steps to arrive at the correct timing for the rotating assembly, cam, and distributor.

1 Inspect Components

A baffling array of parts makes up the hardware that attaches the top timing gear to the camshaft on a Y-block V-8. Left to right: camshaft retainer plate, counterweight (upper), beveled spacer (lower), eccentric, spacer, bolt and washer.

2 Install Cam Spacer

Important!

Cam timing events in my 292 rebuild are trusted to this double-row roller timing chain and gears by Elgin. Double rows of teeth add strength to the timing set while the rollers in the chain links reduce power-robbing friction. When installing the timing chain and gears in the Y-block, the single most important thing to remember is that the camshaft spacer must be installed with the beveled side facing toward the cam.

3 Use Loctite on Plate Bolt

Two bolts hold the camshaft retaining plate against the block. Place a dab of blue Loctite on each bolt before installation.

4 Select Timing Chain Set

This is our Rollmaster timing chain and gearset. The multi-indexed lower sprocket allows for camshaft timing changes as necessary. Retarding camshaft timing provides for more power at the high end of the power curve, while advancing the camshaft increases bottom end power. Note: If you choose to install a timing set with the multi-indexed lower sprocket be sure to read the instructions and note the degree marks engraved next to each slot in the gear.

5 Lubricate Retainer Plate

Lubricate the backside of the camshaft retainer plate with white Lubriplate grease before installation. Torque the retainer bolts at 12 to 18 ft-lbs.

CHAPTER 7

6 Align Cam and Timing Gears

Another of the idiosyncrasies in the Y-block engine series, and for some the most challenging, is the manner in which the camshaft and crankshaft timing gears are aligned when the timing chain is installed. In most engines you align the chain and gears so that the dot on the camshaft timing gear faces straight down and aligns with the dot on the crankshaft timing gear, which faces upward; the Y-block is different.

Align the timing chain and gears so that the 12 link pins on the timing chain separate the dots on the camshaft and crankshaft gears (shown). You can use the bolt holes in the front of the cylinder block as landmark aids to get the alignment correct. It may take several tries to get the timing chain and gears properly aligned; take your time because it is essential to get this step right. Because a multi-indexed crankshaft gear is being used here, it was doubly important to verify the location of the dot on the lower gear when installing the timing set.

7 Install Counterweight

Install the keyed counterweight on the camshaft as you ensure that the timing chain and gears are in proper alignment.

8 Install Spacer

Some Y-block engines use a keyed spacer in place of the counterweight. The important thing to remember here is that one or the other of these components must be in place.

9 Install Eccentric

Next, install the eccentric that activates the fuel pump arm, and accompanying non-keyed washer.

Torque Fasteners

10 Install Bolt and Washer

A bolt and washer hold the entire camshaft gear and related components to the cam. A dab of blue Loctite on the bolt is a good idea. Torque the bolt at 35 to 45 ft-lbs.

102 FORD Y-BLOCK ENGINES: HOW TO REBUILD AND MODIFY

ASSEMBLY

Camshaft Endplay Measurement

You need to measure camshaft endplay so the cam stays in the desired position in the cam tunnel. To measure this, you need to properly mount a dial indicator on the block.

1 Measure Cam Endplay

Measure camshaft endplay in much the same manner as with the crankshaft. Set up a dial indicator with magnetic mount on the cylinder block with the indicator contacting the camshaft gear. Be certain to install the magnetic base so that the pointer of the dial indicator does not contact the front of the cam gear on an angle. Pry the cam forward and backward using a large screwdriver. A spec of .006 inch is the maximum allowable endplay and optimum is .001 to .003.

2 Install Oil Slinger

With the timing chain and gears in place, properly aligned and tightened, and camshaft endplay checked, slide the oil slinger onto the snout of the crankshaft.

Accessory Installation

1 Install Crankshaft Seal

Give the front crankshaft seal a light coating of white grease before installation on both the rubber (seal) portion and the outside where it contacts the timing cover. The latter is done to ease installation.

If you don't happen to own a seal-driving tool, a plastic or rubber mallet is sufficient to install the front seal into the timing cover.

CHAPTER 7

2 Install Cover Gasket

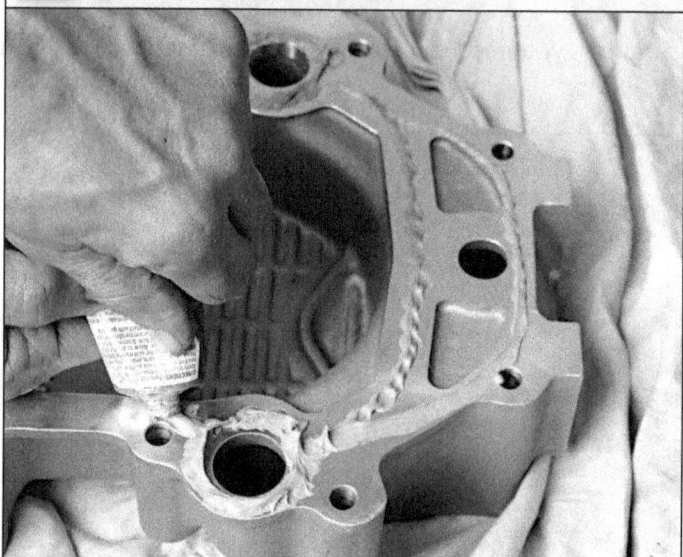

Use sealant on the timing cover gasket, particularly around the water jacket area. RTV gets the job done for both sealing and holding the gasket in place while the cover is being installed. Coat the timing cover bolts with thread sealer to prevent water leaks before you thread the bolts into water jackets in the cylinder block. A thread sealant, such as this product from Permatex, is a must for any bolts or studs that extend into engine water jackets.

4 Install Water Pump

Once the timing cover is in place, you can install the water pump. You should consider installing a rebuilt or new water pump as a worn-out water pump may cause a coolant overheating condition that could damage your newly rebuilt engine. I prefer to use the old-school Indian Head shellac on water pump gaskets.

Torque Fasteners

3 Install Timing Cover Bolts

Replace the timing pointer and then install the timing cover bolts. Snug the bolts and then torque at 23 to 28 ft-lbs.

5 Polish Dampener Snout

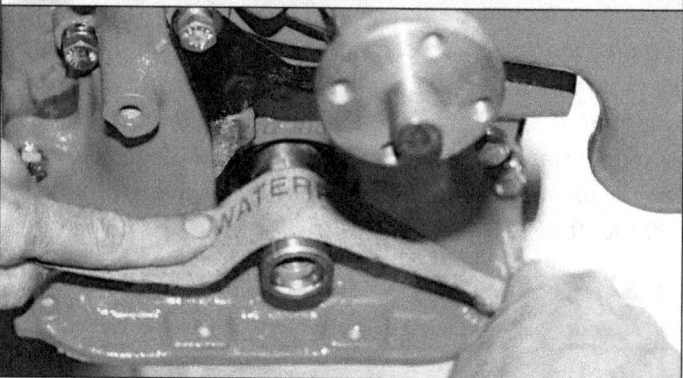

The snout of the crankshaft was a little rough (probably because of improper removal or installation of the dampener in the past) so I used a little emery cloth to smooth it out before installing the dampener.

6 Smooth Woodruff Key

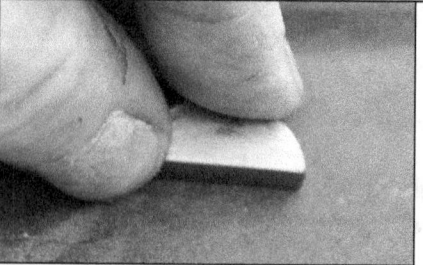

Use emery cloth to smooth the surfaces of the woodruff key that locates the dampener to the crankshaft. A smooth surface here helps with installing the key into its groove on the crankshaft snout and sliding the dampener onto the crank.

FORD Y-BLOCK ENGINES: HOW TO REBUILD AND MODIFY

ASSEMBLY

7 Install Dampener *Important!*

❗ A little white grease applied to the snout of the crankshaft will also aid when installing the dampener. Important: The vibration dampener should slide onto the crankshaft with just a minimum of effort. Do not use a hammer to install the dampener as damage to the dampener and the crankshaft could occur.

8 Torque Dampener Bolt

Mark off the dampener in 90-degree increments from TDC, which assists in setting valve lash both before and after start-up. Torque the bolt securing the dampener to the crankshaft at 85 to 90 ft-lbs. To keep the crankshaft from turning as you torque the dampener bolt, wedge a pry bar or big screwdriver between two old flywheel bolts installed in the rear flange of the crankshaft and your engine stand.

Oil System Installation

1 Choose Oil Filter Adapter

You are getting ready to complete the bottom end of the engine. Here's something to consider if you are working with an early-series Y-block that uses the canister-style oil filter: The adapter shown here is a modern spin on a type of oil filter that saves time when servicing your engine and prevents the leaks that are associated with the canister type. Be sure to grease the O-ring that seals the adapter to the block.

Just to the right of the filter adapter is the oil-pressure sending switch for the idiot light on the dash. If you intend to stay with the light for monitoring your engine oil pressure, the least you can do at this point is to install a new sending unit. Be sure to use thread sealer to avoid leaks.

2 Install Block-Off Plate

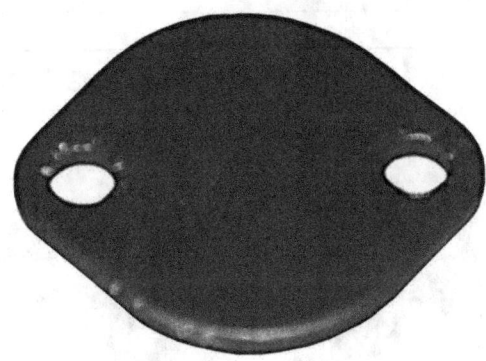

If you are also converting your engine from the road draft tube to a more modern and efficient PCV system, you need a block-off plate such as the one pictured to cover the hole in the side of the block left by eliminating the road draft tube.

FORD Y-BLOCK ENGINES: HOW TO REBUILD AND MODIFY

CHAPTER 7

Professional Mechanic Tip

3 Clean Oil Pickup and Screen

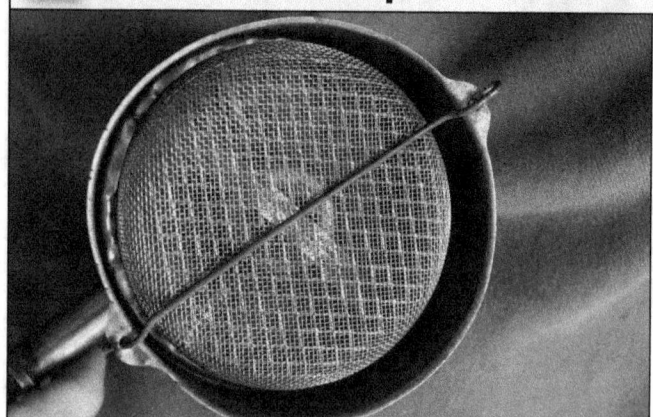

It is imperative that the oil pickup and screen are clean so leftover dirt or foreign particles don't damage the engine. To be doubly sure, replace the pickup screen with a new one. It is held in place by a simple spring clip and is easy to replace. Rich Stuck chose to use an NOS pickup tube on this rebuild.

4 Install Oil Pickup

The oil pickup on the Y-block Ford engine is external. It is fed through a hole in the oil pan from the inside out. Two sealing washers are included in the engine gasket kit for the pickup. One goes to the outside (the thicker one) of the pan and seals the pickup against the pan. The other fits between the large nut and the oil pan. Thread the large nut onto the pickup from the outside but do not fully tighten it at this point.

The oil pan may now be installed. Be sure to use sealer (I prefer RTV) on the gasket; it seals well and also helps hold the gasket in place during assembly. Once you start the numerous oil pan bolts, a speed handle, socket, and extension to snug them up are great time-savers.

5 Install Pickup Tube Seal

The opposite end of the oil pickup tube, which connects to the oil pump, uses a rubber seal that is also included in the engine gasket kit. A light dab of grease helps protect this seal during installation. Some thread sealer on the nut that secures the pickup tube to the pump is also a good idea.

6 Align Oil Pump Gasket

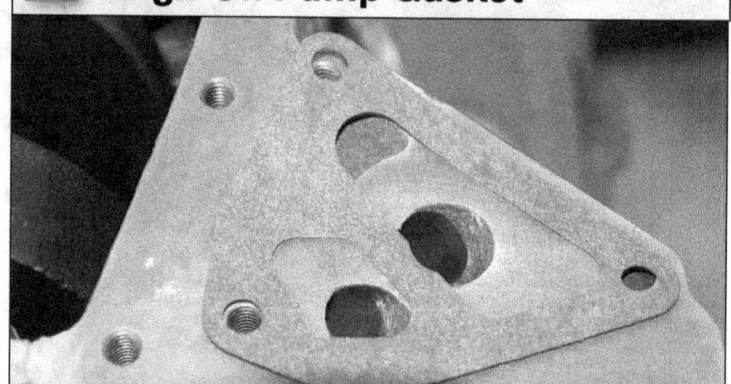

Before the oil pump is installed, check the gasket for alignment with the bolt and oil passage holes in both the block and the pump. No sealer is used on this gasket. I have seen cases where RTV was used here, and the engine was later damaged by pieces of the material that had broken off and become lodged in oil passages.

ASSEMBLY

7 Install Oil Pump

I consider priming the oil pump before installation a must. To install the oil pump, first fit the gasket to the pump, install the pump drive (I highly recommend using this heavy-duty drive from ARP), and then feed the assembly into the block, taking care that the pump drive is in the correct location. A second set of eyes checking alignment of the pump drive from the top (distributor opening) is helpful here.

8 Install Oil Pump Bolts

The oil pump on a Y-block is held in place by three bolts. Once you have the oil pump and drive in proper alignment, use the bolt that enters into the pump from the top to help hold it in place while the other bolts are installed. Do not tighten the bolts at this time.

9 Torque Oil Pump Bolts

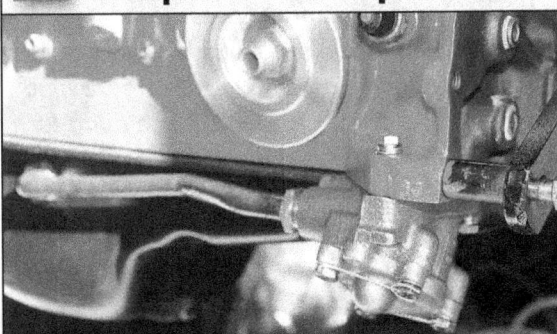

Torque Fasteners

Place the end of the pickup tube into the oil pump. Once you are sure that all components are properly aligned, tighten them. Do not overtighten the nut that secures the pickup tube at the oil pan. The torque value of oil pump to block bolts is 12 to 15 ft-lbs.

Top End Installation

1 Install Cylinder Head Gaskets

The cylinder head gaskets go on the block only one way. Pay attention to the embossed lettering on the gasket that indicates the front. The gasket must face toward the front of the engine even if the lettering faces down when the gasket is in place. Be certain that the locating dowels for the cylinder heads/gaskets are in place and in good condition. If they are not, these parts are the same as those used on later small-block Ford engines; they are available through dealer parts suppliers.

2 Install Lifter Valley Cover

I prefer to use weather strip adhesive to hold the lifter valley cover in place and seal it because there are no slots or dowels to hold the gasket in place during assembly. The lifter valley cover is held in place by two bolts and grommets. Do not overtighten the bolts; doing so bends the cover and creates oil leaks around the cover.

3 Thread-In Head Bolts

4 Choose Engine Gaskets

Because of production variations in the Y-block engine series, your engine gasket set likely includes several different intake manifold gasket sets. Match the correct gaskets to your cylinder heads before installing the manifold.

There is close tolerance between the lifter valley cover and the cylinder heads. Of particular note here: There are both left and right cylinder heads on the Y-block Ford engine. This passenger-side head is identified by the freeze plug located at the back. The driver-side head has a bung for the temperature sender in place of the freeze plug.

Once the cylinder heads are in place and seated on the locating dowels, thread in the head bolts. Remember to put a drop of oil on the threads and under the heads of the bolts. Keep in mind that the Y-block's cylinder-head bolts have different lengths. (The two longer top bolts go on the ends.) It is a good idea to arrange them by length on each side of the engine before proceeding.

Critical Inspection

5 Install Intake Bolts

Carefully set the intake manifold in place. I often fit the bypass hose to the intake first and then install it as a unit. Install the intake bolts snug but do not torque them yet. The intake bolts should thread into the cylinder heads smoothly.

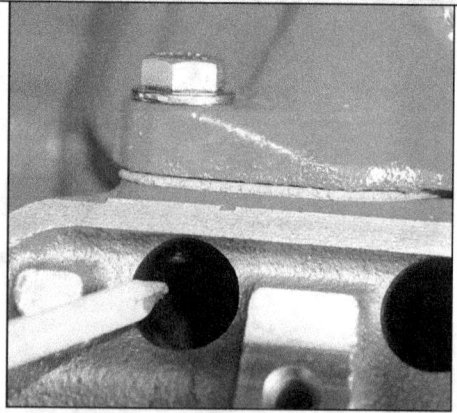

It is important to note that the end intake manifold bolt holes on the Y-block open into the pushrod holes of the cylinder heads. You must use bolts with the correct length. Installing bolts that are too long interferes with the pushrod.

ASSEMBLY

6 Torque Head and Intake Manifold Bolts

Torque the cylinder head bolts in three steps (35, 55, and 75 ft-lbs) following the sequence shown on page 142. Once the cylinder-head bolts have been torqued, go back and torque the intake manifold bolts to 26 ft-lbs, alternating side to side and front to back as you go.

7 Orient Rocker Arm Assembly

When assembling the rocker arm shafts on a Y-block, it is easy to get them in the wrong position. The bottom of the rocker arm shafts has holes drilled in it for oil to pass through. The proper orientation is for the holes in the rocker arm shafts to face downward toward the cylinder head. Failure to get the rocker shafts in the correct orientation results in a lack of lubrication that results in engine damage.

8 Orient Oil Holes

When putting the rocker arm assemblies together, you can keep the oil hole orientation correct by first installing one of the end cotter pins with the open end facing down.

9 Assemble Rocker Arm Parts

Line up the components (rocker arms, spacer springs, and stands) in the correct order and install them on the rocker arm shafts. Lubricate all components with oil before assembly then install each of the components in the correct order, beginning at one end of the rocker arm shaft. This is a good time to refer to the photos you took during the disassembly process.

10 Install Pushrods

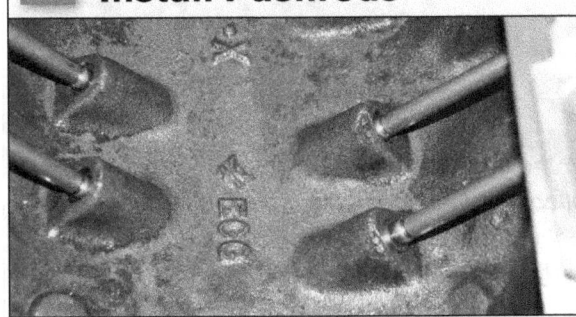

After lubricating both ends of the pushrods with oil, make sure that they are properly seated in the valve lifters when installing them.

CHAPTER 7

11 Install Rocker Arm Assembly

The rocker arm assemblies are now ready to install. An oil-return tube is located at one end of each assembly. The tube on the passenger's side of the engine is located in the front and the driver's side to the rear. The bottom hole of each rocker stand (at the ends of the rocker assemblies) holds the studs to which the valve covers mount. Secure the rocker arm assemblies to the cylinder heads by bolts that extend through the stands.

12 Adjust Valves

The final step is to adjust the valves. Because the specification for "valve lash listed" is hot, set the valves several thousandths wider to allow for the expansion that occurs when the engine heats up. Begin by setting the number-1 cylinder at TDC of the compression stroke. After setting the lash on this cylinder, rotate the engine 90 degrees to the next mark on the dampener (see page 110) and, following the firing order, adjust each set of valves in turn, rotating the engine to the next mark on the dampener as you go.

Use a feeler gauge to determine the gap between the tip of the valve and the face of the rocker arm. Each rocker arm has an adjuster that is turned until the proper gap has been achieved. A slight drag on the feeler gauge should be felt when the lash is correct. Set valve lash again with the engine hot after initial start-up.

When the heads and rocker arms have been installed, the final step is to adjust the valves. The correct valve lash must be set for the engine to run properly.

CHAPTER 8

HIGH-PERFORMANCE Y-BLOCK ENGINE BUILD

The current traditional hot rod movement has generated interest in the venerable Y-block V-8, and the aftermarket has supported it as well as the engine series it replaced, the flathead. Indeed, the manufacturers of speed equipment have developed new performance parts to meet the demand. It seems the old adage is true: "If you wait long enough, everything eventually comes back in style."

Then there are the Y-block stalwarts, my friend Jerry Christenson among them, who have continued to race and modify Y-block engines through the years. Early on, the Y-block faithful were convinced of the engine series' strength and performance potential, despite the lack of performance parts over the decades. These enthusiasts have displayed the true spirit of hot rodding by carefully examining the raw material that Ford gave them and then squeezing every ounce of power from it using little more than ingenuity. The experience and guidance these men have has proved to be invaluable in writing this book.

When I set out to build a proper, modern high-performance version of the Y-block V-8, my approach was simple and straightforward. I wanted it to be the ideal power plant for Richard Stuck's beautiful 1957 Ford Custom, so I selected a combination of traditional and modern performance parts that work well in concert while improving on the original Ford design. A major consideration was the intended purpose for the engine. My goal was not to have a competition-only engine but rather a powerful, reliable, strong street engine.

This engine is based on a 1957 vintage 292-cylinder block. Why not begin with the larger displacement

High-performance and racing Y-blocks have won many NASCAR races, Bonneville speed runs, and other competitions over the years. This 322-ci Y-block features dished pistons so it's compatible with increased cylinder pressures of the supercharger. Here, the short-block is assembled and it's ready to accept the heads, intake, carb, and other related equipment.

FORD Y-BLOCK ENGINES: HOW TO REBUILD AND MODIFY

CHAPTER 8

This 1957-vintage 292 block is the raw material for the performance Y-block engine build. I chose the 292 over the 312 because the 292 has the stronger casting of the two for performance applications. Engineering changes to the main bearing saddle areas of the 312 block resulted in it being weaker than that of its predecessor. After being bored oversize and fitted with a 312 crankshaft, my engine displaces 322 ci.

Rather than depending on 50-year-old hardware, I have chosen to use new, high-quality fasteners, such as these connecting rod bolts by ARP, throughout both engine builds, stock, and performance.

312-cylinder block, you ask? After all, in hot rod circles, isn't the old saying, "There's no substitute for cubic inches?" The reason for my choice is simple: strength of design. When Ford increased the displacement of the Y-block from 292 to 312 ci, it increased the crankshaft's stroke as well as the main bearing journal size. To accommodate the larger main bearing journals, Ford cast and machined a cylinder block that had less beef where it was needed the most: the bottom end.

The advantages of the 292 far outweighed the attributes of using the 312 block. In addition, the longer main bearing cap bolts, which in turn required deeper holes in the casting, resulted in a tendency to develop cracks in the webbing of the cylinder block. Taking into consideration the inherent strength advantage of the 292 cylinder block along with the common and simple modification of turning down the main bearing journals of the 312 crankshaft to the diameter of a 292 journal (instant stroker crank), it all makes sense. Add to this the 292 block's reputation for thick cylinder walls that allow for increases in bore size (unthinkable in later Ford engine series with thin wall castings), and a combination of strength plus cubic inches can be achieved.

Y-Block on a Diet

Here's a quick way to shed ugly, unwanted pounds from your Y-block. As any racer tells you, it's cheaper to remove weight than it is to build the horsepower required to overcome weight. From the standpoint of a drag racer, there is no better place to remove weight than from over the front wheels.

To accomplish this, Rich Stuck equipped his 322-ci-performance version of the Y-block with aluminum cylinder heads that weigh 29 pounds each compared to the stock cast-iron units that tip the scales at 58 pounds each. This cut off 58 pounds.

Another 8 pounds of ugly fat came off when I replaced the cast-iron timing chain cover with an aluminum unit by John Mummert.

I swapped out the OEM cast-iron intake manifold, weighing 41 pounds for one cast-aluminum manifold and saved another 28 pounds.

This brought the grand total of pounds shed on the Y-block diet to 94. Removing this much iron from over the front wheel can go a long way to aid weight transfer and shift the center of gravity to the back of the car, which is exactly where I want it for better traction and handling. ∎

It should be noted that blocks bearing C2AE casting numbers are said to have the thickest cylinder walls of all. For competition engines, additional displacement can be squeezed out of the Y-block with an aftermarket crankshaft used in concert with a camshaft that has been ground on a smaller base circle to provide more clearance for the rotating assembly. For the purposes of my street performance Y-block, an OEM 312 cast-iron crankshaft fills the bill quite nicely.

Rich Stuck has two Iskenderian camshafts from which to choose for these engine builds. Although several aftermarket manufacturers grind camshafts for the Y-block V-8, these particular cams were chosen because they are copies of the original high-performance camshafts offered by Ford in 1957.

Ford Y-Block 285-hp Kit

In 1957 Ford made a performance kit available through the dealer parts system in order to homologate the parts for use in NASCAR competition. The kit consisted of cylinder heads, intake manifold, intake gaskets with blocked heat passages, carburetors, camshaft, and a special air cleaner that contained a high-flow Purolator filter element.

A close look at the air cleaner assembly shows that the Purolator part number has been removed. This was reportedly done because Chrysler had already registered that particular number with NASCAR and was using it on their racing vehicles. The fact that the 285-hp kit was available is a fact and not myth, but whether it was ever available on a production vehicle is in doubt. ∎

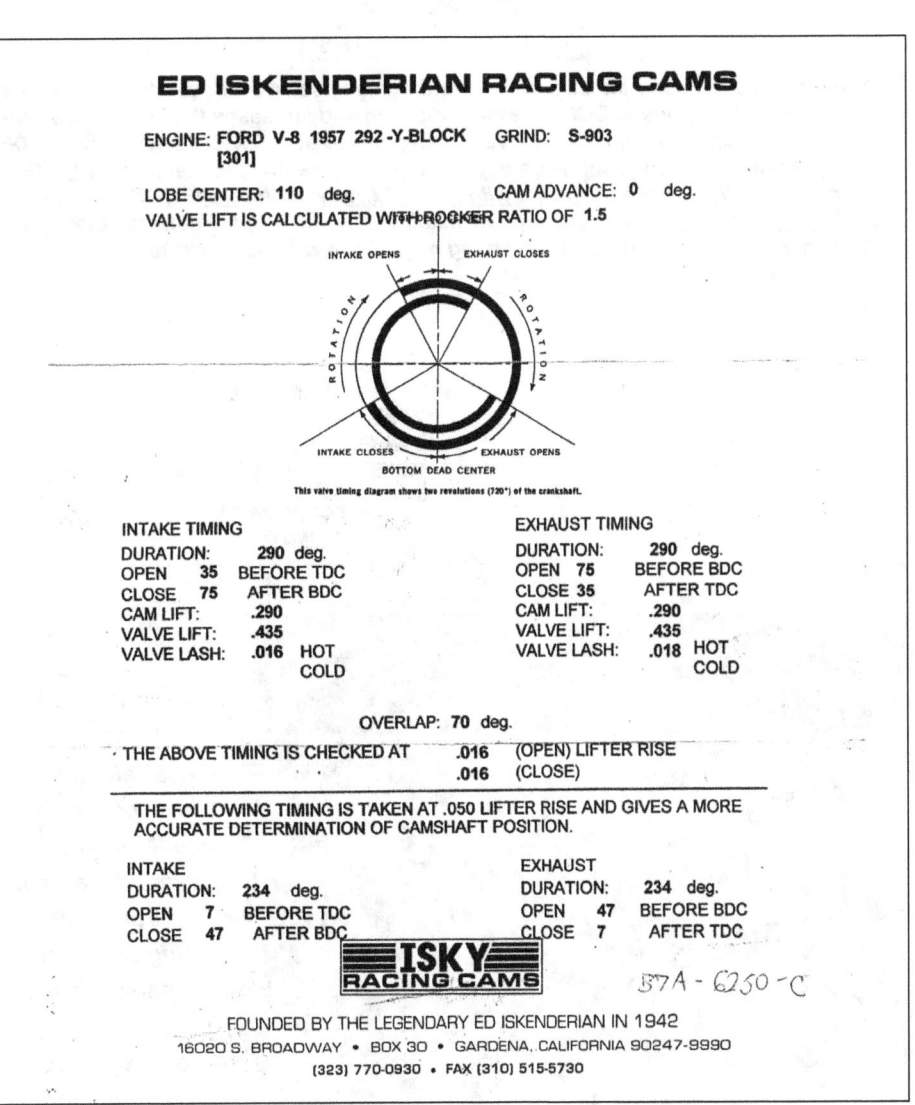

This specification sheet provided with one of the Iskenderian camshafts shows that it is ground to match the Ford B7A-6250-C high-performance cam. Lift is listed at .435 and duration at 290 degrees, and the cam is ground on a 110-degree centerline. (Illustration Courtesy Isky Racing Cams)

CHAPTER 8

Timing Set Installation Instructions

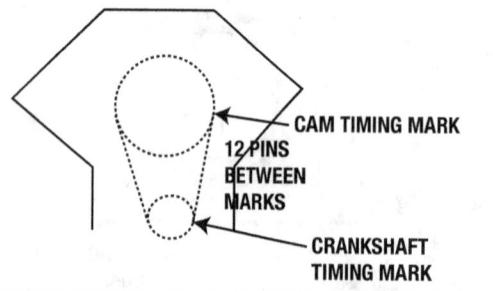

"A" indicates advancing the cam. Installing the timing set A2 reduces the intake lobe centerline by 2 degrees ATDC. "R" retards the cam and increases the intake lobe centerline the specified amount ATDC. If your cam degrees at 110 ATDC and you want 106 degrees, install the timing set A4 degrees. In this case the A4 sprocket tooth is the timing mark. <u>Install the crankshaft gear with the A4 keyway on the crankshaft key and use the A4 tooth as the timing mark.</u> Always install gears with 12 pins between the crankshaft timing mark and the camshaft timing mark. **Cam will be in overlap #1 cylinder.**

Even though the quality of this image is a little suspect, the quality of the information that Rollmaster provides with their multi-indexed lower gear kit is quite helpful.

How sturdy is the cast-iron 312 crankshaft? Jerry Christenson uses one in the engine of his 1956 Thunderbird drag car, and it covers a quarter mile in 10 seconds. Jerry reports that even after machining the main bearing journals to 292 diameter, offset grinding the connecting rod journals to 2.10 inches to gain additional displacement, and running a supercharger delivering 10 to 14 pounds of boost, the crankshaft has stood the test of hundreds of quarter-mile runs with no signs of wear. As a matter of fact, such is the strength and reliability of the engine that Jerry has only had to replace piston rings and wrist pins as part of his race engine's maintenance.

Racing Engines

Enthusiasts and racers from Finland take the Ford Y-block seriously and squeeze every ounce of power from their engines. The Hollowheads Racing Team is at the forefront of getting this venerable engine series to perform its very best. The team fields an Altered dragster, driven by Jyrki Peltonen, that is powered by a 292-ci turbocharged Y-block that is capable of covering the quarter-mile in just over eight seconds; it's one of the fastest Y-block–powered vehicles in the world today.

Most race engine builders agree that a great deal of additional horsepower can be found through modifications to cylinder heads. To this end, the Hollowheads sacrificed a Y-block cylinder head to be cut into several sections to examine its port configurations.

A cast-aluminum timing cover from John Mummert replaced the heavy cast-iron OEM timing cover on the performance engine. Not only does it save weight, it also looks great.

HIGH-PERFORMANCE Y-BLOCK ENGINE BUILD

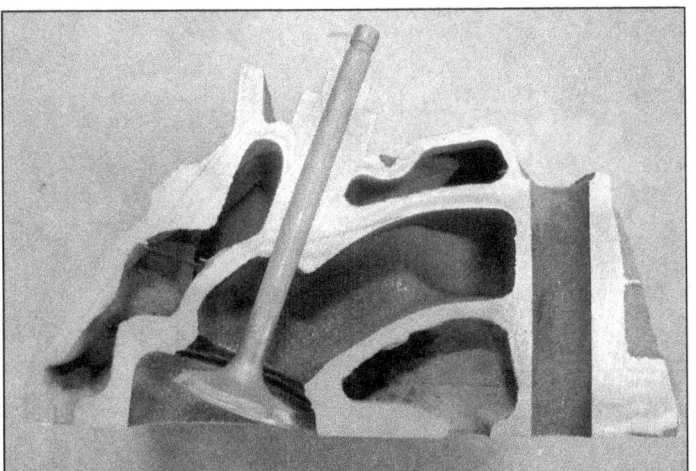 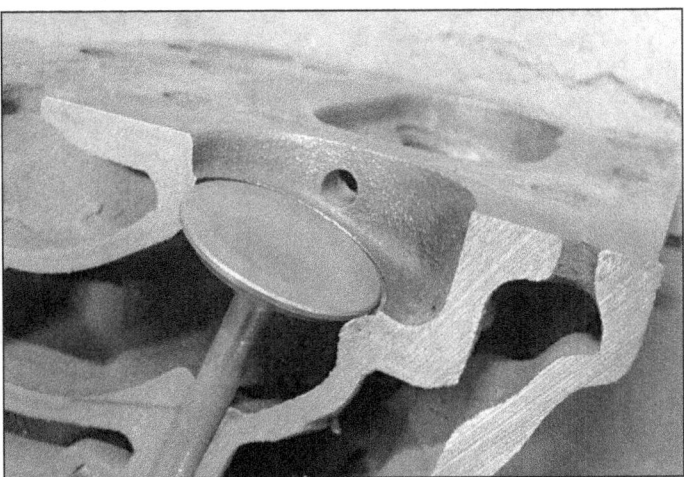

Cutting open the cylinder head reveals the port configuration and allows Crew Chief Seppo Kokko to determine how to best modify the head to attain maximum airflow through the intake and exhaust ports to attain additional horsepower. Based on knowledge gained from sectioning a Y-block cylinder head, Seppo is able to modify the ports in the cylinder heads to be used on the team's race engine.

A look through the modified exhaust ports on this ECZ-C cylinder head casting shows that Seppo has achieved the sought-after result: the straightest possible path between valve and port that provides the maximum amount of horsepower from the head.

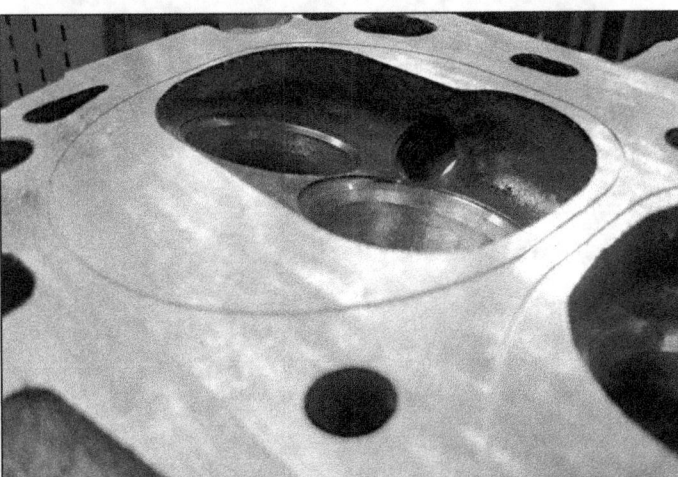 

The Hollow Heads Racing Team are running a turbocharger on their engine, so they needed to find an effective solution to sealing the cylinder heads to the block under the extreme pressures created by this form of induction. To supplement the fire ring in their copper head gaskets, the team had their cylinder head surfaces grooved to accept an O-ring.

CHAPTER 8

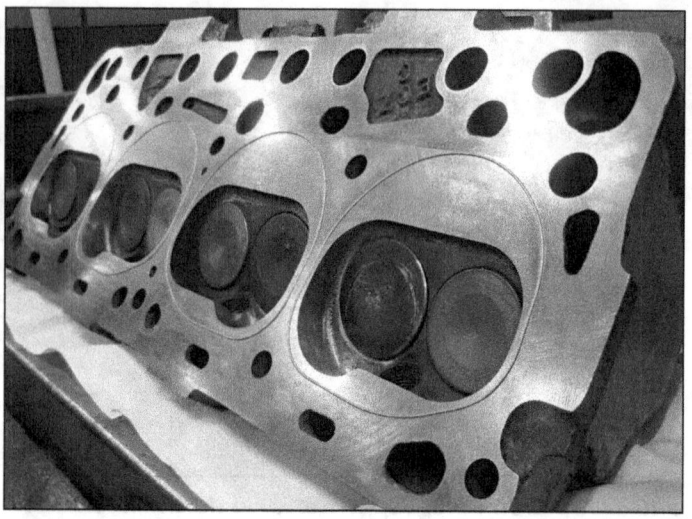
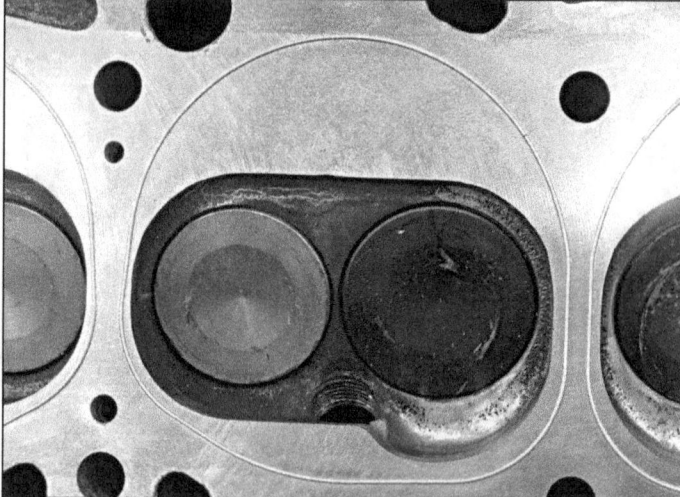

Another cylinder head modification dictated by the use of the turbocharger on this engine was a complete redesign of the standard Y-block cylinder head's combustion chambers.

The addition of a turbocharger to the engine also requires custom-made pistons, as shown here. (Photo Courtesy Seppo Kokko)

RaceTec Engine Parts

The RaceTec piston in this performance engine build is a thoroughly modern design and features an accumulator groove, which, by design, collects any gases that manage to escape (blow by) past the top piston ring. It also prevents the ring from being disrupted; it is allowed to seal properly against the cylinder walls.

This comparison shows the difference between the custom-forged aluminum RaceTec (right) piston and a cast replacement (left) for the Y-block V-8.

HIGH-PERFORMANCE Y-BLOCK ENGINE BUILD

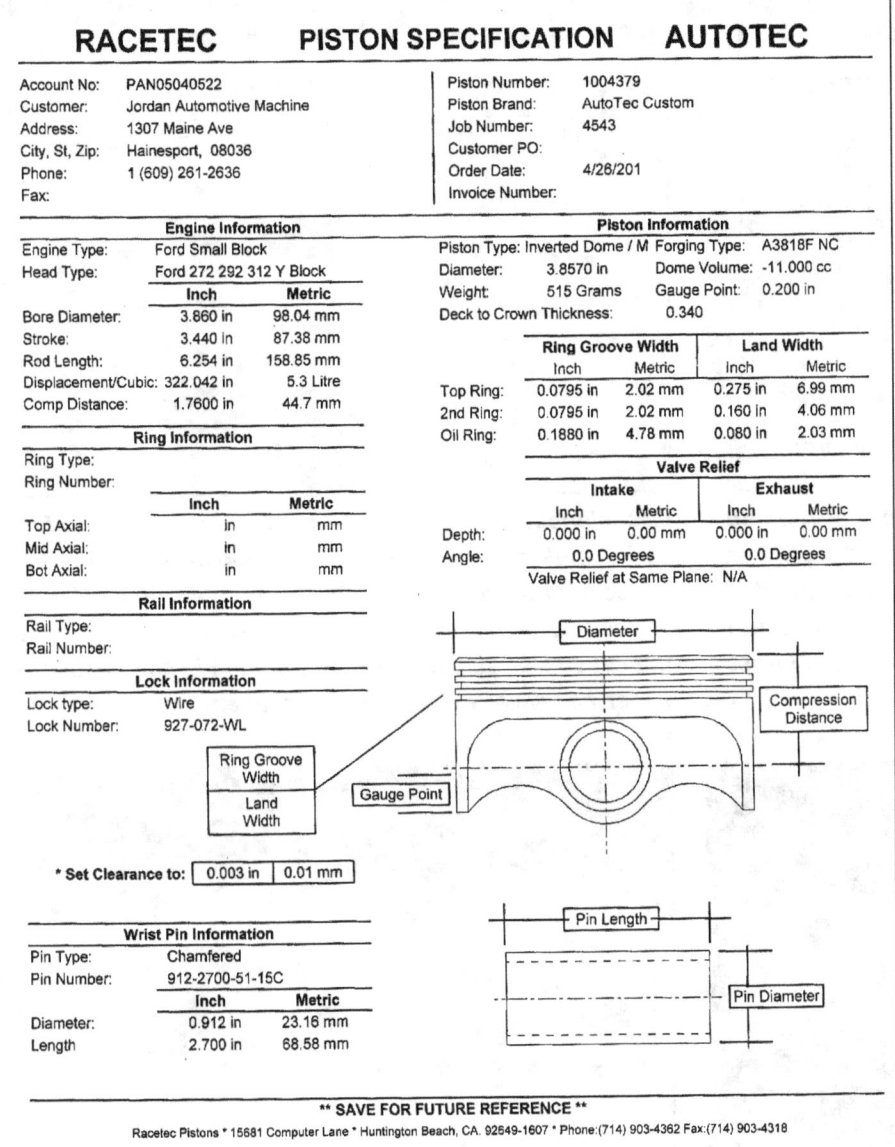

To achieve the optimum compression ratio for the performance Y-block, a custom-made piston was required. I chose RaceTec to provide a set of forged aluminum castings made to my specifications. Because I will run my engine with the original McCulloch supercharger, the compression ratio was kept down to around 9.0:1. Supplying RaceTec with the combustion chamber volume of the cylinder heads, along with cylinder block deck clearance, allowed them to calculate the proper piston configuration for this application.

Although the original supercharged 312 Y-block engines of 1957 had an 8.5:1 compression ratio, I am able to squeeze in another half point because of the aluminum cylinder heads, which dissipate the heat created by combustion more efficiently with modern, higher-octane fuels. This is an example of a RaceTech spec sheet. (Illustration Courtesy RaceTec Pistons)

Not only is the RaceTec piston considerably lighter than OEM or cast replacement pistons, it is of superior design and materials, making it far stronger for use in a performance-oriented engine. Less power-robbing weight in reciprocating mass equates directly to horsepower.

By comparison, the wrist pin supplied with the RaceTec piston (right) is both lighter and stronger in design and material than the OEM part (left). RaceTec wrist pins are the same dimension as those used in later-model small-block Ford V-8 engines. Both are .912 inch in diameter.

FORD Y-BLOCK ENGINES: HOW TO REBUILD AND MODIFY

CHAPTER 8

Top End Components

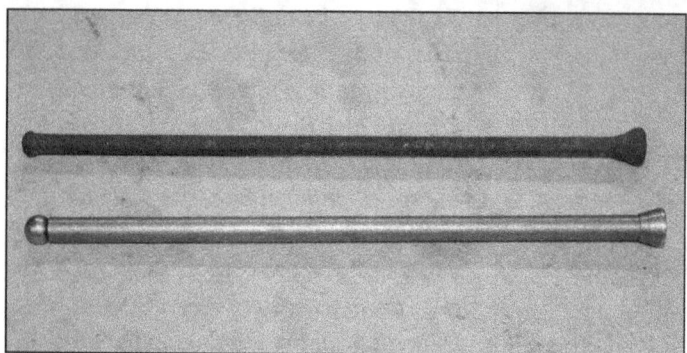

Another upgrade is from the old-style solid pushrod (top) to that of superior tubular design (bottom). Tubular pushrods are hollow, which results in less power-robbing mass; the hollow design makes them inherently stronger. This upgrade is advised for any Y-block engine rebuild, including stock. Tubular Y-block pushrods in OEM length are available from Speed-Pro. For custom lengths, I trust Smith Brothers.

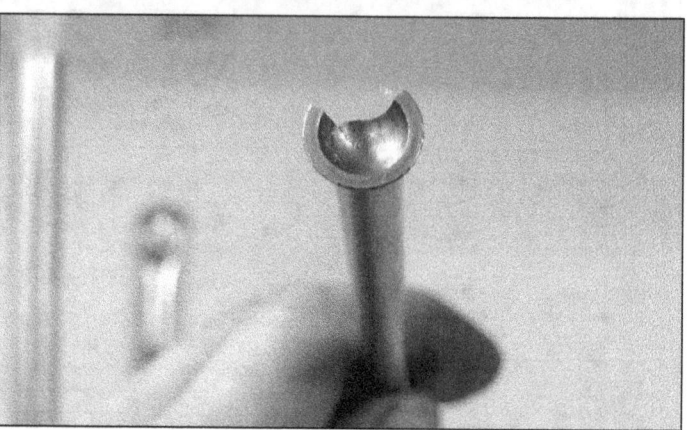

Occasionally, tubular pushrods aren't strong enough for some applications. Valve lash is far too loose, and it could cause the adjuster on the rocker arm to eventually fracture the cup at the upper end of the pushrod. In this instance, the cause was very high-RPM operation in conjunction with super-heavy valvesprings in a racing engine.

The now-assembled 322-ci performance short-block displays the custom dish-top RaceTec pistons, which, by providing a larger combustion volume, supply the desired compression ratio of 9.1:1. This is perfect for use with the factory McCulloch supercharger for this engine. In 1957 the factory horsepower rating for the supercharged 312 was 300. In reality, the engines produced between 340 and 370 hp. Without a dynamometer, I can't be exactly sure, but I am confident that with all the upgrades, my 322-ci engine will deliver in the neighborhood of 400 ponies on pump gas.

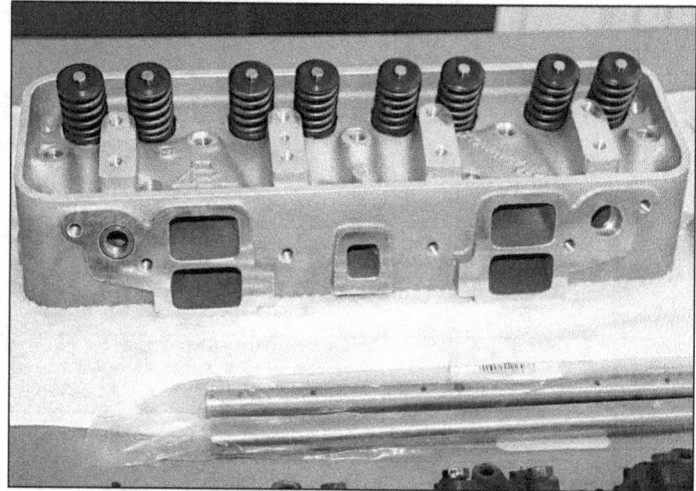

The redesigned aluminum cylinder heads by John Mummert have allowed the venerable Y-block engine series to make a serious leap into the 21st century when it comes to performance. The bare head castings weigh 24.5 pounds each, which is a considerable weight savings over the cast-iron OEM heads. Manganese bronze valveguides and Viton positive-seal valve seals keep oil out of the combustion chambers. As delivered, the Mummert head features a 1.250-inch-diameter valvespring with an installed height of 1.750 inches with 85 pounds of seat pressure on 1.375-inch spring cups. For more aggressive cam profiles that require larger valvesprings, the heads are machined to accept spring cups up to 1.460 inches in diameter.

HIGH-PERFORMANCE Y-BLOCK ENGINE BUILD

When he designed his cylinder head castings, John Mummert thought of everything a true Y-block enthusiast would love, including his logo, the Y-block logo, and the ECG casting letters.

One of the biggest aids to performance, as well as weight savings, came in the form of the cylinder heads that I chose for this 322 Y-block buildup. They are John Mummert cast-aluminum cylinder heads. Modern CNC technology allowed Mummert to redesign the cylinder head ports for maximum efficiency and flow. Fitted with stainless-steel 11/32-inch-stem diameter 1.94-inch intake valves and 1.54-inch exhaust valves, these heads flow 235 cfm at a .550 lift on the intake and 175 cfm at a .550 lift on the exhaust side. The deck thickness is .625, combustion chambers are 60 cc, valve angle is 18 degrees, and the use of 14-mm spark plug holes improves combustion by eliminating valve shrouding that improves flame travel.

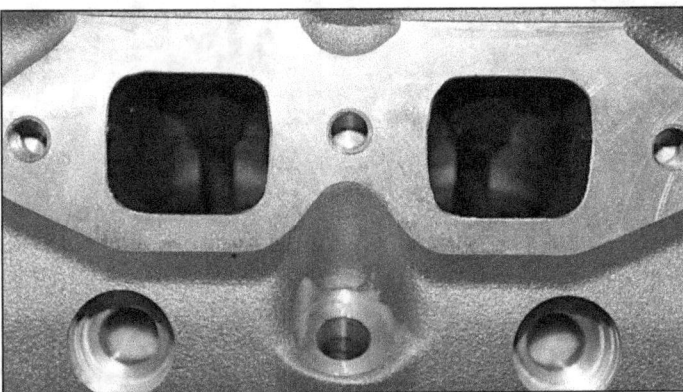

The exhaust port and combustion chamber improvements over the original Ford design found in the Mummert cylinder heads allow you to bolt on instant horsepower to your Y-block without any other engine modifications.

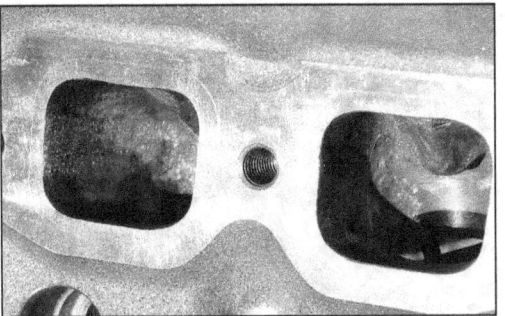

Of course, serious racers, including Jerry Christenson, try to wring every last ounce of power from any cylinder head, even those from Mummert. Evidence of Jerry's port and combustion chamber work are seen here. These modifications include increasing port size and removing material in the combustion chamber to decrease valve shrouding. These changes accommodate Jerry's engine combination and are not necessary for my street performance application.

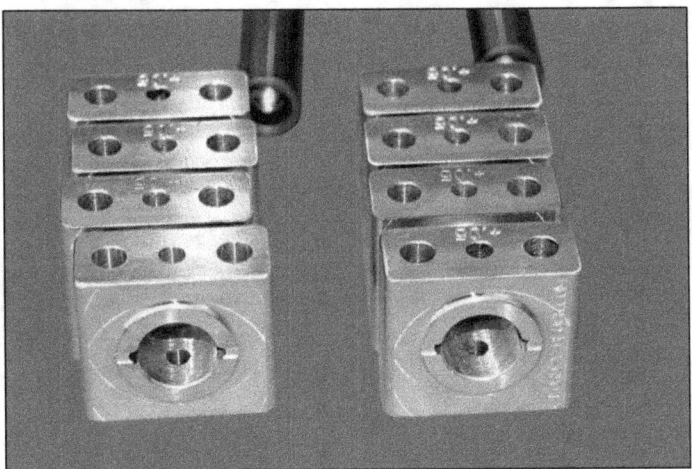

I am using John Mummert's rocker arm stands in concert with ECG rocker arms and hardened rocker shafts for the performance Y-block build. The Mummert stands are fashioned from light, strong billet aluminum and lighter, yet stronger-than-OEM Ford, rocker arm stands.

When mounting aluminum cylinder heads on an engine, it is advisable to use studs in place of the normal head bolts. I am using John Mummert–supplied head studs, nuts, and washers for my engine. The instructions provided with the aluminum heads as to stud installation and torque should be followed closely. Studs are first lightly lubricated with oil and then hand-threaded into the cylinder block. The studs do not get tightened beyond hand-tight. Head gaskets are then slipped down the studs and seated on the deck surface of the block.

CHAPTER 8

I chose Fel-Pro Blue cylinder head gaskets to handle the sealing chores between the cylinder block and aluminum heads. The same gaskets were used in the stock rebuild. These gaskets are far superior to the OEM steel shim head gaskets originally used by Ford on Y-block engines. Again, the head gaskets only mount one way. The markings on the gaskets that read "front" must face the front of the engine.

Top End Components Installation

Torque the hardware that secures the heads to the block. Again, follow the manufacturer's directions and torque specs because these procedures and values may vary from supplier to supplier. They supply torque values as they relate to the use of this stud, washer, and nut combination. The beveled side of the washers must face toward the head of the nuts. Torque specifications are 80 ft-lbs when using oil on the threads of the studs and nuts and 63 ft-lbs when using ARP lube. The tightening sequence for the studs/nuts is the same as on page 142 (top) for all Y-block V-8 engines. It is recommended that you repeat the torque sequence three times to ensure that the fire ring of the head gasket is properly compressed.

The Mummert cylinder heads are installed on the engine, and the intake ports are shown here. I have long wondered why Ford engineers chose this unusual horizontal intake-port configuration for the Y-block cylinder head. The answer is simple: Additional hood clearance, less material required in the head casting, and, my favorite, the orientation of the port does not matter to the engine. All that matters is how directly and efficiently the port transfers the air/fuel mixture to the valve.

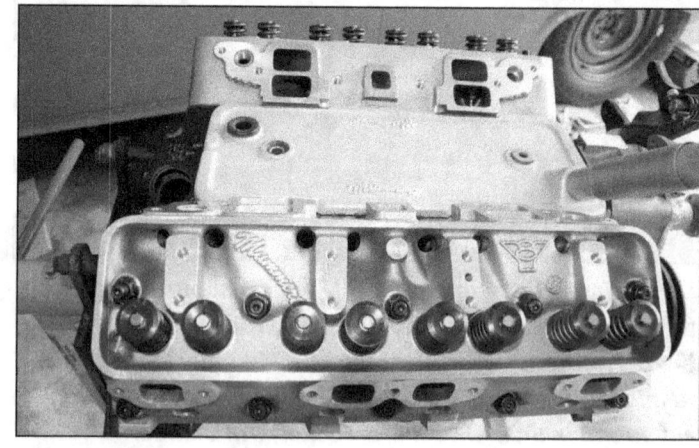

Although not lighter than the stamped OEM valley cover, this cast-aluminum piece looks great and is less likely than an OEM part to leak because of bending from overtightening. Using a proper sealant and snugging the hardware without overtightening keeps the top of the engine dry.

HIGH-PERFORMANCE Y-BLOCK ENGINE BUILD

The 322-ci performance Y-block is now in long-block configuration, and it looks great with the cylinder heads and other aluminum parts installed. I expect it to run as good as it looks.

You do not need to set the valve lash wider to compensate for heat expansion of parts when setting the cold valve lash on an engine equipped with aluminum cylinder heads. Valve lash is set tighter because the aluminum cylinder head castings themselves don't expand at the same rate as cast iron. As an example, the factory specifications for valve lash with the camshaft I am using call for lash to be set at .019 hot. With the aluminum cylinder heads, I set lash at .016 cold.

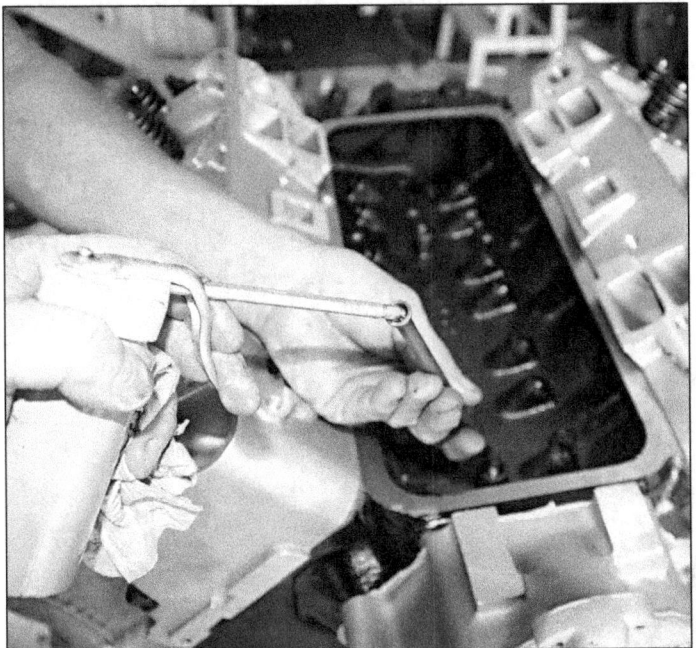

When installing the rocker arm assemblies and pushrods, don't forget to give all components a good coating of oil because it provides protection from friction damage during initial start-up of the engine.

The 322-ci-performance Y-block engine is complete and mounted on a stand showing off the McCulloch supercharger and unique copper-coated Fenton performance exhaust manifolds.

CHAPTER 8

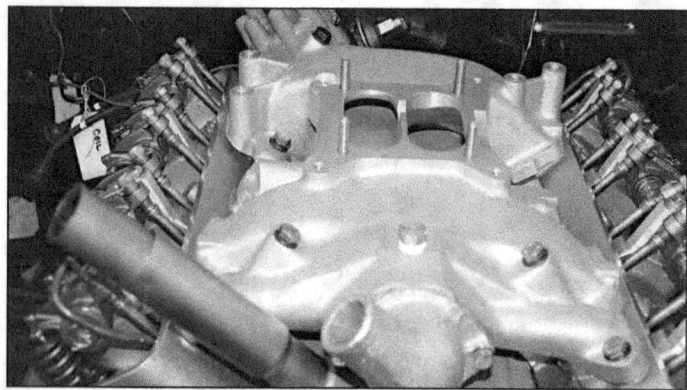

The 322-ci engine is shown mounted in the car without the carburetor and supercharger setup in place. You can see that the Blue Thunder aluminum intake manifold has been cast and machined to accommodate either the original Tea Pot Holley (used with the supercharger) or the later 4160-version Holley carburetor.

Imagine the reaction of any gas-pump jockey who opened the hood of a 1957 Ford to check the oil and was confronted with this sight.

The lettering on the hood of Rich Stuck's 1957 Custom tells the tale. While Ford rated the supercharged 312 engines at 300 hp in 1957, it is well documented that they produced in excess of that number. Suffice it to say that with modern parts and modifications, the engine delivers considerably more than 300 hp now.

This beautiful 1957 Ford Custom, belonging to Rich Stuck of Brick, New Jersey, is the proud recipient of my 322-ci McCulloch supercharged performance Y-block engine.

CHAPTER 9

ENGINE INSTALLATION, START-UP AND BREAK-IN

This chapter takes you through the final phase of your project and consists of the following series of steps: installing the engine into the vehicle, connecting all associated components, start-up, tuning, and break-in.

Installation

After many hours of difficult, dirty work and hard-earned dollars spent, you have finally reached the point where you can reap the rewards of your labors. Reassembly is essentially disassembly in reverse. This is helpful and informative advice indeed. Now is a great time to break out your notes and photographic record of the steps taken during the removal of the engine and give them a careful inspection.

Anyone who has undertaken the removal, rebuilding, and replacement of an engine will tell you that the process isn't quite that simple. However, with proper planning getting the engine back into the car shouldn't be too difficult.

I prefer to leave as many of the bolt-on external accessories off the engine as possible during the installation phase for two reasons. First, without external accessories, the engine is more compact and easier to manipulate. Second, access to important things, such as motor mounts, is much easier with fewer obstructions in the way.

Take the time to prepare the engine compartment to receive the engine by ensuring that all wires, linkages, etc., are safely and securely out of the way. Make sure the car is on a level surface and secure it from

Take your time and methodically lower the engine into the front clip and align it with the motor mounts. Valve covers and exhaust manifolds must be installed later. You spent considerable time and money rebuilding the engine and you don't want to damage fresh paint on the car. Some chose to move the engine on the stand across the garage floor to properly align the engine with the chassis. I find it easier to move the car under the engine, then lower and push the engine into position.

CHAPTER 9

rolling or falling. You must always make safety the highest priority. Never put yourself or your helpers at risk. If you're not comfortable performing a task, take your project to a professional. There is no shame in asking for help, but there could be a lot of pain if you're unable to safely complete the work.

Cover and/or pad any painted or delicate surfaces to avoid damage. Enlisting the help of a couple of friends as the extra hands and eyes make lowering the engine into the car and aligning the motor mounts to the frame much easier. Remember: *Take your time*. There is no need to rush. If something isn't going correctly, reassess the situation, and then proceed. Once the engine is securely bolted into the car you can set about installing the external components and accessories. Referring to your notes and photos on how things came apart is of great assistance here.

Engine Installation

1 Install Fuel Pump

The completed long-block is off the stand and ready to be lifted into the car; this is a good time to install some of the accessories. Shown here is the fuel pump. It is important that you position the top of the pump actuator arm under the eccentric on the front of the camshaft when installed. You have to do this mostly by feel (you feel the tension created by the arm under the eccentric) because you are unable to see inside the timing cover with the pump in the way.

2 Install Motor Mounts

Install new motor mounts and use grade-8 hardware to secure them to the block. (Only rubber mounts are available for the Y-block.) To make sure that the mounts are properly oriented, refer to your photos and notes taken during disassembly.

3 Remove Contaminants

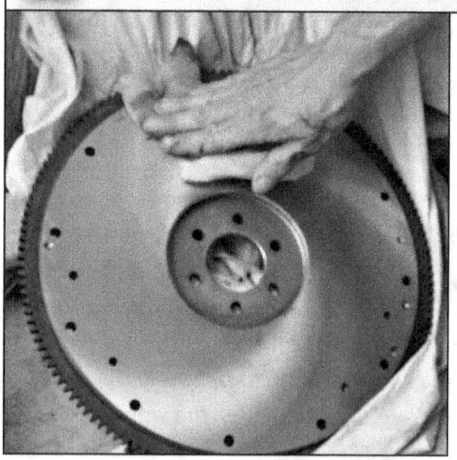

Wipe down the surface with lacquer thinner to remove any contaminants left over from the machine shop before attaching the newly machined flywheel to the engine.

4 Install Flywheel

After aligning the bolt holes in the flywheel with those in the crankshaft flange, tap the flywheel in place with a rubber mallet until it seats flush against the crankshaft flange.

ENGINE INSTALLATION, START-UP AND BREAK-IN

Torque Fasteners

5 Torque Flywheel Bolts

Give the threads on the flywheel bolts some blue Loctite and then torque them at 75 to 85 ft-lbs. You can add a small amount of white grease to the opening in the pilot bushing to aid in installing the transmission.

6 Attach Pressure Plate to Flywheel

To properly align the clutch disc and pressure plate on the flywheel, you can use an old transmission input shaft that has the same spline as the disc. Use only grade-8 hardware of the proper length to secure the pressure plate to the flywheel.

7 Install Bellhousing and Looms

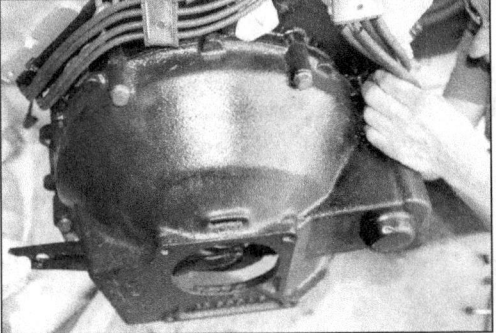

Bolt the bellhousing to the block; the spark plug wire looms can be installed at this time thanks to easy access. It is much easier to install the looms before the engine is in the car.

8 Install Clutch Fork

Install the clutch fork and throw-out bearing in the flywheel. If you haven't already done so, this is a good time to replace your old throw-out bearing; it is much easier to do at this point.

Professional Mechanic Tip

9 Install Starter

It is also much easier to install the starter with the engine out of the car. Installing the starter before dropping in the engine does not create any clearance issues. However, you should always check the clearances around external components before attempting to install the engine.

10 Prep to Install Engine

This engine bay has been cleaned and prepared to receive the engine. Wires and hoses are secured out of the way and the fenders properly protected and padded with fender covers.

11 Install Engine

With the engine secured to the hoist, it's time to lift it into place. This is a two-person operation; one guides the engine while the other operates the hoist. The rule here is to be careful, take your time, and double-check yourself at every turn. Only when the engine is properly sitting in the frame mounts and a floor jack has been placed under the bellhousing to support the back should you go under the car to attach the nuts and washers to the motor mount studs. Do not release the pressure on the lifting chain until the engine has been secured in the mounts with the back supported on a jack.

Once the transmission has been lifted into place and bolted to the bellhousing and the supporting crossmember and mount is installed, you can remove the jack from under the bellhousing. With the engine and transmission secured, you can install other under-car components such as the driveshaft, shift linkage, and exhaust.

Priming the Engine

To avoid potential damage on start-up, it is imperative that the engine has sufficient oil pressure before you make any attempt to start it. Although some people recommend bringing up oil pressure by spinning the engine with the starter (spark plugs out), I disagree. Using this method could cause damage to the starter and may also wipe some of the vital assembly lube off the lobes of the camshaft and faces of the valve lifters before oil reaches these areas during cranking.

Because zinc and its lubricating properties were removed from motor oil because of federal emissions regulations in 2004, I have heard of more and more cases of camshaft failure during engine start-up and break-in because of insufficient lubrication. Joe Gibbs Driven BR Break-In oil and Royal Purple Break-In oil contain zinc dialkyldithiophosphates (ZDDP), and many engine builders use it. Oil pump priming tools are commercially available. These connect to the oil pump via the distributor opening in the cylinder block.

A less expensive means of priming is available if you have an old distributor lying around. (Many Y-block enthusiasts surely have access to the nearly useless pre-1957 distributors that caused so many headaches.) If you happen to have an old distributor, simply remove the gear from the shaft and take the points and condenser off the breaker plate; you have an instant oil-pump-priming tool.

When using any priming tool remember that Ford distributors rotate counterclockwise and, therefore, so should the priming tool. I have found that a variable-speed, reversible drill works well to spin the priming tool. (A speed wrench or even Vise-Grips work if a drill isn't available.)

If your vehicle is not equipped with a mechanical oil pressure gauge that is capable of reading pressure when the engine is not running, I suggest, at the very least, obtaining an inexpensive aftermarket oil pressure gauge from your local auto parts store. The gauge can be temporarily installed in place of the engine's existing oil pressure switch so that you are assured the engine has sufficient oil pressure during priming and start-up. If your vehicle did not roll out of the factory with an oil pressure gauge, as is the case with many

This oil pump primer tool allows you to spin the oil pump to prime the engine's lubrication system once the engine is in the car and oil is in the crankcase, but the distributor is not yet installed.

Use a speed wrench or variable-speed drill to turn the shaft (counterclockwise) until engine oil pressure comes up. With the valve covers off the engine, you should see oil coming from the rocker assemblies as the pressure comes up.

ENGINE INSTALLATION, START-UP AND BREAK-IN

Ford products from the 1950s to 1970s, you should consider installing a quality aftermarket gauge.

While you're at it, consider adding a coolant temperature gauge as well. In the case of Rich's 1957 Custom, into which my 322-ci performance engine was installed, the factory water temperature gauge was found to be reading well into the "hot" zone when the mechanical gauge I installed showed the coolant temperature to be acceptable.

The addition of oil pressure and coolant temperature gauges greatly enhance your ability to accurately monitor these two areas that are so critical to engine function and longevity. Good gauges are a minor investment when the total costs involved in rebuilding an engine are taken into consideration.

Distributor Installation

Once the oiling system has been properly primed, it is time to install the distributor. It needs to be properly timed with the engine's firing order before attempting start-up. Follow this fairly simple procedure to bring your distributor into time with the engine.

Bring the engine up to TDC on the compression stroke of the number-1 cylinder. Install a compression gauge or place a handy thumb into the spark plug hole of the number-1 cylinder. Crank the engine over (a remote starter makes this task simpler) until compression is felt or indicated by the gauge. Caution: Do not confuse compression with the exhaust stroke, which is much weaker, when cranking the engine.

Ensure that the piston is at TDC by checking the alignment between the timing marks on the dampener and pointer. You should also be able to see the top of the piston by looking into the spark plug hole. If there is a slight misalignment between the timing marks, turn the engine over manually and use a socket and breaker bar on the crankshaft bolt until the marks line up.

Now is a good time to take a look at your disassembly photos. (You took photos as recommended, right?) Note the approximate location of the distributor vacuum advance mechanism in relation to other engine components. Then install the distributor in the engine with the contact end of the rotor aligned with the location of the number-1 spark plug wire on the distributor cap.

If you aren't sure of the proper alignment for the number-1 plug wire on the cap, temporarily install the cap on the distributor, note the location of the number-1 plug wire and indicate it on the distributor body by making a small mark with a pencil or marker. This should bring the ignition timing close enough to start the engine with minor movement of the distributor, but you need to set the timing to proper specification as soon after start-up as possible. This should be immediately after the recommended period of time that the engine is run at higher-than-idle RPM to properly break in the camshaft and lifters.

If your distributor is equipped with breaker points, these must also be set to the proper gap for the engine to start. Follow the manufacturer's specifications for setting breaker point gap and ignition timing.

Distributor Installation

1 Install Distributor

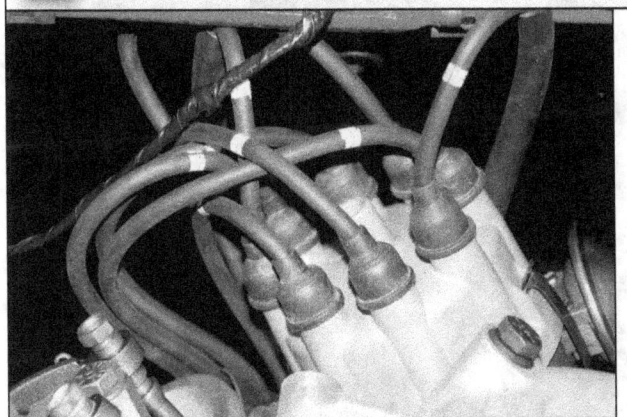

After priming the engine with oil, you can install the distributor. With the engine set at TDC on the compression stroke of cylinder number-1, install the distributor with the rotor pointed toward the location of the number-1 wire of the distributor cap. Mark all the spark-plug wires according to which cylinder they fire.

Point the vacuum advance unit in the general direction it was when the distributor was removed from the engine, and ensure that no obstructions limit its movement when setting the timing after start-up. You may have to advance or retard the distributor slightly when first starting the engine, so don't tighten the clamp holding the distributor yet. As a general rule, if during your initial attempt to start the engine it turns over fast but does not start, chances are the distributor needs to be advanced slightly. If the engine turns slowly or hard, retard the distributor slightly.

FORD Y-BLOCK ENGINES: HOW TO REBUILD AND MODIFY

CHAPTER 9

2 Verify Connections

Having taken the time to tag all the wires with their proper locations before removing the engine from the car pays dividends in time saved once you reach this point. Refer to your notes and photos to ensure that all connections are correct.

3 Verify Alignment

The distributor is timed and in place, the cap and wires are all in order, and the coil is connected and ready to deliver spark when the ignition is activated.

4 Attach Exhaust, Lines and Linkages

Now is the time to attach all the fuel lines, linkages, and exhaust manifolds as required before attempting to start the engine for the first time. I am a firm believer in having the exhaust hooked up before initial start-up so that any inappropriate noises can be more easily identified.

Priming the Fuel System

Your fuel supply should also be addressed before initial start-up. Begin by confirming that there is sufficient fuel in the tank. In the case of modern fuel-injected engines priming the fuel system is not too much of a concern because the car's electric fuel pump provides pressure to the system shortly after being energized by the ignition.

In the case of older engines equipped with a mechanical fuel pump quite a bit of cranking is often involved in initially getting the fuel from the tank to the carburetor. The time-honored method of dealing with this problem is to pour a small amount of fuel through the top of the carburetor to encourage the engine to start.

A word of caution here: Do not pour too much fuel into the carburetor at this point. If the engine

I use an electric fan attached to the engine-side of the radiator to cool this hot Y-block. It is thermostatically operated to activate whenever the coolant reaches a preset temperature.

ENGINE INSTALLATION, START-UP AND BREAK-IN

In addition to adding coolant to the radiator I also add it via the intake manifold. This avoids air bubbles in the cooling system that prevents the system from being properly filled.

The engine is in the car and ready for initial start-up. The supercharger will be installed once the engine has started and has been tuned to my satisfaction.

Break-In

You are quite busy when you start your newly rebuilt engine for the first time, and having a second, or even third, set of eyes on hand to assist with checking vital things, such as oil pressure and coolant temperature readings, fluid leaks, etc., can be a great help.

Keep in mind that foreign particles as small as 32 microns can find their way into critical moving parts of your newly rebuilt engine and cause damage. How small is 32 microns? A human hair's diameter is 40 microns.

For start-up and break-in, it is imperative that you first install a quality oil filter. Break-in lubricants are another important consideration. As of January 2004, the U.S. government mandated that the zinc-phosphorous additive, critical to engine break-in (and particularly camshaft and valve lifter break-in) be removed from all motor oils legal for use in street-driven motor vehicles in order to prevent possible catalytic convertor damage.

Once the engine is started, do not allow it to idle. Run it at approximately 2,500 rpm, varying by a few hundred rpm above and below this number, for the first 20 to 30 minutes. After this initial run, you should change the oil and filter. Although the oil may look clean, keep in mind the size of the particles required to undo all your hard work and the statistic that states: Most of the wear to metal parts in an engine occurs during its first hour of running.

Aftermarket camshaft manufacturers now include a warning and recommendations regarding the type of motor oil to be used exclusively in engines equipped with

does not start immediately, excess raw, unatomized fuel could wash the lubricant from the cylinder walls causing damage to both the walls and piston rings. If the engine does not start almost immediately when cranked, *do not* continue to pour gasoline into the carburetor. If the engine backfires because of incorrect timing, or if any fuel spills onto the intake manifold, a fire could result.

their products in order to avoid excessive wear on metal-to-metal contact surfaces. These recommendations include the use of the assembly lubricant included with the camshaft and motor oils that are designated "For off-road use only," long known to hot rod engine builders as racing oil.

Modern engines with roller-style valve lifters no longer require the additional protection of zinc and phosphorous in their lubricants, but this is not true in the case of classic and muscle cars. Although removing zinc and phosphorous increases the life of catalytic converters and arguably decreases emissions to some degree, classic cars do not use catalytic converters nor are their engines equipped with emissions controls beyond a PCV valve. In addition, as part of its ongoing effort to reduce vehicle emissions, the EPA has mandated that emissions systems must have a service life exceeding 120,000 miles. To meet this requirement, automobile manufacturers have required their oil suppliers to remove additive packages from motor oils that reduce emissions compliance.

A couple of solutions are available to the lubrication problem confronting the owners of classic cars. One is a line of motor oils produced by Royal Purple that contains zinc phosphate (these oils are labeled "for off-road use only"), products with the additive ZDDP, or Cam-shield.

Informational material included with Cam-shield contains the following explanation: "The high-pressure contact zone between the cam lobe and the flat tappet in classic car engines significantly reduces the ability of the oil film to prevent metal-to-metal contact. This requires the engine oil to be formulated with the proper level of antiwear chemistry to prevent metal-to-metal contact. ZDDP has been the predominant camshaft, lifter, valvetrain antiwear chemistry for more than 50 years."

Asking advice on how to break in a freshly rebuilt engine gets you a variety of answers. Some do it one way because that is the way their grandfather did it. Others share the advice that friends or mechanics may have passed along. Although there is no one absolute, written-in-stone way to break in an engine, it is best to err on the side of caution and follow as many of the break-in recommendations provided by the manufacturers of the component parts used in your rebuild as you can.

Start-Up Checklist

Here are some tips on engine break-in from master machinist Gil Jordan that get right to the point. After all his hard work, Gil obviously has a vested interest in my engines and wants to see them run their best. "Starting a new engine is like bringing a baby into the world. There is so much to worry about and do in a very critical, make-or-break period."

- Check timing, oil pressure, and water temperature. Any leaks of any kind?
- Get the idle speed up to break in the cam and lifters. I sure hope they don't decide to wear out prematurely!
- Listen to the engine for any unusual noises. Your engine should not emit any knocking or pinging sounds.
- Double-check the torque on all the bolts.
- How's the water temperature and oil pressure?
- After at least 15 minutes of running the engine at 1,500 to 2,500 rpm, you can idle her down, get the distributor timed, and properly adjust the carburetor.
- If you are satisfied, you can take her out on the road and seat the piston rings next. I always tell customers that the worst thing you can do is let it sit there and idle with no load on the rings to seat them during that critical early period.
- Take the car out on the road, accelerate and decelerate at least 10 times in something lower than high gear to moderately load the engine and seat those rings. No sustained cruising on the interstate, either, because there is not much of a load on the engine there to break in the rings, unless you are packing 4.11:1 rear end gears like the old days. Stop-and-go traffic is a pretty good situation.
- I like to change the oil and filter early and often in the game, because they are a lot cheaper than the investment you've made in the engine.
- Using an oil additive containing ZDDP is probably a good idea with today's off-the-shelf oils to ensure a long life of the flat-tappet cam and lifters, especially if you have a performance cam and valvespring combination. ■

EPILOGUE

Although the great sense of satisfaction you feel the first time that newly rebuilt engine roars to life is certainly well deserved, the story does not end there. To realize the full potential of your Y-block, and have it provide many years of reliable power, there are several matters that must be addressed.

First, keep in mind that the break-in tips are very important to follow as this time is the most critical for that fresh engine.

Second, within those critical 500-or-so miles that you put on the engine it should be checked thoroughly for any leaks or other issues. The state of tune is important at all times; particularly the valve lash and ignition timing settings.

Third, preventive maintenance is not merely a recommendation; it is a must. Within the critical first 500 miles, change the oil and filter again. And while the manufacturer of your head gaskets probably does not require it, I think it is a good idea to go over the cylinder head bolts with a torque wrench one more time just to be sure. From that point forward, it should be paramount to keep your engine on a schedule of regular tune-ups and oil changes, and pay particular attention to all the components in the fuel system since today's available fuels contain percentages of ethanol that have proved to be harmful to the components found in vintage cars. You may want to consider a specialized fuel additive to counteract the effects of ethanol on your fuel system as I do.

Aside from that, all that's left for me to do is wish you the heartiest congratulations for a job well done and many years of trouble-free motoring fun with your Y-block-powered machine.

Our 322-ci performance Y-block engine has proven itself to be powerful and reliable in Rich Stuck's 1957 Custom and continues to log carefree miles, turn heads, and win accolades at car shows and cruise nights.

APPENDIX

Torque Specifications

239, 256, 272 Engine Component	Torque (ft-lbs)	292 to 312 Engine Component	Torque (ft-lbs)
Cylinder head bolts	75*	Cylinder head bolts	75*
Intake manifold	26	Intake manifold	26
Exhaust manifolds	23 to 28	Exhaust manifolds	23 to 28
Main bearing cap bolts	80 to 90	Main bearing cap bolts	95
Connecting rod nuts	45 to 50	Connecting rod nuts	45 to 50
Flywheel to crankshaft	75 to 85	Flywheel to crankshaft	75 to 85
Damper to crankshaft	85 to 90	Damper to crankshaft	85 to 90
Oil pump to block	12 to 15	Oil pump to block	12 to 15
Camshaft thrust plate	12 to 15	Camshaft thrust plate	12 to 15
Camshaft sprocket to cam	35 to 45	Camshaft sprocket to cam	35 to 45
Water pump	12 to 15	Water pump	12 to 15

* Always torque head bolts in three steps: 35, 55, 75.

General Engine Specifications

Year	Engine	Bore (inches)	Stroke (inches)	Standard Compression Ratio (:1)
1954	239	3.50	3.11	7.2
	256	3.62	3.10	7.5
1955	272	3.63	3.30	7.6 (8.5 special police)
	292	3.75	3.30	8.1 (8.5 auto, 7.6 Interceptor)
1956	272	3.63	3.30	8.0 (8.4 Fordomatic)
	292	3.75	3.30	8.1 (8.4 auto)
	312	3.80	3.44	8.4 (9.1 auto)
1957	272	3.63	3.30	8.6
	292	3.75	3.30	9.1
	312	3.80	3.44	9.7 (8.3 supercharged)
1958	292	3.75	3.30	9.1
	312	3.80	3.44	9.7
1959	292	3.75	3.30	8.0
	312	3.80	3.44	8.7
1960	292	3.75	3.30	8.4
	312	3.80	3.44	8.9
1961–1964	292	3.75	3.30	8.0

APPENDIX

Dampener Timing Settings

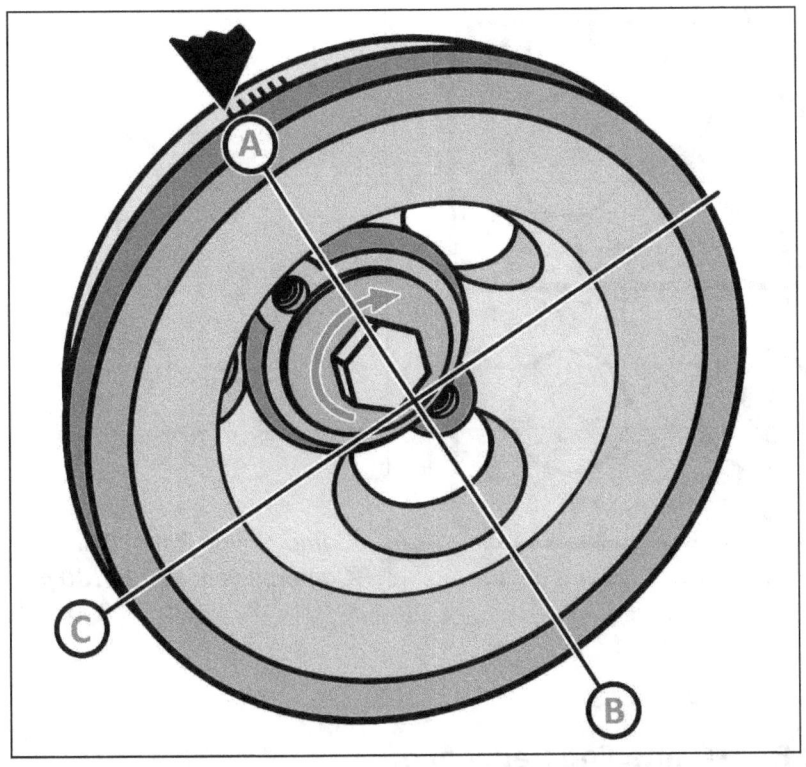

Step 1: Set number-1 piston at TDC at end of compression stroke.
Step 2: Adjust number-1, -4, -5 exhaust and number-1, -2, -7 intake.
Step 3: Adjust number-6, -8 exhaust and number-4, -5 intake.
Step 4: Adjust number-2, -3, 7 exhaust and number-3, -6, -8 intake.

Firing Order and Rotation

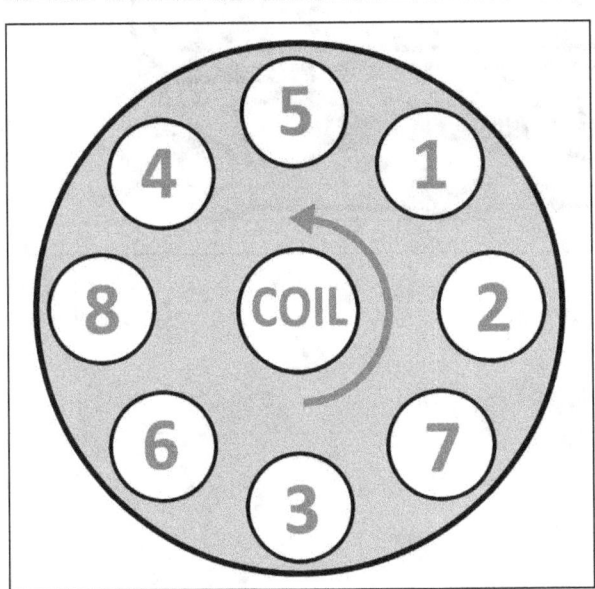

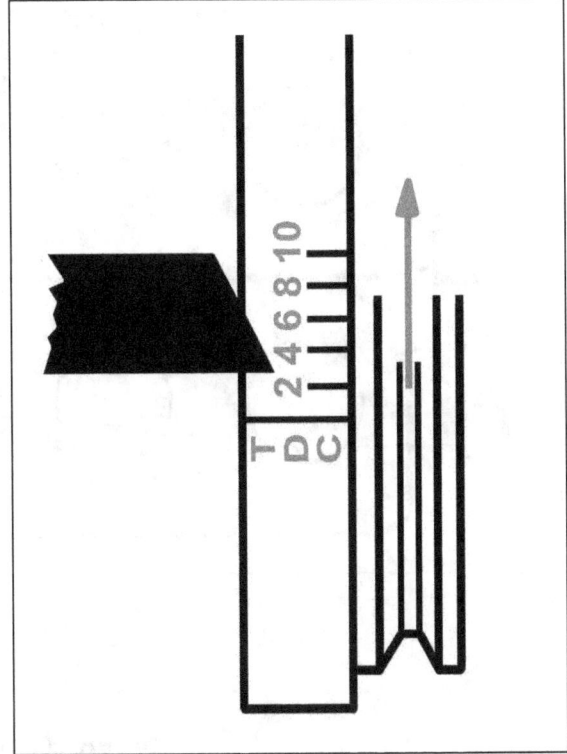

Idle Speed
Standard transmission: 500 to 525
Automatic transmission: 500 to 500 N

Ignition Timing
Standard transmission: 6 degrees BTDC at 500 rpm
Automatic transmission: 6 degrees BTDC at 500 rpm

Dist vac line disconnected.

Ignition Advance at 2,500 rpm
Total: 37 to 45 degrees
Cent. only: 19 to 23 degrees

Rotation: Counterclockwise
Firing Order: 1-5-4-8-6-3-7-2

FORD Y-BLOCK ENGINES: HOW TO REBUILD AND MODIFY

APPENDIX

Cylinder Numbering

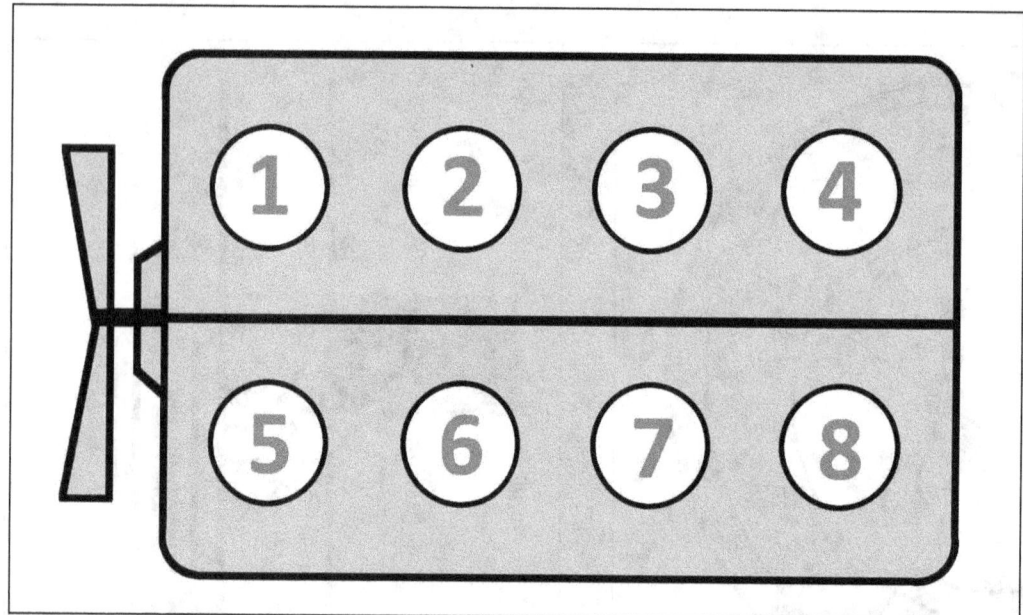

Compression Ratio: 8.3:1
Compression: 120 to 130 psi

Cylinder Head Bolt-Tightening Sequence

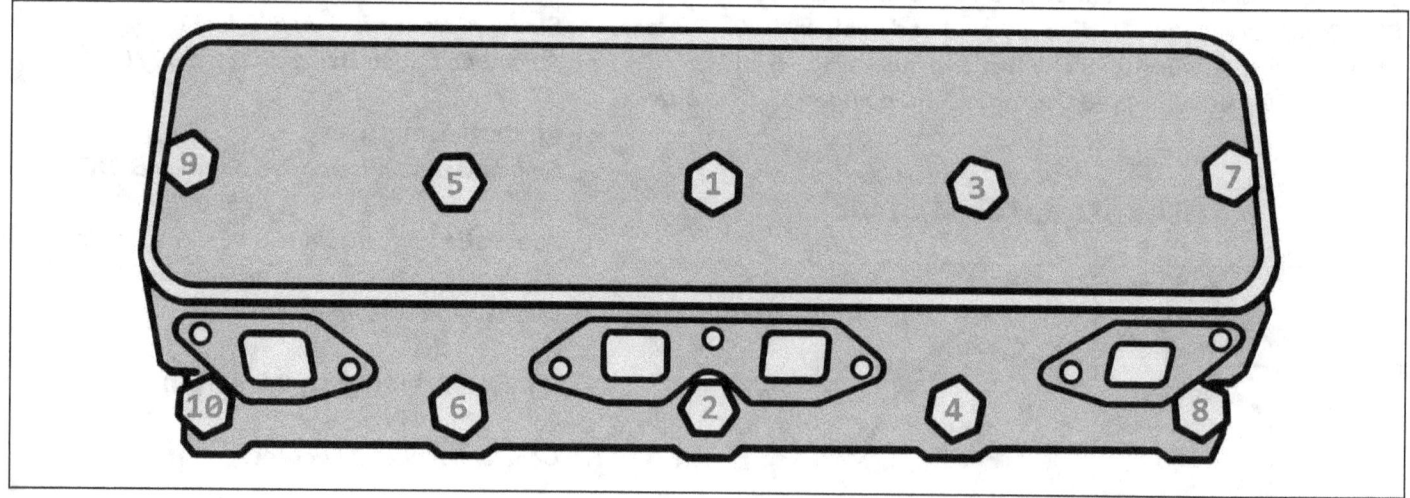

APPENDIX

Cam Timing

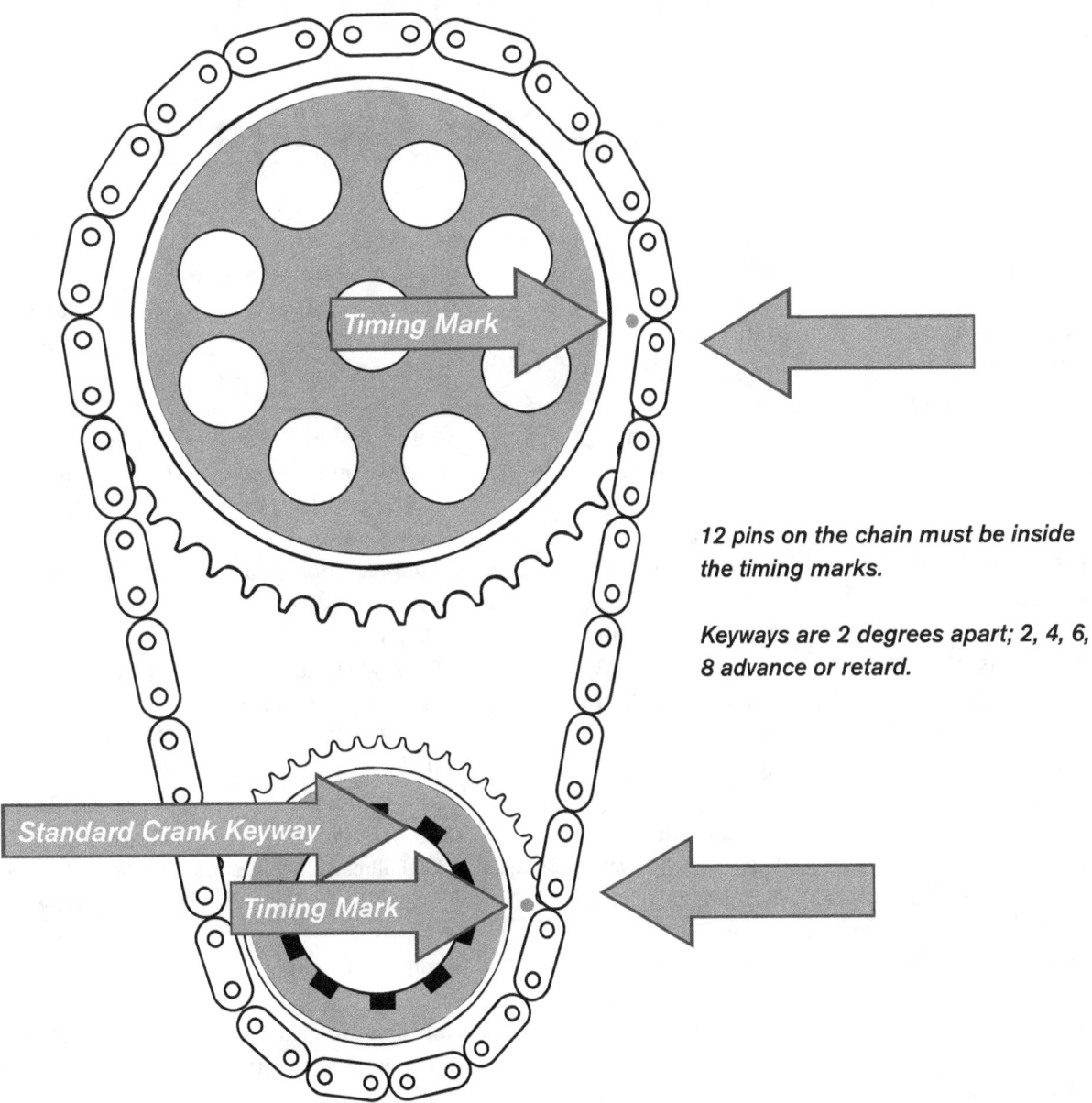

12 pins on the chain must be inside the timing marks.

Keyways are 2 degrees apart; 2, 4, 6, 8 advance or retard.

Source Guide

Advanced Clutch Technology
206 E. Avenue K-4
Lancaster, CA 93535
661-940-7555
advancedclutch.com

AMK Products
800 Airport Road
Winchester, VA 22602
540-662-7820
amkproducts.com

ARP Products
1863 Eastman Avenue
Ventura, CA 93003
805-339-2200
arp-bolts.com

Elgin Cams
1808-D Empire Industrial Court
Santa Rosa, CA 95403
707-545-6115
elgincams.com

Ford Racing Parts
fordracingparts.com

Gardner-Westcott Company
10110 Six Mile Road
Northville, MI 48167
800-897-5025
gardner-westcott.com

Howard's Cams
280 W. 35th Ave.
Oshkosh, WI 54902
920-233-5228
www.howardscams.com

Isky Racing Cams
16020 S. Broadway
Gardena, CA 90248
323-770-0930
iskycams.com

JEGS High Performance
101 JEGS Place
Delaware, OH 43015
800-345-4545
jegs.com

John Mummert
14368 Old Highway 80, Suite C
El Cajon, CA 92021
616-596-0312
ford-y-block.com

Liberty Engine Parts
3250 S. 76th Street
Philadelphia, PA 19153
800-621-4242
liberty-engine-parts.com

Loctite
26235 First Street
Westlake, OH 44145
800-624-7767
loctiteproducts.com

Magnaflux
3624 West Lake Avenue
Glenview, IL 60026
847-657-5300
magnaflux.com

Mallory Ignition
10601 Memphis Avenue, #12
Cleveland, OH 44144
216-658-6413
mallory-ignition.com

Milodon Inc.
2250 Agate Court
Simi Valley, CA 93065
805-577-5950
milodon.com

MSD Ignition
1350 Pullman Drive, Dock #14
El Paso, TX 79936
915-857-5200
msdignition.com

Northern Auto Parts
801 Lewis Boulevard
Sioux City, IA 51106
800-831-0884
northernautoparts.com

Permatex Sealants
10 Columbus Boulevard
Hartford, CT 06106
860-543-7500
permatex.com

RaceTec & AutoTec Pistons
15681 Computer Lane
Huntington Beach, CA 92649
714-903-4362
racetecpistons.com

Red's Headers and Speed Equipment
31-410 Reserve Drive, Suite 4
Thousand Palms, CA 92276
760-343-2590
reds-heders.com

Rollmaster Performance Products
rollmasterusa.com

Sealed Power
26555 Northwestern Highway
Southfield, MI 48033
800-325-8886
sealedpowerpistons.com

Speedway Motors
340 Victory Lane
Lincoln, NE 68528
800-979-0122
speedwaymotors.com

Summit Racing
P.O. Box 909
Akron, OH 44309
800-230-3030
summitracing.com

www.ingramcontent.com/pod-product-compliance
Lightning Source LLC
Chambersburg PA
CBHW081455070526
44586CB00019B/2368